THE ☆ BULLY ☆ OF BENTONVILLE

THE☆BULLY☆OF BENTONVILLE

HOW THE HIGH COST OF WAL-MART'S EVERYDAY LOW PRICES IS HURTING AMERICA

ANTHONY BIANCO

CURRENCY

DOUBLEDAY

NEW YORK   LONDON   TORONTO   SYDNEY   AUCKLAND

A CURRENCY BOOK
PUBLISHED BY DOUBLEDAY
a division of Random House, Inc.

CURRENCY is a trademark of Random House, Inc., and
DOUBLEDAY is a registered trademark of Random House, Inc.

Cataloging-in-Publication Data is on file with the Library of Congress.
ISBN 0-385-51356-9

Book design by Chris Welch

PRINTED IN THE UNITED STATES OF AMERICA

1 3 5 7 9 10 8 6 4 2

For Mara

CONTENTS

ACKNOWLEDGMENTS

The research that led to this book began in the fall of 2003 with a *BusinessWeek* cover story entitled "Is Wal-Mart Too Powerful?" The article was a product of collaboration with Wendy Zellner, then the magazine's Dallas bureau chief, who had covered Wal-Mart for a dozen years. Working with Wendy, one of journalism's most knowledgeable Wal-Mart watchers and a generous colleague besides, was an ideal way to begin trying to understand this most idiosyncratic of corporations. I'd also like to thank Frank Comes and Mary Kuntz, who edited the *BusinessWeek* story and were unflagging in their support of the idea of attempting a critical reappraisal of a famously prickly corporation that had grown accustomed to being treated with the deference due an American icon. I am also grateful to Steve Shepard, the magazine's recently retired editor-in-chief, for supporting the story as strong after publication as before, and for granting me a leave of absence to write this book. Thanks also to Steve Adler, the new editor of *BusinessWeek*, for letting my leave last as long as it needed to.

This book was written without any direct input from Wal-Mart beyond the interviews that Wendy and I did with members of senior management for the *BusinessWeek* piece. However, I did make several trips to Bentonville, and spoke with many current and former Wal-Mart employees all around the country, including some whom I am unable to acknowledge by name. What is more, at no point did I feel that my research suffered for lack of direct access to Lee Scott and other top Wal-Mart executives. In the last two years, Wal-Mart has shed the last remnants of its reticence in stepping forward to practice a very aggressive brand of public relations. Like most political candidates, Wal-Mart executives are always "on message," and that message has been voluminously communicated in speeches and in interviews and on Walmartfacts.com.

Wal-Mart has become a journalistic beat unto itself of late, and I am indebted to the fine work done by many other reporters, particularly Steven Greenhouse of the *New York Times*. Bob Ortega's prophetic 1998 book about Wal-Mart, *In Sam We Trust*, also proved particularly useful in my own research.

I also benefited more directly from the labors of my talented and versatile research assistant, Mielikki Ahti Org, a fellow resident of Brooklyn, New York, who handled all the reporting assignments that I gave her with aplomb. On the West Coast, I was aided by another fine reporter, Chris Lydgate of Portland, Oregon. Thanks as well to Mark Zusman, the editor of *Willamette Week* newspaper, for putting me in touch with Chris. *Willamette Week*, where I got my start as a business writer more years ago than I care to remember, delighted its alumni in 2005 by winning the Pulitzer Prize for investigative reporting. Thanks also to the imaginative Lisa Brasier, formerly of Los Angeles, who contributed a long list of possible titles for this book before vanishing into the wilds of upstate New York.

In Québec, I received all the help I needed to overcome my deficient French. Diane Berard, the feisty editor of *Commerce* magazine, traveled with me to Jonquière and allowed me to benefit from her abundant journalistic skills. In Sainte-Hyacinthe, the resourceful Halina Carter was pressed into double duty as interviewer and translator after a wrong turn on Highway 20 left me disastrously behind schedule. Carlo Tarini went above and beyond the call of his professional duties as a PR man in otherwise helping me get where I needed to go in Québec. Back in New York City, two first-rate translators—Claudia Lieto-

McKenna and Chloe Mathieu, transplanted Canadians both—put my Québec interviews into useful form.

I am also beholden to the always helpful and very well-connected Terri Thompson, director of the Knight-Bagehot Fellowship Program at Columbia University, and to Susan Zegel, a *BusinessWeek* librarian who knows how to find whatever I cannot find. Mark Stein, an editor at the *New York Times,* did yeoman's work helping whip the book into its final shape.

My special thanks to my daughter, Marissa, who showed patience beyond her years in putting up with my preoccupation with this book, and to Mara Der Hovanesian, who reinforced my morale whenever it wavered and who read the manuscript at several junctures and made invaluable suggestions upon each reading.

That my agent, Esther Newberg of ICM, believed strongly in this project from the beginning helped convince me to take it on. Last but certainly not least, I'd like to acknowledge the vital contribution made by Roger Scholl, the editorial director of Doubleday Currency, who set this project in motion by urging me to write a book on Wal-Mart. Roger's attention and energy never flagged, and he retained his good humor through even the tightest spots, of which there were more than a few.

THE☆BULLY☆OF BENTONVILLE

CHAPTER ONE

THE CASE AGAINST WAL-MART

H. Lee Scott Jr. looks every inch the chief executive of America's biggest and most powerful corporation as he strides through the lobby of the Omni Los Angeles Hotel on his way to make the most important speech of his career. Wearing an expensive, well-tailored suit on his stocky frame, his hair carefully coiffed, and his corporate game face on, Scott shows no sign of his natural fear of public speaking. To the contrary, the fifty-four-year-old executive appears eager for the chance to justify his company, Wal-Mart Stores, to the 500 business and community leaders who await him in the Omni's ballroom.

The Omni—a luxury high-rise located in a solidly pro-union, politically liberal city—is an unlikely venue for the chief executive of an Arkansas-based corporation that is famously frugal, deeply conservative, and Southern-fried to the core. Wal-Mart already has 180 stores in California, but its ambitious expansion plans call for it to quadruple this total while moving from the outskirts into the heart of Los Angeles and the state's other big cities. In many Golden State locales, Wal-Mart was being denied the zoning and other clearances it needed, and so Scott has flown out on this February day in 2005 to make the case for himself and his company in person at a luncheon sponsored by Town Hall Los Angeles, a nonpartisan group that immodestly but not inaccurately bills itself as a forum "for the most important thinkers and leaders on Earth."[1]

Scott takes the stage to polite applause and opens with an aw-shucks flourish reminiscent of the late Sam Walton, the disarmingly folksy "Mr. Sam," who founded Wal-Mart in the remote Ozarks hill town of Bentonville in 1962. "I know that Town Hall Los Angeles has a national reputation for hosting conversations on the issues that matter—talks that feature prominent figures from the worlds of government, business, the nonprofit sector, and the arts," Scott says. "It's a little humbling for a shopkeeper from Arkansas to follow such folks to Town Hall's distinguished podium."[2]

Scott soon discards the faux humility to offer a ringing defense of the embattled company where he has worked for twenty-six years. By selling vast quantities of goods at its trademark "Every Day Low Prices," Wal-Mart has single-handedly raised America's standard of living, saving consumers about $100 billion a year, he contends. "These savings are a lifeline for millions of middle- and lower-income families who live from payday to payday," he says. "In effect, it gives them a raise every time they shop with us." As Scott tells it, Wal-Mart also provides good jobs for hundreds of thousands of equally deserving employees, offers even part-time workers generous health insurance and other benefits, and contributes hefty tax payments to thousands of towns and cities from sea to shining sea. "I believe that if you look at the facts with an open mind," he says, "you'll agree that Wal-Mart is good for America."[3]

Scott accuses greedy labor unions, inefficient supermarket chains, and other Wal-Mart opponents of distorting "the facts" to suit their own purposes, undermining not only the company but also the nation. In so many words, the CEO contends that Wal-Mart *is* America and that to oppose the company's advance into California

and other growth markets is to oppose progress itself. "When someone builds a better mousetrap, it's not the American way to deny
average folks the chance to use it to improve their lives," he says. "The
horse and buggy industry wasn't permitted to crush the car. The can-
dle lobby wasn't allowed to stop electric lights." To deny Americans
"the higher living standards that Wal-Mart's business efficiency can
bring is to make a mockery of American ideals under the guise of
pursuing them."[4]

Hold it right there. When America's largest corporation conflates its
self-interest with life, liberty, and the pursuit of happiness, alarm bells
should go off in every city hall, statehouse, and union hall in the land.
The outcry against Wal-Mart is rooted in the arrogance of its pre-
sumption that selling vast quantities of cut-rate merchandise entitles it
to behave as if it represents the best interests of the American people.
Scott likes to call Wal-Mart an "agent" of the consumer, but this seems
far too mild a description of a company of such size, power, and right-
eous zeal. Its critics would argue that intimidator, enforcer, coercer,
tyrant are more apt. In the name of the shopper, Wal-Mart systemati-
cally bullies its workers, its suppliers, and the residents of towns and
cities disinclined to submit to the expansion imperative of a company
currently opening new stores at the rate of 1.45 a day.

Who among us does not crave a bargain? But we Americans—
including the financially strapped folks Wal-Mart claims as its own—
are not defined by how much money we save down at the Supercenter.
We are a nation of workers *first* and shoppers second; as the saying
goes, "You got to work to eat." We also are a nation of citizens entitled
to vote as we choose, even if it means going against our financial self-
interest as defined by Wal-Mart.

Today, Wal-Mart is besieged by critics on all sides, but perhaps the
greatest threat it faces is from within—from unhappy, demoralized
employees who are quitting at the rate of hundreds of thousands a

year and who have dozens of class-action lawsuits pending against the company. On the very day that Scott was extolling Wal-Mart's virtues at the Omni, a ragtag group of his low-level employees gathered 850 miles to the east to bite the hand that barely feeds them. Joined by dozens of supporters, they stationed themselves across the street from a Wal-Mart Supercenter in Loveland, Colorado—a fast-growing exurb of Denver—to loudly cheer on a drive to unionize the store's tire-and-lube shop. Joshua Noble, the twenty-one-year-old leader of the rebellion against his virulently anti-union employer, is an epileptic who had to move back in with his parents because he could not afford to live on his Wal-Mart paycheck. "Always the low price means always paying your workers less," Noble declares.[5]

The average Wal-Mart hourly employee makes substantially less than the $12.28 average for retail workers in the United States; although the exact amount is debatable, the highest figure, Wal-Mart's own, is a mere $9.68 an hour. And starting wages are several dollars an hour less. Scott—who received $12,593,493 in salary, bonus, stock awards, and other compensation in 2004—defends Wal-Mart's pay scale by rounding off the hourly average to $10 and noting that it is almost twice the federal minimum wage of $5.15. Even so, the typical employee working full-time at Wal-Mart makes just $17,600 a year, well below the $19,157 poverty line for a family of four.

Because Wal-Mart is so big, it has dragged down wages throughout the country. Economists at the University of California at Berkeley found that Wal-Mart's expansion during the 1990s cut the income of America's retail employees by 1.3 percent—or by $4.7 billion in 2000 alone.[6] What is more, the depressing effect of Wal-Mart's expansion on payrolls extends well beyond retailing. According to a 2005 analysis by economists at the Public Policy Institute of California, take-home pay per person fell by 5 percent across the board following Wal-Mart's entry into a county. The evidence "strongly suggest(s) that Wal-Mart stores lead to wage declines, shifts to lower-paying jobs (or less skilled workers), or increased use of part-time workers," the authors concluded, adding that the company's impact on local labor markets was particularly pronounced in the South, where its stores are most numerous and where they have been open the longest.[7]

And the health insurance that Scott touted in his speech? Only 44 percent of Wal-Mart's 1.3 million U.S. workers have signed up for even the least-expensive medical benefits that the company offers.[8] Many simply cannot afford even the minimum $1,000 deductible and the $35 monthly premium for individual and $141 for family coverage. The result? To make ends meet, many employees see no alternative to going on the dole. An astounding 46 percent of the children of Wal-Mart workers are uninsured or on Medicaid.[9] "For being such a big company, Wal-Mart has a very poor benefits plan," complains Noble, who pays nearly $200 a month for his health insurance plus another $100 for the prescription medicine that prevents his epileptic seizures.[10]

Unhappy Wal-Mart workers complain as much about being overworked as underpaid. The company deliberately understaffs its stores to hold down payroll costs on one hand, and yet is absolutely allergic to paying hourly workers overtime on the other, putting its store managers in the position of finding ways to reconcile the irreconcilable or suffer the career consequences. The obvious, though generally illegal, solution is to force employees to work extra hours without pay, either by eliminating meal and rest breaks or by having them punch out and keep working "off the clock." To a certain unquantifiable extent, Wal-Mart's labor cost advantage is the product of playing fast and loose with its own stated policies at its employees' expense.

In 2000, Wal-Mart did its own audit of one week's time-clock records for 128 stores employing 25,000 hourly workers in total. What they found was shocking—three apparent violations for each worker: 60,767 instances of rest breaks not taken, 15,705 instances of meal breaks forgone, and 1,371 instances of minor-age employees working excessive hours or at inappropriate times (during school hours, for example). Despite this, the company took no corrective action whatsoever, and instead disavowed its own audit after it was leaked to the *New York Times* in 2004, claiming that it had no way of knowing whether workers hadn't simply forgotten to sign out as they came and went. "Our view," said a spokesman, "is that the audit really means nothing."[11] Others do not agree—federal and state authorities have repeatedly cited and fined Wal-Mart for labor-law violations, including hiring outside contractors who employ illegal aliens.

Wal-Mart insists on describing itself as "pro-associate, not anti-union," but it is ruthless in trying to suppress any and all attempts by unions to organize its stores. One of the company's standard-issue manuals for store-level supervisors is the *Managers' Toolbox to Remaining Union-Free*, which urges managers to keep an eye open for such telltale signs of incipient unionism as "frequent meetings at associates' homes" or "associates who are never seen together . . . talking or associating with each other." By some accounts, Wal-Mart headquarters conducts covert surveillance of employee telephone calls and e-mails. Whenever it does detect pro-union sentiment at a store, the home office dispatches a "labor relations team" by private jet to cajole and intimidate dissident workers into toeing its strict anti-union line.

In a rare instance of defiance, workers in a store in Jonquière, Québec—North America's staunchest bastion of trade unionism— voted in the fall of 2004 to join the union that Wal-Mart considers its archenemy, the United Food and Commercial Workers. In apparent retaliation, Wal-Mart, to the outrage of the people of Québec, shut down the store, which still had sixteen years to run on its twenty-year lease, and put 190 workers on the street in an area with one of Canada's highest unemployment rates.

Without a union to protect them, aggrieved Wal-Mart employees are turning to the courts. In 2005, the company faced more than forty class-action suits in thirty states alleging that it forces employees to work extra hours without pay, including a case in Texas brought on behalf of 200,000 workers who claim that Wal-Mart owes them $150 million for forcing them to work through their fifteen-minute breaks over a four-year period. In Massachusetts, lawyers representing 55,000 workers claim to have documented 7,000 different instances of managers deleting large blocks of time from payroll records. Wal-Mart settled one such case in Colorado in 2001 by distributing $50 million in unpaid wages to 69,000 employees. A year later, an Oregon jury delivered a guilty verdict against the company in the first of these so-called wage-and-hour cases to go to trial.

Scores of other lawsuits allege that Wal-Mart routinely violated laws against discrimination in denying women, black, and Hispanic workers raises and promotions. A sex-discrimination case certified in mid-2004 by a federal judge in California is the largest civil rights class-action suit in history by several orders of magnitude. The case, *Dukes v. Wal-Mart*, encompasses the claims of every woman who has worked at Wal-Mart since late 1998—1.6 million workers all told.

In its attempts to prevent the case from broadening beyond the six original plaintiffs, Wal-Mart claimed that each store was "different" from the others and that at worst there were only a few "bad apples" among its store managers. Its own records tell a different story: Since 1997, female employees were paid 5 percent to 15 percent less than men working the same jobs in every part of the country, despite having higher performance ratings and more seniority on average. Women comprise two-thirds of all hourly workers but received only one-third of all promotions to management positions. At Wal-Mart, a mere 33 percent of managers are women, compared with 56 percent at the company's top twenty competitors, according to a study commissioned by the plaintiffs. The depositions of hundreds of female employees filed in support of the case are liberally spiced with tales of good ol' boys behaving badly: the home-office exec who routinely told mixed-gender groups of employees they should strive to make customers feel as if they could trust them "with their wife and their wallet"; the Midwestern district manager who liked to hold business meetings at Hooters; the "Spirit Committee" of a Wisconsin store that brought in a stripper to perform at a staff session in celebration of the manager's birthday.

Wal-Mart workers are quitting in far greater numbers than they are filing lawsuits or signing union representation cards. Turnover among hourly employees is nearly 50 percent a year, about double the rate of Costco, which long ago supplanted its much larger rival as America's big-box employer of choice. To replace the workers who are voting with their feet and leaving, Wal-Mart must hire about 600,000 new employees a year in the United States alone—a figure without precedent in the annals of business. In addition, the company filled 125,000 new positions in 2005—a figure that will only grow as it continues to add 280 to 300 new stores a year.

Viewed from the Olympian heights of Bentonville, high turnover in Wal-Mart's stores is not all bad. The constant churn sharply reduces the number of employees eligible for raises and promotions—holding the average wage down—and also assures that the great majority of workers do not stick around long enough to have the chance to vote in a union election or file a discrimination suit. Still, an awful lot of warm bodies are needed to keep the Wal-Mart sales machine humming. How long can the company sustain its manic hiring pace before it cycles through the entire blue-collar population of America? And at what cost? Hiring and training a replacement worker costs Wal-Mart $2,500 on average, or about $2 billion a year.

The reason Wal-Mart's behavior toward its employees, the communities in which it operates, and its manufacturing suppliers is so important is that it casts such an enormous shadow over the American economy. In the business world, there is big, and then there is Wal-Mart Stores. The "shop" that Scott keeps will ring up more than $300 billion in revenue in 2005, more than any corporation in history. Wal-Mart's sales are greater than the next five biggest U.S. retailers combined.[12] By itself, Wal-Mart is China's fifth-largest trading partner, ahead of Germany and Great Britain. "If we were a country," Scott has said, "we would be the twentieth largest in the world. If we were a city, we would be the fifth largest in America."[13] Every week, 138 million shoppers visit Wal-Mart's 3,750 stores in the United States and its 2,400 outlets in nine foreign countries. It employs 1.6 million people, four times as many as McDonald's, the world's second-largest private employer. Three hundred thousand more Americans now wear the Wal-Mart uniform than are currently on active duty in the Army, Navy, Air Force, and Marines combined.

Wal-Mart is larger than any company has ever been. But the economic influence it wields is disproportionate even to its size. Because of the breadth of its product offerings, Wal-Mart is centrally positioned within the U.S. economy to a degree unmatched by any retailer in history. With a 25 to 35 percent share of the market in everything from toothpaste, dog food, and detergent to DVDs, jewelry, and toys, Wal-Mart dominates across the full spectrum of consumer goods and can make or break even the largest and most diversified of the manufacturers that supply it.

Wal-Mart's blue, gray, and rust color scheme is a familiar sight throughout the country, but the foundation of its dominance—the reason it is so damn big—is hidden from view. Wal-Mart can routinely underprice other discounters and still make big money because it pursues cost efficiency with a zeal bordering on the maniacal. In part, this is because Wal-Mart's selling and general administration costs—wages mainly—are fully 25 percent below those of other big-box chains. Equally vital is Wal-Mart's mastery of the technology-driven discipline of logistics: It moves merchandise from factory loading dock through to cash register with a speed and precision no one else comes close to equaling. The combination has made Wal-Mart the most formidable consumer-business machine in the history of capitalism.

In the 1960s and 1970s, when mass discounting was young, Wal-Mart was welcomed almost everywhere it wanted to go. A shiny new Wal-Mart discount store at the edge of town became an emblem of economic progress throughout the South. It was not unusual for towns to send delegations to Wal-Mart headquarters bearing tax subsidies and other inducements to attract stores. Many got their money's worth, for Wal-Mart put its first few hundred stores into small, remote communities that the dominant retail chains of the day either shunned or exploited through rip-off pricing. While a new Wal-Mart store was not the powerful economic engine that a new factory would have been, it did bring jobs and tax revenue to communities in desperate need of both while enabling shoppers to stretch each hard-earned dollar further than ever before. Let's give Wal-Mart its due and concede that it is indeed the best, most sincerely devoted corporate friend that the budget-minded American shopper has ever had.

Today, there still are plenty of communities across the country so keen to get their own Wal-Mart that they are willing to subsidize a giant now coining $10 billion a year in profits. But these days, the company has to fight its way into town as often as not. In cities big and small, Wal-Mart's advance is sparking "site fights" that tend to escalate into the municipal equivalent of civil war. "I've been here forty-four years and I've never seen such division and intense passion on both sides," says Kay McKay, a civic leader in Flagstaff, Arizona (population 50,000), where Wal-Mart won a referendum in 2005 by a margin of just 365 votes out of more than 17,100 cast.[14]

The growing resistance Wal-Mart faces is deeply rooted in a changing American landscape. In Sam Walton's heyday, the consumer suffered because of a lack of real competition among merchants and the city was just beginning to burst its long-established boundaries and flood the surrounding landscape with new roads, housing subdivisions, and shopping centers. But by the 1990s, the country had sprawled its way from a shortage to a surplus of retail stores of most sorts. A new Wal-Mart still brought cheaper prices to Anytown U.S.A., but no longer was even a modest spur to economic growth, making the subsidies that the company continued to extract at every opportunity into a bad deal indeed for local taxpayers. For years now, Wal-Mart's expansion has been essentially a zero-sum game: It grows by wresting business away from other retailers large and small. In hundreds of towns and cities, Wal-Mart's entry put ailing Main Street shopping districts into intensive care and then ripped out the life-support system.

Environmental objections also figure prominently in the growing grassroots backlash to Wal-Mart expansion. As the novelty allure of big-box bargain-hunting has faded, millions of affluent Americans have decided that they value the look and feel of their neighborhoods over the opportunity to buy cheap underwear closer to home. One particularly inflammatory issue throughout the country is the heavy auto traffic that a high-volume, low-margin operation like Wal-Mart is destined to attract. "What Wal-Mart has got to understand is that it's not about low prices anymore—it's about what people want in their neighborhoods," contends David Birdsall, a developer who has run into intense opposition in building a half-dozen Wal-Mart stores in Ohio, Indiana, and Michigan. "It's great to get low prices, but, frankly, am I going to wipe out this, this, and this to save 50 cents on a gallon of milk?"[15]

What the various anti–Wal-Mart factions usually share by the end of a fight over a new site is resentment of the company's heavy-handed intrusion into the affairs of local government. Heaven help any community that turns down a Wal-Mart building plan. America's largest corporation does not hesitate to throw its weight around in even the smallest town to get what it wants, even if it means going over the heads of elected officials to wage referendum campaigns juiced by heavy ad spending.

In 2004, when Wal-Mart tried to win support to build a Supercenter on a choice sixty-acre site in Inglewood, a black and Latino community in central Los Angeles, the company succeeded in putting on the ballot a highly technical seventy-one-page referendum designed to "throw out all the local planning laws and make themselves a little Wal-Mart city,"[16] as one critic put it. Despite outspending its opponents by 10 to 1, Wal-Mart's ballot measure was crushed, 61 percent to 39 percent. From Bentonville, the company issued a

defiant statement: "We are disappointed that a small group of Inglewood leaders together with representatives of outside special interests
were able to a convince a majority of Inglewood voters that they don't
deserve the job opportunities and shopping choices that others in the
L.A. area enjoy."[17] Translation: "'The people' want what *we* say they
want." And where does a relentlessly for-profit corporation based in
Arkansas get off demeaning any other party to a Los Angeles political battle as an "outside special interest"?

Like politicians or four-star generals, a Wal-Mart boss never apol-
ogizes. But CEO Scott later came close in acknowledging the errors
of Inglewood. "I think we came across as a bully who would get their
way regardless," Scott said a few days before his L.A. speech. "Our
size causes us, when we do something inappropriate, which is usually
done out of stupidity, to come across as being done out of arrogance.
And people just won't stand arrogance."[18]

Wal-Mart set a new standard of stupidity in the referendum battle
in Flagstaff three months later. One beautiful May morning, Flagstaff's
residents opened their newspapers to find a full-page ad paid for by
Wal-Mart and featuring a 1933 photograph of a mob of Nazi supporters piling books onto a bonfire in Berlin. "Should we let government
tell us what we can read? Of course not," the copy read. "We can read
what we choose because of the limits the Constitution places on government's ability to restrict our freedoms. So why should we allow local
government to limit where we can shop? Or how much of a store's floor
space can be used to sell groceries?"

It's hard to say which was more offensive: Wal-Mart comparing
Flagstaff's elected officials to Nazis or its equating freedom of speech
with the freedom to shop.

In 2004, the University of California at Santa Barbara convened a
gathering of academics who made a persuasive case that Wal-Mart's
aggressively low-cost, low-wage business model has made it "the tem-

plate business for world capitalism," in the words of Nelson Lichtenstein, a labor historian who organized the conference. The enormous
influence that Wal-Mart wields over even other megacorporations is
rooted in part to its mastery of so many business fundamentals (labor
and community relations excepted). In 2005, Wal-Mart ranked fifth
on *Fortune* magazine's annual survey of the American corporations
most admired by other American corporations. Mainly, though, Wal-
Mart coerces emulation. Its utter domination of the U.S. trade in
consumer goods—the world's richest market—leaves many competitors and suppliers alike with no real alternative but to adjust their
business models to conform to Wal-Mart's.

The so-called Wal-Martization of the U.S. economy certainly has
its pluses. In applying relentless pressure on its 61,000 vendors to
make the manufacture and distribution of most everything we consume more cost-effective, it has done more to boost U.S. productivity—a key indicator of the nation's economic vitality—than any other
corporation. An oft-cited study by McKinsey Co. found that a
remarkable one-eighth of the surge in U.S. productivity from 1995 to
1999 can be explained by only two syllables: Wal-Mart.[19] Similarly, in
bringing their prices down to compete with Wal-Mart, rival retailers
radiate the economic benefits of "Every Day Low Prices" throughout
the ground floor of the U.S. economy. The net effect is to suppress
inflation, making every dollar spent in America go further than it
would otherwise.

From 1985 through 2004, Wal-Mart's expansion brought an overall decline of 3.1 percent in consumer prices in America, as measured
by the Consumer Price Index, according to a study that the company
commissioned from Global Insight, a prominent economics forecast-
ing firm. In 2004 alone, Wal-Mart saved U.S. shoppers $263 billion,
or about $895 per person. Even after adjusting for the decline in
workers' incomes also caused by the company's growth, Americans still
came out $118 billion ahead, substantially more even than the $100
billion boost in disposable income that Scott had cited in his speech

in Los Angeles nearly two years before Global Insight released its findings at a Wal-Mart–sponsored economics conference in late 2005.

But what Wal-Mart giveth, it also taketh away. What in an economist's language sounds like a bloodless program of national self-improvement is in fact a brutal, Darwinian struggle spilling blood in every shopping mall and factory. Failure to measure up to the demanding efficiency standards set by Wal-Mart has crippled thousands of businesses—not just corner grocers and family hardware stores, but also the billion-dollar likes of Kmart, Toys 'R' Us, and Winn-Dixie. "The principal strategic question for every American retail and consumer goods manufacturer is 'What's my relationship to Wal-Mart?'" observes Peter J. Solomon, one of Wall Street's top retail experts.[20]

Although Wal-Mart does not gain from putting suppliers out of business, it enfolds them in a bear hug so powerful that it can suffocate them just the same. A classic example is pickle-maker Vlasic Foods, which came to grief agreeing to Wal-Mart's demand for a gallon jar of dills that it could sell for $2.97, or for less than most grocers sell a quart. In no time, Wal-Mart was selling 240,000 jars a week, monopolizing Vlasic's production. The problem was not only that Vlasic made just a penny or two of profit per jar, but also that demand plunged for spears and chips, its most lucrative items. The more Wal-Mart sold, the less Vlasic made. When Vlasic begged Wal-Mart to let it raise the price, Wal-Mart stubbornly refused, threatening to stop carrying all Vlasic products if it discontinued producing the economy jar. Finally, Wal-Mart relented and allowed Vlasic to switch to a half-gallon size priced at $2.79. "The Wal-Mart guy's response was classic," recalled Steve Young, a former Vlasic executive. "He said, 'Well, we've done to pickles what we did to orange juice. We've killed it. We can back off.'" Wal-Mart's reprieve came too late for Vlasic, which filed for bankruptcy protection in 2001.[21]

The biggest category of business cost suppressed by the Wal-Mart Effect is the wages and benefits of the very blue-collar workers who are the company's best customers. Naturally, this painfully ironic impact is most pronounced in Wal-Mart's own industry, retailing. Adjusted for inflation, the wages paid by Wal-Mart have declined by about 35 percent since 1970, about in line with the decline in the real value of the minimum wage over this period. Overall, U.S. retail wages today are only about one-third of those earned by union workers in manufacturing, compared to one-half in 1960, before Wal-Mart began its rise to economic preeminence.

The extreme pricing pressure that Wal-Mart applies to its vendors also hurts industrial workers everywhere by greasing the free-trade skids by which tens of thousands of U.S. manufacturing jobs a year are moving offshore to China and other low-wage countries. Wal-Mart certainly cannot be blamed for the huge wage disparity that exists between the United States and China, where the average industrial worker earns about 40 cents an hour and loosely regulated sweatshops still abound. However, as China's largest corporate trading partner, Wal-Mart has done more than any company in the world to establish the "China price" as the price American suppliers must beat. Consumer goods manufacturers that are unable to deliver the China price to Wal-Mart (and, in many product lines, few can) face three choices: shrink, close, or set up shop in China to exploit all that cheap labor.

By some estimates, more than 80 percent of the 6,000 factories in Wal-Mart's current database of suppliers are located in China and 70 percent of the nongrocery goods it sells today are made in China. Wal-Mart alone accounted for more than 11 percent of the United States' $162 billion trade deficit with China in 2004.[22] "Wal-Mart's growth as an economic force is inseparable from China's rise as a manufacturing giant," concludes Ted C. Fishman, author of *China Inc.* "No company in the world has embraced China's potential more vigorously than Wal-Mart, and no company has been a bigger catalyst in pushing American, European, and Japanese manufacturers to China."[23]

As enormous as Wal-Mart is, it is getting bigger—and fast. At its current pace of growth, it will double in size in the next five years, becoming the first half-trillion-dollar corporation by 2010. It will reach this milestone even sooner if it makes a large acquisition over-seas or if it finally is allowed to enter consumer banking in a big way at home, as it has been lobbying to do. Its main growth vehicle, the Supercenter, combines a full-size supermarket and a regular-size dis-count store under one roof covering 200,000 square feet, or about seventeen football fields. Over the last decade, Wal-Mart has built 1,750 of these colossal combination stores, and the company sees room for at least 4,000 more in the United States alone. This would entail ringing every major city in the country with a suburban fringe of Supercenters situated just a few miles apart.

Wal-Mart acknowledges no theoretical limit to its growth, except perhaps the sum total of humankind's disposable income. In his 2005 annual letter to shareholders, CEO Scott estimated the company's share of the global retail market at a mere 3 percent. "In other words," he added portentously, "about 97 percent of the retail business around the world is not being done at Wal-Mart today." And tomorrow? "Could we be two times larger? Sure," Scott said in 2003. "Could we be three times larger? I think so."[24]

From time to time throughout the modern history of American capitalism, one giant corporation has been elevated to preeminence by the magnitude of its power and the ways in which its exercise excites the hopes and inflames the fears of its age. Standard Oil Co., the Pennsylvania Railroad, the Great Atlantic & Pacific Tea Co., General Motors, IBM, and Microsoft have all filled this standard-bearer role. Today, for better and mostly for worse, the mantle has passed to Wal-Mart, the Bully of Bentonville.

CHAPTER TWO

THEY CALL ME MR. SAM

Fourteen years after Sam Walton's death, he remains an inescapable presence within Wal-Mart's sprawling headquarters in Bentonville. Photographs of the company's late founder are hung by the dozen in lobbies, anterooms, and hallways. Mounted on the wall of each of the seventy-seven rooms where Wal-Mart's buyers negotiate with vendors is Walton's picture, along with placards listing "Sam's Rules for Building a Business." (There are ten of them, just like that other set of commandments.) The keys still hang in the ignition of Walton's last pickup truck, which is on display a short drive from the home office in the Wal-Mart Visitors' Center, along with a replica of his office exactly as it looked on his final day of work. Not since the passing of Mao Zedong has a leader remained as posthumously present as Chairman Sam.

Lee Scott pays homage to Walton constantly, both inside and outside the company—and not just because he was schooled at "Mr. Sam's" knee. Walton's heirs, who still own 40 percent of Wal-Mart's shares, insist on it. "After Dad was gone, we made a real strong commitment to keeping his name and his philosophy in the tops of minds around the company . . ." Chairman Rob Walton, Sam's eldest son, declared in a rare public pronouncement in 2003. "Interestingly, it has gotten even stronger over the years."[1] In effect, Sam Walton doesn't just haunt Wal-Mart headquarters; he still runs the place.

This is not to say that Wal-Mart hasn't evolved in important ways since Sam Walton succumbed to bone cancer in 1992. It was only after his death that the company made its massive push into the grocery business at home and its equally large-scale expansion abroad. However, all of the elements that now define Wal-Mart's business approach and corporate personality—its virtues as well as its increasingly evident faults—were present from the start. Wal-Mart is what Walton made it, and he made it largely in his own image. Although Mr. Sam was more complex a character than he let on, first, last, and always he was an Ozarker. One cannot understand the man—or the world-beating company he begat—without also decoding the Ozarks. Geography is not always destiny, but in Wal-Mart's case it most definitely has been.

Few have traveled farther in the business world without leaving home than Samuel Moore Walton. From the sleepy little Ozarks town of Bentonville in northwest Arkansas, Walton built a penny-pinching backwoods chain of discount stores into America's largest corporation, while amassing a family fortune that currently exceeds $80 billion. Yet he never seriously considered pulling up roots and forsaking the remote Ozarks hill country for the bright lights of Little Rock, St. Louis, or Dallas, much less Chicago, Los Angeles, or New York. That Walton's colossal achievements in capitalism were deeply grounded in the Ozarks seemed paradoxical to most everyone but the man himself. "The best thing we ever did was to hide back there in the hills and eventually build a company that makes folks want to find us," Walton observed late in life. "They get there sometimes with a lot of trepidation and problems, but we like where we are."[2]

Of the thirty-two stores that Walton had opened by the time Wal-Mart Stores first floated its shares on the public market in 1970, twenty-nine were located in the Ozarks, in towns far too insignificant and inaccessible to attract much bigger chains like Sears, Kmart, or Woolco. Going public put Wal-Mart on a path to massive growth but did not immediately blow Walton's hinterlands cover. Wal-Mart was not yet large enough to rank among the country's seventy top discount chains. The minority on Wall Street who were even aware of the company's existence tended to airily dismiss it as "a couturier to the hillbillies." The assessment was accurate as far as it went, but grievously underestimated Walton's ambition and abilities, and the latent power of the Ozarks-centric business model that he was busily devising through trial and error.

The Ozarks, which consist of 50,000 square miles of elevated plateaus and mountains, comprise the only extensive area of rugged topography between the Appalachians and the Rockies. Encompassing all of southern Missouri and northern Arkansas and bits of Oklahoma and Illinois, the Ozarks are roughly the size of Florida. Despite impressive percentage gains over the last three decades, the region's population today is only about 800,000, or one-twentieth of the Sunshine State's— and fully 150,000 of its inhabitants are concentrated in its largest city, Springfield, Missouri. And the Ozarks remain what they have been ever since the dispossession of the Indian: one of the whitest, least ethnically diverse parts of America. As late as 1930, the total black population of the Arkansas Ozarks amounted to fewer than 1,000; more than half of its fifteen counties lacked a single black inhabitant. In Benton County, home to Bentonville, blacks have accounted for less than 1 percent of the population since the Civil War.

For a century or more, the Ozarks were a textbook example of what historians call a "semi-arrested frontier." The area was settled in the 1800s by successive waves of descendants of the English and Scots-Irish Protestants who colonized Virginia and the Carolinas. Few hill-country farmers could afford to own slaves, and the Ozarks' thin soil and clannish social order hardly tempted free blacks after Emancipation. Like most of the South's rural interior, the region was barely touched by the great Catholic and Jewish migration from Southern and Eastern Europe of the late nineteenth and early twentieth centuries. Insulated from the complex, fast-moving central currents of the evolving American experience, the Ozarks become a backwater characterized by poverty, ignorance, intolerance, superstition—and fierce individuality. "The typical Ozarks hillman . . . is almost insanely jealous of his independence and his personal liberty, and will fight to the death in defense of whatever he happens to regard as his rights," the famed Ozarks folklorist Vance Randolph observed in a 1931 book.

For generations, the popular image of the Ozarks veered between two extremes. Periodically, it was romanticized as an unspoiled rural redoubt of a vanishing "wholly American" lifestyle. Muralist Thomas Hart Benton (a grandnephew of the U.S. Senator after whom Bentonville and Benton County were named) dubbed the area "America's Yesterday" in a travel magazine article he wrote in 1934. More often, though, the Ozarks were mocked as America's Dogpatch, a "place where hounds amble along dirt roads, chickens pick for bugs in the yard, and well-to-do families flaunt Sears washing machines on their front porches."[3] The 1930s comic strip "L'il Abner" (set in the fictional Dogpatch) and the hit 1960s television sitcom *The Beverly Hillbillies* poked gentle fun, but the Ozarks were the butt of much nasty commentary, as well. The mere fact that Sam Walton was a native Ozarker meant everything in a region where outsiders were automatically viewed with suspicion, especially "city fellers." Walton's backwoods brethren collectively may have ranked far below average in every national measure of affluence and accomplishment, but the society of the hill country was as exclusive in its way as that of any of America's elite urban enclaves. In the Ozarks, as in medieval Europe, native status was conferred strictly by birthright. A man of Walton's generation could live his entire life in the hills and still be considered a "furriner" by the natives if his father or grandfather was not Ozark-born.

Descended from family with patrilineal roots in the region dating back to 1838, Sam Walton was a true hill-country aristocrat who knew the landscape of the Ozarks intimately. He studied its intricately variegated topography from the air, as a pilot who spent more than two decades scouting new store locations in a little twin-engine plane with his younger brother and fellow pilot, James "Bud" Walton. "I'd get down low, turn my plane up on its side, and fly right over a town," Sam recalled. "Once we had a spot picked out, we'd land, go find out who owned the property, and try to negotiate the deal right then."[4] On his own, Sam logged countless additional air miles keeping tabs on the stores he had planted like so many plasterboard saplings throughout the Ozark hills, often visiting four or five in a day—and surviving many a harrowing landing on backwoods runways. He put in so many miles that on night flights home he could identify the towns in the darkness below by the pattern of their twinkling lights.

Walton perused the Ozarks no less intently on foot, tramping many of its hills and valleys in a relentless lifelong quest for quail. ("He hunted," one of Walton's three sons once remarked, "like Sherman marched through Georgia."[5]) During hunting season, Walton liked to knock off work by three or four o'clock in the afternoon, load his bird dogs into his pickup truck or his two-seat plane, and go off in search of a new patch of backcountry to hunt. Walton was always careful to ask the landowner's permission—often sealing the deal by giving him a box of chocolate-covered cherries—not only because it was the proper, neighborly thing to do, but because it helped drum up business down at the store. "When these farm folks would come to town to shop, they'd naturally do business with that fellow who hunted their land and gave them candy," Walton recalled in the early 1990s. "I still meet folks today who tell me their father recalls me coming out to hunt their land in those days."[6]

Securing scores of long-term property leases throughout the Ozarks was an achievement in its own right, for transacting business in the hill country was difficult, even for a native like Walton. "It is almost impossible for an old-time Ozarker to enter into the simplest business agreement without a long series of debates and hypothetical questions and false starts," Randolph wrote. "Try to buy something from one of them, and it is only with the greatest difficulty that you can get him to put a definite price on it; accept his offer at once and he is terribly 'sot back,' sure that he could have easily obtained at least twice the amount mentioned, and feeling somehow insulted besides!"[7]

Like many native Ozarkers, Walton was sensitive to the slights of outsiders. "Most media folks—and some Wall Street types, too—either thought we were just a bunch of bumpkins selling stocks off the back of a truck, or that we were some kind of fast-buck artists or stock scammers," he complained in his autobiography. For the most part, though, Walton hid his feelings behind a shrug and a smile and did what he could to exploit to his commercial advantage the tendency of city folks to underestimate him and his company. Throughout Wal-Mart's fledgling years, he traveled the country, charming better-established retailers into surrendering their secrets. "He came to my office in New York City and told me he was a country boy from Bentonville, Arkansas," recalled Herbert Fisher, a pioneering discounter. "He asked if I could be of help to him and then he proceeded to write down every idea I presented."[8]

Walton's rube routine took burlesque form in a story known within Wal-Mart as the "Chicken Report." It was based on a presentation that a Wal-Mart executive named Ron Loveless made, with Walton's encouragement, to an unsuspecting audience of Wall Street analysts during the company's annual meeting. "People often ask us how we predict market demand for discount merchandise," Loveless began. "You've heard a lot of numbers today, but there is more to it than that. We raise a good many chickens in Northwest Arkansas and we've come to depend on them for what we call the Loveless Economic Indicator Report. You see, when times are good, you find plenty of dead chickens by the side of the road, ones that have fallen off the truck. But when times are getting lean, people stop and pick up the dead chickens and take 'em home for supper. So in addition to traditional methods, we try to correlate our advance stock orders with the number of dead chickens by the side of the road."

As recounted by Bethany Moreton in her essay "It Came from Bentonville," Loveless then displayed an elaborate series of charts and graphs with Monty Pythonesque aplomb. He explained away one anomalous spike in a trend line as the result of a head-on collision between two chicken trucks near Koziusko, Mississippi, and kept a straight face while showing slides of uniformed "Chicken Patrol" officers inspecting a bird carcass on a two-lane country road. Nobody laughed, a delighted Loveless told Moreton: "The audience sat there nodding and frowning and writing it all down!"[9]

In his maddeningly impersonal autobiography, *Made in America*, Walton had little to say about his forebears other than his parents. What information can be gleaned from census records and other public documents about the first two generations of Waltons to inhabit the Ozarks mostly serves to underscore their ordinariness and their grit. The Waltons were industrious folk who pretty quickly cleaned the dirt from under their fingernails and moved off the farm to do business in town as postmasters, storekeepers, and bankers. Until Sam came along, though, the family produced no truly standout citizens—no mayors, military officers, judges, physicians, or business tycoons.

Sam was named after his paternal grandfather, Samuel W. Walton, who was born in 1848 in Lamine, a small but prosperous Missouri farm community at the northern edge of the Ozarks. Samuel, a farmer's son, prefigured the family's grand destiny in a modest way, opening a little general store in Lamine in 1869. Eleven years later, Samuel's life took a tragic turn when his wife died at age thirty-two giving birth to their seventh child. Samuel closed his store, packed up his children and his belongings, and headed south into the sparsely settled highland interior of the Ozarks. In Webster County, the enterprising Walton created the nucleus of a new town known today as Diggins. Here, deep in the backwoods of the Ozarks, Walton opened his second general store, served as the local postmaster, and also built a thriving lumber wholesaling business.[10]

In Diggins, Walton remarried and fathered three more children. The youngest, Thomas Gibson Walton, would grow up to father America's richest man. However, there was nothing fortuitous about his start. In 1894, forty-eight-year-old Samuel and his young wife died within months of each other, apparently perishing in a flu epidemic. Thomas, who was just two years old, was sent to live with his grandmother in the little Ozarks burg of El Dorado Springs. Years later, he moved to Kingfisher, Oklahoma, where his two older brothers had grown up under the care of one of their Walton uncles. In Kingfisher in 1917, Tom Walton married Nannia Lee Lawrence, the daughter of a well-off farmer. With his father-in-law's help, Tom bought a piece of property and started farming himself.

It was on the farm that Nan gave birth to Samuel Moore Walton on March 29, 1918. "Sammy," as he was known throughout his boyhood, had not yet turned four when his mother gave birth to another boy, James L. Walton, better known as "Bud." Although Sammy and Bud were born in Oklahoma, they were Oklahomans in name only. To their Walton relatives back in Missouri, they were Ozarkers born in temporary exile, it being a peculiarity of Ozark culture that "the children of native parents are native, no matter where they are born."[11]

Standing just five feet five, Tom Walton was a wiry, hard-bitten, handsome bantam rooster of a man who worked hard but fancied himself a wheeler-dealer. "[He] loved to trade, loved to make a deal for just about anything: horses, mules, cattle, houses, farms, cars. Anything," Sam would later recall. "Once he traded our farm in Kingfisher for another one, near Omega, Oklahoma. Another time he traded his wristwatch for a hog. . . . He was the best negotiator I ever ran into."[12] Even so, Tom's attempts at clever dealing never added up to more than a lower-middle-class living for himself and his family. "Dad never had the kind of ambition or confidence to build much of a business on his own, and he didn't believe in taking on debt," Sam wrote in *Made in America.*

The elder Walton succeeded nonetheless in instilling a ferocious work ethic in Sam and Bud. "The secret is work, work, work," Tom once proudly told a journalist. "I taught the boys how to do it."[13] He also imparted to his sons a frugality that verged on the pathological. As one of Tom's longtime acquaintances put it: "He could squeeze a Lincoln until the president cried. I'll bet he had the first 95 cents of the first dollar he ever made."[14]

In 1923, Tom and Nan Walton sold almost everything they owned and headed back to the Ozarks with their two young sons. Officially, the Waltons left because they wanted to assure that their young sons would start school in Springfield, Missouri, a much larger and more educationally advanced place than Kingfisher. Nan, who had dropped out of college to marry, laid great emphasis on education as a vehicle of advancement for her sons. In Sam's own estimation, his outsize ambition was mainly his mother's doing. "Our mother was extremely ambitious for her kids . . ." he recalled. "She just ordained from the beginning that I would go to college and make something of myself."[15]

Tom jumped at the chance to go to work for the bank that William E. Walton, his father's oldest brother, had founded in the 1880s in Butler, a little town along the western edge of the Ozarks. William, who'd married but never had children, groomed one of Tom's half brothers, Jesse B. Walton, to succeed him as president of Walton Trust Company and its affiliate, the Walton Mortgage Company. Jesse hired Tom to open a loan office in Springfield, which was home to various and sundry Waltons. As an adult, Sam's earliest memories would be of Springfield, which is where he not only started school but also moved decisively into the Walton family orbit.

The Waltons hadn't lived in Springfield more than a few years before Tom was transferred to Marshall, a town of 5,000 a bit north of the original Walton family homestead in Lamine. The family continued to move about central Missouri until 1933, when they landed in Columbia, a bustling college town of 30,000 in the Ozark foothills.

Nan insisted on the move, arguing that the Columbia address would help her boys gain admission to the University of Missouri.

Throughout the 1930s, Tom Walton was often on the road, looking to collect on delinquent mortgages from farm families, foreclosing if need be. Sam occasionally accompanied his father, witnessing at close range the deep misery of dispossession that the Great Depression inflicted on rural Missouri. For their part, the Waltons owned no property to lose; they, too, struggled to make ends meet. "We never thought of ourselves as poor, although we certainly didn't have much of what you'd call disposable income lying around, and we did what we could to raise a dollar here and there," Sam recalled. From the age of seven, Sam helped out by selling magazine subscriptions, delivering newspapers, and raising pigeons and rabbits for sale. The Walton household was not a happy one, and money worries were only partly to blame. "The simple truth is that Mother and Dad were two of the most quarrelsome people who ever lived together," Sam recalled in his autobiography.

All through his school years, Sammy Walton was the all-American boy in overdrive. Quiet, handsome, and well-mannered, he was, in fact, a bit of a momma's boy. He cringed at cusswords, slicked his hair unfashionably straight back, and wore sweaters and corduroy pants to elementary schools where most boys wore overalls. But Walton also was an amiable, even-tempered youth who excelled at sports and was effortlessly popular. "People just sort of flickered toward him even when he was young," his Shelbina classmate Everett Orr remembered. "How such a shy guy could become a leader, I just can't understand."[16] At thirteen, Walton became the youngest Eagle Scout in the history of Missouri and validated the honor by diving into a fast-moving river to rescue a drowning classmate. In high school, he was president of his senior class and twice led his team to state championships in football as an undersized (five-foot-nine) but fearless quarterback. "It never occurred to me that I might lose," recalled Walton, who, in fact, never played on the losing side of a football game in his life. "To me, it was almost as if I had a right to win."[17]

In 1937, Walton enrolled at the University of Missouri, majoring in economics. His sports career was over, but he made himself into a big man on the Mizzou campus just the same, shedding the last remnants of his boyhood reserve in what amounted to a continuous—and successful—campaign for president of the senior class. "I learned early on that one of the secrets to campus leadership was the simplest thing of all: speak to people coming down the sidewalk before they speak to you . . ." Walton recalled. "Before long, I probably knew more students than anybody in the university."[18] While waiting on tables, lifeguarding, and working other part-time jobs, Walton joined scores of campus organizations and held a leadership position in most of them, including the Reserve Officer Training Corps. In 1940, the year he graduated with a degree in business, the newspaper of his fraternity teasingly profiled him as "Hustler Walton," noting that he was "one of those rare people who knows every janitor by name."

As an undergrad, Walton had dreamed of going on to the Wharton School of Finance at the University of Pennsylvania, but in the end did not even apply, lacking both the money and the desire to prove himself all over again at an elite Eastern grad school. Although he'd hustled good grades all the way through school, he was neither intellectually inclined nor academically curious. A born salesman and proud of it, Walton started work as a J. C. Penney management trainee in a store in Des Moines, Iowa, just three days after receiving his diploma. James Cash Penney himself visited the store one day and instructed the future mogul in the proper technique of wrapping a package with a minimum of paper and twine. "I loved retail from the very beginning," Walton recalled.[19]

Like many a lifelong love affair, this one was interrupted by war. As a Reserve Officer Training Corps graduate, Walton fully expected to be in the thick of the fighting after the attack on Pearl Harbor put the United States into World War II in late 1941. But because of a relatively minor malformation of the nerves in his heart, he was disqualified from combat and classified for "limited duty." Walton took it hard. For the first and last time in what was an exceptionally well-ordered life, he spun off track. In April 1942, he abruptly left J. C. Penney and headed south to Oklahoma with, as he put it later, "some vague idea of seeing what the oil business was like" as he awaited his inevitable call-up to a stateside Army posting.

Walton never offered a convincing explanation of this odd episode, except to say that he was "down in the dumps" after flunking his Army physical. However, it later came to light that he had been dating a cashier in the same store named Beth Hamquist, in violation of Penney's strict anti-fraternization policy (which Wal-Mart would adopt). Walton maintained that he left Penney's voluntarily, but it's possible that his boss uncovered his transgression and forced him out. By some accounts, Walton had asked Hamquist to marry him, only to change his mind after she accepted. In hightailing it to Oklahoma, it appears that Walton not only was fleeing the brokenhearted Hamquist but also was setting off in pursuit of the woman he ultimately did marry, Helen Robson.

Robson, who also had gone to college in Columbia, hailed from Claremore, a small town eighteen miles from Pryor, where Walton got a job in a big gunpowder factory. Within a few months, they were engaged. "My whole family just fell in love with him," Robson recalled, "and I always said he fell in love as much with my family as he did with me." Sam would be the first Walton to marry into money. Helen's father, Leland S. Robson, was not only wealthy but well-connected—a self-made lawyer, rancher, and banker. Robson, who'd started out as an itinerant peddler of pots and pans, had made Helen and her three older brothers equal partners in his 18,500-acre cattle ranch. Walton was indeed smitten with his future father-in-law, who was everything his own underachieving father was not.

By the time that Walton was called up to active duty as an officer in the Army Intelligence Corps in July 1942, he had "two things settled:

I knew who I wanted to marry and I knew what I wanted to do for a living—retailing." He wed Robson in Claremore during a Valentine's Day furlough in 1943. For three years, Walton helped supervise security at prisoner-of-war camps, aircraft factories, and the like, mostly in California. In any of the sixteen different locations in which he and his bride lived during the war, Walton might have come across the sort of retailing opportunity that would have compelled his return as a civilian. There would have been no better place to start a business at war's end than California, which would be transformed by America's phenomenal postwar boom into the seventh-largest economy in the world. But after Walton was discharged in 1945 with the rank of captain, he went home to the Ozarks.

Left to his own devices, Walton would have joined with a college buddy to buy a Federated department store in St. Louis from Butler Brothers, a large regional retailer that owned the Ben Franklin five-and-dime chain. But Walton needed a loan from his father-in-law to swing the deal, and his wife refused to bless it. "I'll go with you any place you want so long as you don't ask me to live in a big city," Helen told him. "Ten thousand people is enough for me." Walton returned to Butler Brothers and asked if it had anything in a small town. Wearing his Army uniform, he caught a train down to Newport, Arkansas, a cotton town of about 7,000 on the southeast edge of the Ozarks, and in the summer of 1945 put $25,000 down to acquire the floundering local Ben Franklin store. Sam and Helen invested $5,000 and borrowed the rest from Leland Robson.

Ben Franklin had all sorts of policies and procedures that it required its franchisees to follow, which was just as well, because Walton didn't know the first thing about running a variety store. He was a quick study, though, and took himself to graduate school in casing a competing Sterling Store directly across the street that was doing twice the sales volume of the Ben Franklin when Walton bought it. For much of his five years in Newport, Walton worked seven days a week, stopping at ten o'clock on Saturday night and returning first thing Sunday morning, leaving his aggrieved wife to ready their four young children for Sunday school. "It's true that we had less time with Sam after Wal-Mart," Helen said. "But don't get the idea that he wasn't working most of the time before that."[20] Bud Walton, who'd returned from heroic service as a Navy bomber pilot in the Pacific, soon joined Sam in Newport as his assistant manager.

Within two years, Walton had doubled his store's sales and paid off the loan from his father-in-law. When he heard through the grapevine that the Sterling Store was planning to take over the lease of an adjoining grocery store, Walton impulsively blocked his rival's expansion play by talking the grocer's landlord into renting the space to him instead. "I didn't have any idea what I was going to do with it," he later admitted, "but I sure knew I didn't want Sterling to have it." Walton started a department store called Eagle Store, which competed for business with not only Sterling but his own Ben Franklin. After hours, he hustled between his two stores, pushing cartloads of merchandise, hoping that what hadn't sold in one might sell in the other.

Although the Eagle never made much money, the Ben Franklin thrived. According to Walton, it generated more revenue and profit than any other franchise within its six-state Ben Franklin region and was the largest variety store of any sort in Arkansas. Yet Walton's inaugural business venture ended badly. In his eagerness to acquire the Ben Franklin franchise, he'd made the rookie mistake of neglecting to have an automatic option for renewal written into his lease. When the lease expired in 1950, Walton's landlord essentially forced him into leaving. "It was the low point of my business life," Walton recalled. "I felt sick to my stomach."[21] Walton had two choices if he was to continue in retail: take a job in Newport with another merchant or uproot his family and start over in a new town. He left, seething over the unfairness of it all.

Tucked into the northwest corner of Arkansas, Bentonville was not easily accessible by car from Newport. It required an eight-hour drive filled with corkscrew turns leading up and over the Boston Mountains, which contain the highest peaks in the Ozarks. (It was this trip, which Walton made scores of times as he simultaneously wound down his business in Newport while starting up in Bentonville, that convinced him that the Ozarks were best traveled by piloting his own plane.) Bentonville did offer the geographic advantage of proximity to Claremore, still the Robson family's locus, and was ideally situated for quail hunting. As Sam put it, "With Oklahoma, Kansas, Arkansas, and Missouri all coming together right there it gave me easy access to four quail seasons in four states."[22]

With a population of 2,912, Bentonville was the smallest of the many towns that the Waltons scouted throughout northwest Arkansas, and so musty and sedate a place that it gave even Helen pause. "Bentonville really was just a sad-looking country town, even though it had a railroad track to it . . ." she recalled. "I remember I couldn't believe this was where we were going to live."[23] To Sam, the strongest argument in Bentonville's favor was circumstantial: The owner of an antiquated five-and-dime store on the town square was willing to sell to him. Walton had emerged from the Newport misadventure with $55,000 cash, more than enough to swing the deal, but relied on his father-in-law to negotiate the acquisition of Harrison's Variety Store and a lease to an adjoining barbershop. Walton knocked down the wall between the two properties and essentially built a new store, twice as big at 4,000 square feet and entirely up to date. He called it "Walton's 5c & 10c," though he remained a Ben Franklin franchisee.

Walton hit Bentonville like a boulder dropped into a pond from 10,000 feet. He hustled the town just as he'd hustled the University of Missouri campus, operating in perpetual meet-and-greet mode—"He would yell at you from a block away, you know," marveled one of his clerks. "He would just yell at everybody he saw"—and joining every civic group in sight.[24] He simultaneously served as president of the Rotary Club and the Chamber of Commerce and was elected to the city council and the board of the local hospital. He helped organize a

Little League baseball program, sponsored the local high school football team, and even taught Sunday school.

Walton's 5c & 10c offered a wider selection of merchandise at better prices than did Bentonville's other two variety stores, which soon went under. At the time, the typical retail store in America did not allow shoppers direct access to most types of merchandise. Clerks behind counters took goods down from shelves and rang up transactions at cash registers scattered throughout the store. In Bentonville, Walton experimented with the brand-new concept of "self-service." He piled merchandise on island counters and in barrels all around the floor and stationed a handful of cashiers at the front of the store. It worked, but it wasn't pretty. "Elderly ladies would come in and bend way down over into those barrels," recalled Charlie Baum, a Ben Franklin manager who worked with Walton. "I'll never forget this. Sam takes a look, frowns, and says, 'One thing we gotta do, Charlie. We gotta be real strong in lingerie.' Times had been hard, and some of those under things were pretty ragged."[25]

Walton got his start as a storekeeper at a time when country merchants throughout America generally were inclined toward peaceable coexistence. In the typical rural community of the 1940s, there were as many as four or five stores selling groceries, but perhaps just one or two dealing in hardware, appliances, drugs, or general merchandise. On most items, prices tended to be higher in the country than in the cities, where the clustering of chain stores served to intensify competition. The disparity between town and countryside was particularly marked in the Ozarks, where driving to a good-sized, well-provisioned city like Springfield or Columbia simply was not an option for most hill folk. Pre-Walton Bentonville was a classic example, supporting three listless little variety stores where a single robust one would have sufficed. "We found almost no spirit of competition," Walton recalled. "A few retailers were scattered around the square, but each of them had sort of carved out their niche, and that was that."[26]

The Ozarks held scant appeal for major retailers. Nowhere in

America did rural antipathy to the chain store run deeper than farm country spanning the Ozarks and the eastern sections of Oklahoma, Kansas, and Texas. As Yale University's Bethany Moreton has noted, this area "hosted the nation's most vigorous populist protest against huge economic 'combinations'"—as epitomized by Standard Oil at the turn of the twentieth century and by the A&P grocery chain during the 1920s and 1930s. While often tinged with racism and anti-Semitism, the "distrust was often honestly come by," Moreton wrote. "The sections of the country that opposed chains most vociferously had suffered at the hands of northern railroads, eastern banks and industrial monopolies that demonstrably extracted wealth in a semi-colonial relationship with the hinterlands."[27]

If Ozarkers remained skeptical of "foreign-owned" chain stores into the 1940s and 1950s, the feeling was mutual. In a postwar America booming with economic opportunity, why would an A&P or a Woolworth invest in the Ozarks, which were as impoverished as ever and losing population to boot? During the Depression, thousands of families had fled the poverty of the hill country to find work in the big city or in the fields of California. (Route 66, the famed transcontinental highway that carried "Okies" and "Arkies" to the San Joaquin Valley, passes right through the heart of Wal-Mart country.) World War II added to the outflow, and most enlistees never returned. After the war, the dream of the family farm turned into a nightmare in the Ozarks as mechanization transformed the production of milk, eggs, chickens, and other commodities into capital-intensive agribusiness far beyond the means of most mountaineers. By 1960, the population density of the most rural of the Ozark counties had dwindled to thirteen people per square mile, insufficient to support even rudimentary retail commerce. "A symbol for Arkansas in the 1950s was the abandoned rural store . . . its windows barred with iron to deter the rural poor and surrounded by a weed patch," noted one historian.[28]

For Walton, these discouraging demographics were irrelevant. In rooting himself in Bentonville the way he did, he'd left himself a choice between building a business in his backyard or not building a business at all. Walton, a natural promoter as well as a born merchant, overwhelmed the nominal disadvantages of time and place with the sheer fervency of his pursuit of the underserved consumers who still inhabited the Ozarks. They were his people and he knew how to appeal to them. And it helped enormously that he would be left alone in the hills for years to tinker with his business model before having to go up against Sears, J. C. Penney, Kmart, and the numerous other retail chains that dwarfed Wal-Mart in its early years.

For Walton, expanding his business was as natural and as necessary as breathing. In 1952, he opened a second Walton's 5¢ & 10¢ on the square in Fayetteville, which was thirty miles south of Bentonville and the seat of Washington County. After Walton learned to fly in 1957, the pace of his expansion quickened. He opened a few stores on the outskirts of Kansas City, near the Ben Franklin warehouse that supplied him with much of his merchandise. Mainly, though, he hop-scotched from one obscure Ozarks hamlet to another—Springdale, Siloam Springs, Lebanon, Versailles, Waynesville—as fast as his limited supply of capital would carry him. Each of these new outlets was a franchise operation organized as a separate partnership among Sam, his brother, his father—retired now and still living in Columbia—and Helen's brothers, Nick and Frank Robson.

Walton's eureka moment came early in 1962, when he and Bud decided to experiment by building a variety store twice as large as usual in St. Robert, a Missouri Ozarks town even smaller than Bentonville. In short order, this 13,000-square-foot variety store—the first of three Walton Family Centers—became the Waltons' most profitable outlet and the second-highest-grossing Ben Franklin store in the country. Like the fictional Ozarks mountaineer Jed Clampett, who had discovered oil with an errant rifle shot ("up from the ground came a-bubblin' crude"), the brothers Walton had happened on a backwoods bonanza. As Sam put it, "The first big lesson we learned was that there was much

much more business out there in small-town America than anybody, including me, had ever dreamed of."[29]

Even as the new store in St. Robert was opening Walton's eyes to the magnitude of business to be done in rural America, he arrived at a second prophetic insight: the old five-and-dime variety store was history. The fact that all sixteen of the stores Walton owned were variety establishments might have doomed him, too, had he not figured out that discounting was destined to be the next big thing in retailing. Walton flew to Chicago in 1962 to try to persuade Butler Brothers to partner with him in starting a discount chain aimed at rural America. "I was used to franchising, and I liked the mind-set," he recalled.[30] In a presentation to a group of senior Butler Brother executives, the forty-four-year-old Walton radiated enthusiasm, offering the booming start of the new store in St. Robert as evidence of the sales potential of the sort of small towns that Kmart and most other discounters were ignoring. Butler Brothers would have to cut its usual 20 to 25 percent markup of merchandise in half, but he assured the executives that they would more than make up in increased volume what was lost in profit margin. It was a good pitch, but Butler's brain trust turned him down flat.

Next, Walton flew to Dallas to call unannounced on Herbert Gibson, the gruff, self-important founder of Gibson Discount Stores. Gibson was an Ozarker—"a barber from over at Berryville," in Walton's description—who had moved to Dallas in 1935 and made it big as a wholesale distributor of health and beauty aids. Gibson, who was nearly twenty years older than Walton, beat his fellow Ozarker to the punch in recognizing the potential of discounting. In the late 1950s, he launched a regional chain of franchised discount stores under the motto "buy it low, stack it high, sell it cheap." Like Walton, Gibson had defined his retail business as "a country operation" and zeroed in on budget-conscious shoppers in towns of 20,000 to 50,000. In two such cities in Arkansas—Fayetteville and Fort Smith—Gibson had opened discount stores that were taking business from Walton's 5c &

10c's. "We knew we had to act . . ." Walton recalled. "I was probably one of the few out here who understood what he was up to."[31]

Walton, who went to Dallas hoping to buy a discount-store franchise or two, spent five hours fidgeting in a waiting room before he was finally summoned into Gibson's presence. "Do you have one hundred thousand dollars?" Gibson demanded. Walton confessed that he didn't. "Well, we buy in carload lots. Takes a lot of money to do that," Gibson said. "You're not fixed to do business with us. Goodbye."[32]

Walton screwed up his courage and decided to go it alone into discounting. He and Helen pledged their house in Bentonville and everything else they owned as collateral for a bank loan that Sam used to build a 16,000-square-foot store in Rogers, a slightly larger town next to Bentonville. Wal-Mart Discount City opened on July 2, 1962. Racks of clothes hung from metal pipes; most of the other merchandise was stacked on tables. There were three checkout stands, one of which was labeled "Express." The store had twenty-five employees, mostly women, earning just 50 cents to 60 cents an hour. Walton ran newspaper ads promising "Every Day Low Prices in all departments," amounting to as much as 50 percent off the manufacturer's suggested retail price. Much of the merchandise was not first quality, but it all was priced to move. A bottle of Geritol, regularly $1.19, was marked down to 97 cents; a Wilson baseball mitt, listed at $10.80, went for $5.97; a Sunbeam iron, available elsewhere at $17.95, was $11.88.

Wal-Mart No. 1 did well, but not as well as that Walton Family Center in St. Robert. Hedging his bet on discounting, Walton next opened two more family centers, one in Bentonville and another in Berryville (no doubt intended as a stick in the eye of local favorite son Herb Gibson). In 1964, Walton added a second Wal-Mart, putting it in Harrison, a little mountain town eighty miles east of Bentonville, not far from the future site of the ill-fated Dogpatch U.S.A. amusement park. The Harrison store survived an opening day straight out of "L'il Abner." Walton put a donkey ride in the parking lot and a huge stack of bargain-priced watermelons on the sidewalk. The watermelons popped in the heat and the juice flowed into the parking lot, where it intermingled with donkey excrement to form a foul mixture that shoppers tracked all over Walton's floor. "It was the worst retail store I had ever seen," recalled David Glass, an ambitious young discount-drugstore executive who was weighing a job offer from Walton and had driven down from Springfield to check him out. "He was a nice fellow, but I wrote him off."[33]

The Harrison opening-day fiasco did no long-term damage to the store's prospects or to Walton's relationship with Glass, a future Wal-Mart CEO. Furthermore, it illustrated one of Walton's great strengths as a merchant: a flair for down-home retail showmanship that offered Ozarkers relief from drudgery along with bargain buys. "We tried literally to create a carnival atmosphere in our stores," he recalled. "We'd have bands and little circuses in our parking lots to get folks to those sales. We'd have plate drops, where we'd write the names of prizes on paper plates and sail them off the roof of the stores. . . . At store openings, we'd stand on the service counters and give away boxes of candy to the customers who had traveled the farthest to get there. As long as it was fun, we'd try it."[34]

Although Walton added a few more variety stores in the coming years, he decisively shifted his focus to discounting in the mid-1960s. He opened another Wal-Mart store in 1965, four more in 1966–67, and five apiece in 1968 and 1969. The next year, Walton combined his variety and discount stores into a publicly traded company called Wal-Mart Stores, which started with eighteen discount stores and fourteen variety stores. Over the next five years, he phased out the variety operation entirely, closing down some stores and converting others into Wal-Marts. Meanwhile, Ben Franklin and other variety chains failed to follow suit, sealing their doom.

CHEERLEADER-IN-CHIEF

The sun was still an hour from rising in Bentonville when Sam Walton lifted his twin-prop Cessna off the runway and headed east. About 7:00 he was in Memphis, Tennessee, peering through the front window of Wal-Mart store No. 950, which was not set to open for another hour. Walton took his microcassette recorder from the breast pocket of his plaid blazer and rapped gently on the store's front window. He was wearing the standard Wal-Mart badge, with his first name in capital letters, and his ever-present Wal-Mart mesh ball cap. The employee who looked up and saw Walton through the plate glass recognized him instantly and rushed to unlock the door.

"Good mornin', Mr. Sam, welcome to Memphis."

"Good mornin', Doug, great to be here," Walton replied. "I want to walk around a little bit, and then we'll get everybody up front. But I'd like to get all your department heads and assistant managers up here in the snack bar, and I'd like to see your P&L

and your merchandising statements, and I want to see your thirty-, sixty-, and ninety-day plans, all right?"

As Doug rushed off to do the boss's bidding, Walton started strolling through the store, eventually arriving at the pharmacy. "Hello, Georgie," he said. "I like this Equate Baby Oil here for $1.54. I think that's a real winner."

"That's my VPI," Georgie replied. (VPI stands for volume-producing item, a gimmick Walton had devised years before to boost sales and help inculcate his merchandising philosophy in employees. The idea is that every store is filled with scores of obscure items that will fly off the shelves if shrewdly and energetically promoted. Each department manager picks a VPI, and whoever generates the biggest sales wins a bit of cash.)

Walton took out his tape recorder. "I'm here in Memphis at store 950, and Georgie has done a real fine thing with this end-cap display of Equate Baby Oil. I'd like to try this everywhere," he said, causing Georgie to blush a deep pink.

A manager rushed up with an employee in tow. "Mr. Walton, I want you to meet Renee," he said. "She runs one of the top pet departments in the country."

"Well, Renee, bless your heart," Walton said. "What percentage of the store [total sales] are you doing?"

"Last year it was 3.1 percent," Renee said. "But this year I'm trying for 3.3 percent."

"Well, Renee, that's amazing. You know, our average pet department only does about 2.4 percent. Keep up the great work."

Walton strode over to a cashier's stand and picked up a speakerphone and, without bothering to identify himself, summoned everyone to the front of the store. Within minutes, the entire staff had coalesced around him. Walton invited them to sit while he dropped to one knee, like a football coach in chalk-talk mode.

"I thank you," Walton said. "The company is so proud of you, we can't hardly stand it. On top of everything else, you went through the trauma of remodeling and still came through with 0.8 percent shrinkage." (Shrinkage refers to loss of inventory due to customer or employee theft. Wal-Mart pays a bonus to stores that keep shrinkage below a certain threshold. Each of these associates recently had received a check for several hundred dollars.)

"But you know, that confounded Kmart is getting better, and so is Target. So what's our challenge? Customer service, that's right. Are you thinking about doing those extra little things? Are you lookin' the customer in the eye and offering to help? You know, you're the real reason for Wal-Mart's success. If you don't care about your store and your customers, it won't work. They like the quality and they like the attitude here."

Walton asked, "How many of you own Wal-Mart stock?" Most everyone put a hand up. "Well, I hope you realize we're just getting started," he said. "But we've got to continue to improve. You're up over 8 percent [in sales for the year] at this store. I wonder if you can continue. We'd like to see 10 percent."

Walton scrambled to his feet and closed by leading the group in the call-and-response company cheer. "Give me a W," he shouted. "W," came the thunderous response. "Give me an A." And so on through T. He called the hyphen "a squiggly" and crouched low and twisted his hips back and forth as he called it out.

Walton followed the spelling drill by shouting, "Whose Wal-Mart is it?"

The response came fast and loud: "It's my Wal-Mart."

Next followed a question beloved by high school and college coaches everywhere: "Who's number one?"

"The customer! Always! Umph!"[1]

CHAPTER THREE

ROCKEFELLER OF THE OZARKS

W hen Bentonville staged a Sam and Helen Walton Appreciation Day in 1983, Ozarkers from miles around gathered in the town square to celebrate one of their own, a man who may have piled up hundreds of millions of dollars in the bank but still drove an old Chevy with canine teeth marks on its padded steering wheel and ordered the barbecued chicken every Friday night at Fred's Hickory Inn. "There's an expression in Arkansas that I had never heard before: 'Common as anybody,'" recalled Fran Pickens, a longtime friend of the Waltons who'd moved to Arkansas from Texas. "That's what they all said about Sam, and that's the greatest compliment the country folks can pay you."[1] Toward the end of the hometown celebration in his honor, Walton returned the compliment from a reviewing stand set up in Bentonville's town square across from the 5¢ & 10¢ store he'd opened in 1950. "Y'all are real good," he somewhat abashedly told the crowd. "We couldn't have done it without your support and without your buying a little merchandise from that old five-and-dime."[2]

Sam Walton may have been as unpretentious and down home a

man as ever kissed a pig, but he was hardly common as a business-man. Fascinated by the minutiae of in-store merchandising, he knew in the most fine-grained way what made one product sell and not another. A prime example of what is known in the retail trade as an "item man," Walton loved to recount his triumphs with ladies' panties ("two-barred, tricot satin panties with an elastic waist," to be precise), Moon Pies, Bedmate mattress pads, and the like. Walton was just as attentive to the demand side of the equation: the customer. "He'd always talk to us about how important it was to talk to the customers about their chickens, their pigs, their cows, their kids," said Charlie Cate, one of Walton's first clerks.[3] Walton was a consummate merchant who knew his customers' wants and needs as well as he knew his own and was utterly devoted to satisfying them.

However, the creative flair that Walton displayed as a merchandiser did not extend to corporate strategy and management. Wal-Mart did not pioneer self-service, deep-discount pricing, warehouse club stores, big-box superstores, or any of the other retailing concepts that it came to dominate and epitomize. Even the name Wal-Mart was somebody else's contribution.[4] The one big, seminal idea that Walton could call his own—that there was a whole lot more business to be done, at a price, in rural America than anybody thought—was not a thesis he set about proving but a realization that had dawned gradually, after years of grinding effort to make the most of Wal-Mart's humble founding circumstances.

Walton may not have been a particularly creative thinker, but he was a relentlessly diligent student of the retailing scene in America. He read the trade press voraciously and walked the aisles of hundreds of variety stores in the 1940s and 1950s, interrupting many a family road trip to check out a Newberry, Woolworth, Kress, or T.G. & Y glimpsed from the driver's seat. When Walton read about two Ben Franklin stores that had eliminated most of their clerk positions to experiment with something called self-service, he jumped on an overnight bus to Minnesota to investigate in person. He insisted that his managers be as familiar with the offerings of competing stores as with their own, even if it meant rummaging in garbage bins after hours to find price tags and invoices.

Sam Walton adopted the innovations of other merchants so quickly and so emphatically that he effectively made them his own—and usually improved them in the process. He saw no shame in his voracious "borrowing"; he happily gave credit wherever credit was due. "If [a competitor] had something good, we copied it," he acknowledged.[5] Walton's object was not to win prizes for originality, but to attract business to his stores—often by taking it away from those very competitors whose ideas large and small he had so shamelessly lifted.

Walton did not attract much national attention outside the retail trade until 1982, when his name popped up at number seventeen on *Forbes* magazine's first list of the 400 richest Americans. "I could kick your butt for ever running that list!" Walton complained to *Forbes*, which only added to his mortification by publishing his rejoinder. By 1985, Wal-Mart's soaring stock value had elevated Bentonville's hometown hero past oil heir Gordon Getty and into the number-one ranking on the *Forbes* list, with a fortune estimated at $2.8 billion. Walton bristled at what he took to be the condescending tone of much of the coverage of his achievement, complaining that "the media usually portrayed me as a really cheap, eccentric recluse, sort of a hillbilly who more or less slept with his dogs in spite of having billions of dollars stashed away in a cave."[6]

In fact, most billionaires would have killed for Walton's press clips. He came across not as a bumpkin weirdo but as a plainspoken man so deeply rooted in the verities and virtues of a bygone America that he seemed not only admirable but also mysterious. In a country obsessed by getting and spending, how was it that the richest American showed so little interest in the luxury and status that money buys? If anything, the news media did Walton a favor. In wearing out the thesaurus in search of synonyms for "folksy" and "unpretentious," the press skipped lightly over the issue of how he'd made all that money, leaving Walton free to credibly present himself as a homespun embodiment of the American dream. "Ours is a story about the kinds of traditional principles that made America great in the first place . . ." he wrote in his foreword to *Made in America*. "More than anything it proves there's absolutely no limit to what plain, ordinary working people can accomplish if they're given the opportunity and the encouragement and the incentive to do their best."[7]

People have compared Wal-Mart's founder to all sorts of archetypal Americans, from Horatio Alger and P. T. Barnum to James Cash Penney and football coach Tom Landry. One writer even likened him to Benjamin Franklin, with whom he was said to share "the common touch to an uncommon degree," among other traits.[8] Above all, though, Walton was an implacably driven business-builder. Wal-Mart was not the happy accident of virtue colliding with opportunity, but a product of vaulting ambition and Herculean effort. In the ruthlessness with which Walton sought and exploited competitive advantage and in the boundlessness of his ambition to dominate an industry, Walton is best compared to John D. Rockefeller, the founder of Standard Oil Co. Like Rockefeller, Walton built a company that defined its era and changed the way business was done in America as much through sheer bullying force as through the inspirational power of its example.

Walton and Rockefeller also were personally alike to a surprising degree. Each man was the product of a rural upbringing shadowed by chronic money worries; each had an almost pathological frugality seared into his soul as a result. Like Walton, Rockefeller lived far below his means while shunning high society and ostentation in all its forms. His wife frequently had to remind him to buy a new suit when his current one got too shiny; Walton's business attire (and everything else he wore) came off the rack at Wal-Mart. Walton and Rockefeller both were early-rising, abstemious teetotalers who married once and for life, affirming Flaubert's famous line about a character in *Madame*

Bovary: "To be fiercely revolutionary in business, he needed to be utterly conventional at home."

In some ways, though, Walton suffered by comparison to Rockefeller. The Standard Oil chief was a pious and committed Baptist "drawn to the church, not as some nagging duty but as something deeply refreshing to the soul," according to biographer Ron Chernow.[9] Walton, too, was reared a Christian, but he was not a true believer. Walton was a Methodist until he and his wife moved to Newport, where, for purely circumstantial reasons, he joined the Presbyterian congregation. For Walton, religious practice was a vehicle of secular advancement; he attended church every Sunday for the same basic reason he went to Chamber of Commerce meetings every Wednesday. "Church is an important part of society, especially in small towns," he philosophized. "Whether it's the contacts and associations you make, or the contributions you might make toward helping other folks, it all sort of ties in together."[10]

Long before Rockefeller founded Standard Oil and got rich, he scrupulously honored the obligations of Christian charity by donating a significant portion of his income every week. At once America's greediest and most philanthropic man, Rockefeller gave of his time as generously as his money—and not merely as a donor but also as a founder of great educational and social institutions. Walton was as averse to giving money away as to spending it on himself. He held tight to every share of Wal-Mart stock he ever owned and made little use of his vast fortune beyond securing his family's control of the company. To be fair, in his later years Walton did redirect a portion of the vast flow of dividend income from his Wal-Mart stock into philanthropy, but the sums he gave amounted to a minute fraction of the Walton family's net worth and were narrowly concentrated in northwest Arkansas.

Rockefeller, in Chernow's estimation, "derived a glandular pleasure from work and never found it cheerless drudgery"[11]; yet in his mid-thirties he installed a telegraph at home so he could leave the office at lunchtime several afternoons a week. He retired from Standard Oil altogether when he was just fifty-eight years old. Walton, father to three sons and a daughter, continually tested the limits of the Protestant work ethic as Wal-Mart grew and grew. For most of his working life, he started work at 4:30 in the morning, except on Saturdays, when he was at his desk by 2:00 or 3:00 A.M. to prepare for the weekly management meeting that he insisted on holding when most of his subordinates would have rather been tending their gardens or coaching Little League. "His idea of coming home was to have dinner, and come in to sit down, and read and read and read. It was difficult," Helen Walton acknowledged. "I tried to make it so the children wouldn't miss their dad."[12]

Yet Walton was celebrated as "an American folk hero" while Rockefeller was reviled, in President Theodore Roosevelt's resonant phrase, as "a great malefactor of wealth." The disparate eras in which the two moguls lived had a lot to do with it. Rockefeller caught the brunt of the great popular backlash against the egregious corporate abuses of the Gilded Age, while Walton came to the fore at a time when big business was hailed as the munificent source of vast stock-market wealth bestowed on the middle-class masses. Also, Walton was simply much more likable than Rockefeller, who was no less charismatic than Wal-Mart's chief but who progressively walled off his private self by "train(ing) his face to be a stony mask" and adopting "the soundless movements and modulated voice of an undertaker."[13]

Most important, Rockefeller and Walton took opposite approaches to their shared goal of market domination. An industrial virtuoso, Rockefeller spun out organizational structures and commercial arrangements of staggering complexity. Standard Oil's creator was an ingenious administrator who did as much as anyone to pioneer the form of the modern corporation even as he concocted countless devious schemes to advance his self-interest at the expense of free and open competition. By contrast, there was nothing nefarious about

Walton, who did business with all the subtlety of a fullback hitting a hole off tackle. Relishing the sort of head-on competition that Rockefeller went to great conniving lengths to avoid, Walton created a business model that was no less brilliant in its contrarian simplicity.

Utimately, it was Walton's unshakable belief in cut-rate pricing that defined him as a merchant and Wal-Mart as a company. Most retailers price to demand. But the notion of charging whatever the traffic would bear was alien to Walton, in part because he understood that his fellow Ozarkers were chronically pinched. Clarence Leis, an early Walt-Mart store manager, was flummoxed at first by the boss's unconventional approach: "Merchandise would come in and we would just lay it down on the floor and get out the invoice. Sam wouldn't let us hedge on a price at all," Leis recalled. "Say the list price was $1.98, but we had only paid 50 cents. Initially, I would say, 'Well, it's originally $1.98, so why don't we sell it for $1.25?' and he'd say, 'No, we paid 50 cents for it. Mark it up 30% [to 65 cents], and that's it.'" Walton routinely would forgo a markup altogether and price an item at or below cost to beat a competitor's price. "What we were obsessed with was keeping our prices below everybody else's," he recalled. "Our dedication to that idea was total."[14]

Pricing to cost would have ruined most merchants (and later did destroy many a retailer that tried to compete with Wal-Mart). However, Walton was a discounter by temperament long before he officially adopted discounting as a strategy. The deprivations and hard work of his youth had left him obsessively mindful of the value not merely of a dollar but of each of its components. "When a penny is lying out there on the street, how many people would go out there and pick it up? I'll bet I would. And I know Sam would," Bud Walton declared at a time when he and Sam both measured their net worth in nine figures.[15] Rockefeller was famous for passing out newly minted currency to children. Walton was famous for constantly cadging cash from friends and employees. William Enfield, a county judge who was Walton's oldest friend in Bentonville, took to carrying a roll of dimes when he traveled with Walton. "Every time we'd land some-where, Sam wanted to call back to his office to see how things were going. He never had any money for the phone," Enfield said. "He's always broke."[16]

Wal-Mart could underprice its competitors and still enjoy superior profit margins only because Walton instilled a fanatical devotion to cost control in his company as thoroughly and enduringly as if it were effected through DNA transfer. Walton's aversion to spending more than $1 per square foot for leased space caused him to put Wal-Mart No. 8 in Morrilton, Arkansas, into a defunct Coca-Cola bottling plant outfitted with used fixtures strung by baling wire from the ceiling. Walton decreed that the expenses of the buying trips he and his managers made should never exceed 1 percent of the value of goods purchased, which, in a place like New York or Chicago, meant doing without cabs and crowding three or four to a room in budget-priced hotels and working from six in the morning until midnight to keep the trip as short as possible. Walton once pitched a fit when he returned to Bentonville from a trip to find that carpeting—which he considered a damnable extravagance—had been installed in Wal-Mart's home office.

Walton was equally relentless in his penny-pinching when it came to workers' wages. When Charlie Baum was made manager of Walton's Fayetteville store in 1955, he'd been appalled to learn that the members of his almost entirely female labor force were making just 50 cents an hour. Baum took it upon himself to give everyone a raise to 75 cents—the federal minimum wage at the time—and soon got a telephone call from Walton, who told him that the maximum raise allowable was a nickel an hour. Baum, a favorite of Walton's, ignored the boss and stayed with 75 cents an hour "because those girls were earning it," as he put it.[17] (In 1956, Uncle Sam hiked the minimum wage to $1, putting Wal-Mart again below par.)

For more than a decade, Walton took questionable advantage of an exemption in federal law that allowed small businesses to pay less-than-minimum wages. In the late 1950s, the U.S. Department of

Labor finally ruled that Walton's enterprise was too big to qualify for exemption and ordered him to take his employees' salaries up to the federal minimum. Walton fought the order in court for as long as he could, arguing that because each of his stores was organized as a separate entity on paper, his business was small enough to deserve exemption. He lost, and the federal minimum wage became the new maximum wage at Wal-Mart well into the 1980s.

Surely, no mogul of equal stature has ever romanced his workers as ardently as did Sam Walton. He spent the larger half of every workweek out among them, improvising merrily as he flew from town to town, usually accompanied only by his favorite bird dog, Ol' Roy. Field visits by CEOs tend to be stilted, nervous-making affairs tolerated at best by workers afraid of doing or saying the wrong thing. But Walton's visits were joyous, even raucous occasions. A reporter who accompanied Walton on a trip marveled that when he announced his presence over the public address system workers began to "shriek as if Elvis Presley had risen from the dead."[18]

Walton's brilliance as an employee motivator was much envied by his CEO peers, most of whom would never have dreamed of leading a corporate cheer or, for that matter, donning a grass skirt and doing a hula down Wall Street, as Walton did in 1984 to settle a wager. The fun and games were critical to Wal-Mart's success, for it was Walton's incandescent common touch that reconciled the contradiction at the heart of the company's approach to the labor-intensive enterprise of retailing. That is, Wal-Mart's business model worked well only if its hourly workers were both poorly paid and highly inspired—a combination often found among inner-city public school teachers or disaster-relief volunteers but exceedingly rare in the world of big business.

Walton's success in building a company in his own can-do, rah-rah image began with the selectivity in hiring facilitated by the stunted labor market of the Ozarks. The postwar decline of row-crop agriculture and a simultaneous curtailment of the regional forest products industry created a glut of unskilled labor. In the 1950s and 1960s, poultry processors, men's shirt makers, and other non-union, low-wage manufacturers built new factories that sopped up some of the surplus, mainly by hiring women who left the farm to bring in sorely needed income for their families.

Sam and Helen, who often helped with the screening of job candidates in the early years, wanted employees who conformed to their image of Wal-Mart as the epitome of "small-town friendly"—that is, cheerful, presentable, industrious, and devout, in every sense. "We make no bones about the fact that we believe in God, that we think everybody should," declared Jack Shewmaker, an Ozarker who joined Wal-Mart in 1970 and later became its president.[19] Walton artfully spun the Christian fundamentalism prevalent in the Ozarks—known to some as "the buckle on the Bible Belt"—into a corporate culture infused with the virtues of devotion and self-sacrifice. "Wal-Mart publications are full of stories of hard-pressed associates, once down on their luck, who find redemption, economic and spiritual, through dedication to the company," noted an historian who has studied the company. "Selfless service to the customer, the community, and Wal-Mart will soon reap its own reward."[20]

A high school diploma was optional at Wal-Mart, but a college degree was an obstacle to employment in the company's formative years. The handful of university graduates who did land jobs "had a heck of a time fitting in at first and could probably tell some real horror stories," Walton acknowledged.[21] Walton, a college man himself, tried to pass off the company's aversion to the well-educated as a "tremendous prejudice" of his store managers. The deeper reality was that he indulged the traditional anti-intellectualism of the Ozarks, where the one-room schoolhouse predominated into the 1950s and the school year traditionally was six months long at most because children were needed to help with the spring planting and the fall harvest. Poor, uneducated, pious country folk who "came across the Red River barefooted and hunting a job," as one early Wal-Mart applicant described himself, were more likely than college grads to accept poverty-level wages and still find inspiration in Walton's constant exhortations to put on a happy face while moving the merchandise.

The Wal-Mart store replicated the division of labor found on the Ozarks farm: "dozens of waged women in smocks, overseen by a salaried store manager in a tie."[22] Often, the manager had been trained by some of the very female employees he now bossed. Rare was the woman who rose above department manager, an hourly position that served as a springboard for many a less experienced male co-worker. Early editions of *Wal-Mart World*, the company newsletter for employees, featured photographs of boys a few years out of high school presenting service pins to women who could be their mothers or even their grandmothers. Judging by the smiles all around, "the ladies" seemed to be content working for Walton even so.

Wal-Mart's early labor force also mirrored the Ozarks in its racial homogeneity, which is to say that it was almost entirely white. The first decade and a half of Walton's retailing career coincided with the last, heaving gasp of de facto segregation in Arkansas. In Little Rock, the state capital, the "White" and "Colored" signs weren't removed from drinking fountains until the early 1950s.

Even so, many historians contend that integration aroused less hostility in Arkansas than in Deep South states like Alabama or Mississippi. As one put it, "Nearly all white Arkansans were committed to white supremacy by habit or conviction, but few were extremists."[23]

There is no reason to think that Sam Walton was any more or less progressive in his racial attitudes than were his peers. He does not appear to have been politically active on either side of the racial divide, and had nothing to say on the integration issue in his autobiography even in passing. Walton's silence was understandable. He was a businessman, not a reformer, and the racial agitation of the civil rights era made it increasingly difficult for Arkansas merchants to simultaneously please both a white and a black clientele. In the Ozarks, it was easy: There were no black customers. But as Walton expanded into the racially heterogeneous towns of southern Arkansas in the 1970s, he walked a fine line between courting the segregationist dollar and honoring the strictures of the U.S. Civil Rights Act of 1964.

Walton did hire black workers, but mostly for behind-the-scenes jobs as stockers or janitors. In Magnolia, a predominantly black cotton town in southern Arkansas, there were only a half-dozen black workers allowed on the floor of Wal-Mart No. 83, according to Austin Teutsch, a white Arkansan who worked in the store for a time in the 1970s and later wrote a generally admiring biography of Walton. "Walton would hire a black man or woman and put that person on the floor as a sales trainee with duties to stock the shelves," Teutsch recalled. "They were instructed to wait on a black customer and leave the white customer to the white clerk. If there wasn't a white clerk present, they should wait until the white customer asked for assistance. Walton allowed the white customer to select his clerk, knowing full well many of the citizens wouldn't ask for, much less buy, a garment from a black clerk."[24]

In sum, Walton built a business by hiring less talented and less ambitious versions of himself, and he did not want any labor union coming in and messing up a good thing. The traditional Southern aversion to labor collectivism was especially strong in Arkansas, which in 1944 became the first state to impede union organizing by enacting a right-to-work law. Hatred of unions was virtually a birthright in the Ozarks, where the natives were so protective of their independence (and so suspicious of one another) that they were loath to join forces even to build roads or cooperatively market farm products.

Organized labor took a first run at Walton in 1970, when the Retail Clerks tried to sign up workers in a newly opened store in the Ozarks burg of Mexico, Missouri. It was a halfhearted attempt at best, but Walton sounded a red alert and called in John E. Tate, one of America's foremost union-busting lawyers. Tate easily repulsed the Retail Clerks in Mexico and also prevailed in a brief subsequent skirmish down the road in the town of Clinton. Walton was so relieved and impressed with Tate that he appointed him to Wal-Mart's executive committee and its board of directors. However, this battle-hardened lawyer cut short the victory celebration by advising his client that Wal-Mart would remain an irresistible target for organizing drives unless he changed his attitude. "I told him, 'You can approach this one of two ways,'" Tate recalled. "'Hold people down, and pay me or some other lawyer to make it work. Or devote time and attention to proving to people that you care.'"[25]

Helen Walton had been saying much the same thing for years, but now, suddenly, the message got through. By his own account, Walton underwent a kind of Ozark version of the conversion on the Road to Damascus that inspired him to grant workers the status of partners. "I would love to tell you that from the very beginning we always paid our employees better than anyone else paid theirs, and treated them as equals. I would love to tell you all that, but unfortunately, none of that would be true," Walton wrote in *Made in America*. "In the beginning, I was so chintzy I really didn't pay my employees very well. . . . It wasn't that I was intentionally heartless," continued Walton, now in full breast-beating mode. "I was so obsessed with turning in a profit margin of 6 percent or higher that I ignored some of the basic needs of our people, and I feel bad about it."[26]

In truth, Walton never ceased being margin-obsessed or chintzy, in the sense of continuing to pay the lowest possible hourly wages to store workers. However, in the early 1970s he did cut the rank and file in on some of the financial incentives formerly reserved for managers, including a retirement plan funded by profit sharing, bonus programs tied to a store's financial results, and the right to buy shares in the company at a 15 percent discount to their market price. The company invested virtually all of the profit-sharing money that it held in trust for workers in Wal-Mart stock, a self-serving approach that greatly benefited employees just the same. The meteoric rise of Wal-Mart shares throughout the 1970s and 1980s created hefty six- and even seven-figure retirement accounts for hourly employees who persisted in their low-wage servitude.[27] A down-home quote from a fanatically loyal millionaire cashier or home-office secretary became a staple of the many admiring news stories about Wal-Mart.

Shortly after Tate knocked the scales from his eyes, Walton also instituted the "We Care" program, which assured even the lowliest worker the right to take a grievance all the way up the corporate ladder to the top if need be, without fear of retribution from a supervisor. Walton also instructed his managers to open the books to workers and regularly disclose all the key measures of their particular store's performance, including profits. Underscoring Wal-Mart's new egalitarianism, Mr. Sam decreed that employees henceforth were to be called "associates," a term that he lifted from J. C. Penney Co. "Because you are our partner," Walton told his associates, "we have an open door, and we listen to you, and together we can work out our problems."[28]

Although Walton got an earful during his store visits, he also encouraged associates to telephone him if need be, or even to show up on his doorstep in Bentonville unannounced. His door really was open and so was his mind—his implacable opposition to collective bargaining aside. He would not hesitate to rebuke or fire a manager who disrespected a worker. A clerk in Texas once telephoned Walton in Bentonville after his store manager humiliated him by peremptorily ordering him to stop what he was doing and remove a piece of paper from the floor. Walton told the clerk to mark the spot with tape. The next day, Walton flew to Texas and invited the manager, who was new to Wal-Mart, to join him on a walk-around. When they came to the telltale bit of tape, Walton laid a crumpled sheet of paper atop it and sarcastically demonstrated the proper removal technique by picking it up himself. He then took the manager out behind the store and fired him. Reports of this and other instances of Walton's intervention on behalf of persecuted associates reverberated far and wide through Wal-Mart, burnishing Mr. Sam's populist credentials.

Even so, the bigger the company grew, the harder it was for Walton to sustain even the semblance of a personal relationship with tens of thousands of workers scattered over a few dozen states. He maintained a manic schedule of store tours, but also devised various inspirational gimmicks that did not require his presence. The most notable was the Wal-Mart cheer, which workers in every store were required to perform at the start of every shift. It was introduced in 1975, after Walton returned from a trip to South Korea, where he'd witnessed factory workers doing morning calisthenics punctuated by mass chanting of their employer's name. Walton also cooked up "Sam's Pledge" to encourage compliance with "The Ten-Foot Rule." The pledge varied in the recitation, but usually went something like this: "From this day forward, I solemnly promise and declare that every customer that comes within ten feet of me, I will smile, look them in the eye, and greet them. So help me Sam!"[29]

Shrewdly, Walton softened the Orwellian edge of all this mandatory good cheer by also sanctioning goofiness in the vein of his own grass-skirted hula down Wall Street. "We're constantly doing crazy things to capture the attention of our folks and lead them to think of surprises of their own," he noted in his autobiography.[30] On a dare, a male Wal-Mart vice president put on pink tights and a blond wig and rode a white horse around the town square in Bentonville. Unlike Walton, David Glass was a reserved man, but he was shamed into putting on overalls and a straw hat and riding a donkey in mock punishment for his candid comments to a reporter about the opening-day fiasco in Harrison. Numerous stores staged pig-kissing, poetry-reading, Moon Pie-eating, or baby-serenading contests, as well as women's fashion shows "using ugly old men from the stores as models," as Walton put it.

To Walton, these wholesome hijinks were not just a technique of employee motivation but also a defiant affirmation of Wal-Mart's small-town roots, of its Ozark soul. "We know that our antics—our company cheers or our songs or my hula—can sometimes be pretty corny, or hokey," he declared. "We couldn't care less."[31]

Although Wal-Mart paid its hourly workers less than did the competition, it was more generous in rewarding store managers than were most discount chains. Because managers received a bonus pegged to store profits, there was no theoretical limit to their earnings. By the 1980s, the manager of a thriving store could take home as much as $175,000 to $200,000 a year, which went a long way in a small town. This was good money, but not easy money; running a Wal-Mart store was a burnout job from the company's earliest days.

With few exceptions, managers were required to work through two, eight-hour shifts six days a week and to be on emergency call twenty-four hours a day. Bentonville set ambitious sales and profit goals for each store, and a manager could not fall short many times and expect to keep his job (though demotion was more likely than dismissal). A manager also had to walk a fine line between pushing workers to be more productive and antagonizing them to the point where they started burning up the phone lines to the home office. If disgruntled workers started muttering about the need for a union, headquarters was inclined to axe the store manager first and ask questions later.

In Wal-Mart's formative years, many a clerk or stock boy worked his way up through the ranks to store manager without ever leaving his hometown. This tended to happen fast if he had even a modicum of talent and drive, because most of his colleagues—all of the women, that is—were effectively disqualified from rising above department manager. But as Wal-Mart became a sizable company, it professionalized store management in a way that not only blocked the traditional path upward but also created a two-tier caste system consisting of an elite of highly mobile, overwhelmingly male managers and an underclass of dead-ended hourly workers that was predominantly female.

In the late 1970s, Wal-Mart started a management training program, making an undergraduate degree a prerequisite for admission. The company even began recruiting management trainees on college campuses, concentrating on small schools in the South and Midwest.

Walton so thoroughly reversed the company's early prejudice against the educated that he and his wife contributed a large sum to the University of Arkansas to create a Walton Institute within its business school in Fort Smith. Wal-Mart sent its brightest managerial prospects to Fort Smith for advanced training.

Qualified hourly workers were free to apply to the training program at their store—and many did—but it was an awful lot like enlisting in the U.S. Army. If you survived basic training, the company might send you anywhere it had a store to fill an assistant manager vacancy. To get a store of your own, you'd almost certainly have to move at least two or three times more and keep right on moving even after you'd grasped the golden ring as store manager. Bentonville strongly preferred to entrust the opening of a new store to an experienced store manager. As the pace of new openings accelerated, this effectively put managers on a six-month rotation. "Traditionally, we've had this attitude that if you wanted to be a manager at Wal-Mart, you basically had to be willing to move on a moment's notice," Walton said. "You get a call that says you're going to open a new store 500 miles away, you don't ask questions. You just pack and go, then sometime later you worry about selling your house and moving your family."[32]

For his first dozen years in business, Walton was unable to take full competitive advantage of his obsessive frugality. As a Ben Franklin franchisee, he was required to buy at least 80 percent of his merchandise from Butler Brothers at a hefty 25 percent markup. Chafing under this requirement from the start, Walton routinely hitched a trailer to his car and drove from Newport into Tennessee, where he found wholesalers willing to sell at better prices than was Butler Brothers. Although founding Wal-Mart freed Walton from franchisor-imposed price constraints, he remained at a serious disadvantage to bigger retailers when it came to buying goods directly from manufacturers like Procter & Gamble, RCA, or Eastman Kodak. Most big consumer products companies were loath to sell through discount stores for fear of cheapening their brands, and they more or less dictated the price of the merchandise they did deign to provide to small fry like Wal-Mart Stores. "I don't mind saying that we were the victims of a good bit of arrogance from a lot of vendors in those days," Walton later complained, in what for him was a strong rebuke. "They didn't need us, and they acted that way."[33]

As Wal-Mart gained size and strength, Walton gradually reversed the dynamic of his one-sided relationship with suppliers. By the late 1970s, Walton had the upper hand and he used it unsparingly to extract price and other concessions from even the largest vendors. To save money, Wal-Mart stopped sending buyers out on sales calls and insisted that vendors call on them in Bentonville. "[He] is tough as nails," said George Billingsley, a Bentonville Realtor who was a close friend of Walton's. "Just ask any vendor: He's as cold as a Sunday night supper."[34]

Walton took all the song and dance out of procurement, forbidding his buyers from accepting any of the gratuities that lubricate commerce in America: expense-account meals, golf outings, cases of wine, Super Bowl tickets, and so on. Buyers were not even allowed to bring sales reps into their offices at headquarters, but instead had to meet with them in the small, windowless interview rooms that lined both sides of a hallway just off the lobby. Nor did Walton allow his employees to be distracted by talk of cooperative advertising, return management fees, and the other additives vendors customarily use as deal sweeteners. For Wal-Mart, it all boiled down to a single price on an invoice, and the boiling had better be quick or a recalcitrant visitor would find himself back in the parking lot in a hurry. Wal-Mart is "the rudest account in America," a senior consumer goods executive once complained (anonymously) to a reporter.[35]

For years, the cost advantage that Wal-Mart held over other retailers was purely a matter of Walton's fanaticism in stretching a dollar any way he could. Operationally, Wal-Mart was something of a mess, even by Walton's own description. "We didn't have systems. We didn't have ordering programs. We didn't have a basic merchandise assortment. We certainly didn't have any sort of computers," he conceded in *Made in America*. "In fact, when I look at it today, I realize that so much of what we did in the beginning was really poorly done."[36]

Then, too, the Ozarks put Walton's fledgling company at a significant cost disadvantage when it came to distribution. None of the wholesale distributors and trucking companies that catered to the big, established retailers offered regular delivery service to Ozarks towns as small and as distant from major highways as those where Wal-Mart put its stores. Instead of centralizing merchandise orders to facilitate volume purchasing, each Wal-Mart outlet placed its own orders with salesmen and usually had to pay extra for special delivery by common carrier. Walton did buy some items in bulk, taking delivery in Bentonville, where, in a rented garage, laborers repacked the orders into store-sized loads. Walton improvised madly to get these goods out to the stores. His oldest son, Rob, had just got his driver's license the first time he was drafted to haul a truckload of something to a store one night.[37]

In the late 1960s, Walton recruited a handful of smart, experienced executives from Ben Franklin, Newberry, and other retailers to begin building the distribution, computer information, and communications systems that Wal-Mart so conspicuously lacked. By building its own network of warehouses and its own fleet of trucks to make deliveries to stores, the company was able to consolidate its ordering and buy in volume just like the biggest retailers. What is more, by taking on the rigors of systems development itself instead of outsourcing it to third parties, as did most every other retailer, Wal-Mart brought to bear its compulsive pursuit of cost advantage to a vast new area of chain-store management. In distribution, as in procurement, Wal-Mart succeeded in transforming initial weakness into enduring competitive edge.

Even so, this aspect of the business did not come naturally to Walton, because it was not a simple matter of minimizing expense but instead required making heavy investments in technology to streamline the flow of merchandise and information. Wal-Mart's founder was perfectly capable of understanding the rationale for investing $70 million in an automated distribution center the size of twenty-three football fields or sinking $24 million into a private satellite network, but he required serious persuasion when it came to actually parting with the cash. "All these guys love to talk about how I never wanted any of this technology, and how they had to lay down their life to get it," Walton conceded. "The truth is, I did want it, I knew we needed it, but I just couldn't bring myself to say, 'Okay, sure, spend what you need.'"[38]

Walton gave the lion's share of credit for Wal-Mart's back-office prowess to Glass, who finally succumbed to Walton's recruiting pitches in 1976 (and would succeed Walton as CEO in 1988). In some ways, Glass was Walton cloned. Born and raised in the backwoods Ozarks city of Mountain Home, not far from the Walton family's Webster County stronghold, Glass grew up on a farm without electricity or indoor plumbing and was well-acquainted with the taste of rabbit and squirrel. Born in 1935, Glass was a bit young to bear the scars of the Great Depression in memory the way Walton did, but he was as tight with a dollar as his predecessor and no less rigorous an enforcer of corporate frugality. Like his predecessor, Glass was an unpretentious man for whom the bright city lights held no allure. "He's still the same old kid he always was, and I'd just whup him if he weren't," his mother, Myrtle Glass, told a reporter in 1992.[39]

Although Glass was not without talent as a merchant, he was, definitively, a master back-office technician and he looked the part, with his quizzical half-smile and his beetling, peaked eyebrows and long dark sideburns. Diffident and dry-witted, Glass was Walton's opposite temperamentally (certainly no one ever thought to call him "Mr. Dave") and had none of Walton's genius for connecting with regular folk or delivering stem-winding speeches. Glass would succeed Walton as Wal-Mart's CEO without ever replacing him as its inspirational leader.

Glass made himself so useful to Walton that he survived the bungling of one of his first big assignments, the construction of Wal-Mart's first fully mechanized distribution center in Searcy, Arkansas, in the late 1970s. The Searcy "DC" did not entirely eliminate the human element, but its 700 employees mostly tended machines of one sort or another. The colossal warehouse was equipped with eight miles of high-speed, laser-guided conveyor belts and was linked by computer to stores and to suppliers, the better to track inventory levels and to speed reordering. The Searcy facility was the prototype of dozens of DCs to come, but getting it working right was a struggle. According to Glass, the company began shipping freight before the building had a roof or working toilets.

Even with Walton's reflex miserliness slowing the pace of Wal-Mart's progress, the company managed to get the jump on its competitors in virtually every area of the digital revolution that has transformed retailing over the last three decades, establishing a technological edge that it has yet to relinquish. Wal-Mart was one of the first retailers to use computers to track inventory (in 1969), adopt the now-ubiquitous product bar codes (1980), and implement electronic data interchange to speed purchase orders to suppliers (1985). In 1987, Wal-Mart began building what is now America's largest private satellite-communication network to move data through space faster and in greater volumes than is possible over telephone lines. Piece by piece, Walton and company were putting together a seamlessly integrated system that "would give its executives a complete picture, at any point in time, of where goods were and how fast they were moving, all the way from the factory to the checkout counter."[40]

In Walton's view, Wal-Mart's expansion in the 1970s and 1980s—the climactic decades of his career—was simply a matter of "rolling out the formula" to hundreds of new locations outside of Wal-Mart Country. His world-beating formula in a nutshell was this: an affinity for underserved small-town locations plus a low-paid but highly motivated workforce and ultra-efficient distribution equals "Every Day Low Prices" that few consumers could resist and that no competitor could match. The amplitude of Wal-Mart's growth curve during

Walton's last two decades of running the company he had founded was simply astonishing. Wal-Mart went from 32 stores in 1970 to 276 in 1980 to 1,726 in 1990. The company's sales in these milestone years totaled $31 million, $1.248 billion, and $25.881 billion, respectively. Wal-Mart's common stock split so many times over this period that 100 shares purchased for a total of $1,650 in the 1970 initial public offering grew to 51,200 shares worth $3.2 million by 1990.

Wal-Mart's ascendance was not nearly as easy as Walton and colleagues made it look, for it is an exceptional company that can maintain its discipline while growing at a geometric rate. Discounting's other pioneers were a particularly pertinent case in point. A few hundred entrepreneurs around the country had gone into the business before Walton had, but very few of them survived the entry of Kmart and other established chains into the field in the 1960s. Walton took special satisfaction in the demise of Gibson Discount Stores. In his view, "guys like Herb Gibson" were sloppy, unfocused operators who had only themselves to blame. "Most of these early guys were very egotistical people who loved to drive big Cadillacs and fly around in their jets and vacation on their yachts."[41]

Ever since the advent of mass merchandising in the latter decades of the nineteenth century, the conventional strategy for building a national retail chain had been to open as many stores in as many big cities around the country as fast as possible. This was essentially what Kmart did in discounting, saturating the suburbs of America's large and midsized cities at a furious clip; by 1980, Kmart had 2,300 outlets, none of which were located in towns of less than 50,000. By contrast, Wal-Mart methodically moved out from its base in Bentonville in a pattern described by a series of slightly overlapping, adjoining circles. At the center of each circle was a distribution center capable of supplying 150 stores within a radius of about 250 miles, or the approximate distance that a truck could safely travel to and from a DC in a day. "We were always pushing from the inside out," Glass explained. "We never jump [locations] and then backfill."[42]

The initial thrust of Wal-Mart's expansion beyond the Ozarks was southwest into Oklahoma, Louisiana, and Texas. It then pushed east across the Deep South, eventually extending all the way to Florida, Georgia, and the Carolinas. Next, the company worked its way north and east through the Midwestern states while simultaneously pushing west across the Great Plains to the Rockies. Wal-Mart maintained its small-town focus but edged its way within sight of the gates of such cities as Tulsa, Kansas City, and Dallas.

Wal-Mart finally entered the big city in launching its Sam's Warehouse Club division in 1983. At 130,000 square feet on average, Sam's outlets were twice the size of a Wal-Mart discount store and even more minimally furnished. Catering to small-business owners and other bulk buyers, these bare-bones outlets charged wholesale prices for a wide variety of brand-name merchandise but required payment of an annual membership fee.

With a markup of just 9 percent to 12 percent, a Sam's Club had to do $25 million a year in sales to break even, and this was possible only in a sizable, urban market. Within two years of opening the first Sam's Club on the outskirts of Oklahoma City, Walton had branched into sixteen other big cities stretching across the Southern quadrant of the country from Houston, Texas, and Wichita, Kansas, all the way to Charleston, South Carolina, and Jacksonville, Florida. (Sam's Club was founded as a self-contained division with Wal-Mart, with its own procurement and distribution networks.)

Walton admitted to lifting the Sam's Club concept wholesale, so to speak, from Sol Price, a pioneering California discounter who had founded Fed-Mart in 1955 (a tour of its Houston store helped convince Walton to shift into discounting) and Price Club in 1976. Over the years, Walton had spent many hours walking the aisles of Price's stores, surreptitiously whispering notes about merchandise and prices into the little tape recorder he always carried with him. One day in a Price Club in San Diego, a security guard caught Walton and confiscated his machine. Unabashed, Walton attached a note to Robert

Price, Sol's son, asking that the tape be returned to him because he didn't want to lose comments he'd recorded before hitting Price Club. Sam's Club quickly eclipsed Price Club (now part of archrival Costco) and would grow into a big business in its own right, with 550 stores and $37 billion in sales by 2005.

Walton was hugely successful, but hardly infallible. Aside from Sam's Club, all of Wal-Mart's other attempts at diversifying in the 1980s flopped resoundingly. The failures included Discount Drugstores, Save Mor home-improvement centers, Helen's Arts and Crafts stores, and Bud's Closeout outlets. (Luckily, Sam had only one brother and one wife after whom to name new ventures or there might have been more failures. He was content to honor Ol' Roy with a private-label dog food.)

Ironically, by far the most expensive of Walton's flops—Hypermart USA—put the company on a path to a new-format triumph of such magnitude that in time it would eclipse even the Wal-Mart discount store. Walton took the hypermart concept from Carrefour, a big French retailer that had opened the first *hypermarché* just outside of Paris in 1963. It combined general merchandise of the sort that Wal-Mart sold with fresh food and other groceries at a discount on a truly colossal scale. At 220,000 square feet on average, the *hypermarché* was about four times the size of a typical Wal-Mart. By 1973, Carrefour and its imitators had run so many small shopkeepers out of business that the French government enacted legislation to slow their expansion.

Walton first encountered the *hypermarché* in Brazil in the early 1980s and was amazed to see the great throngs that Carrefour attracted. On a subsequent swing through Europe, Walton checked out the *hypermarché* on its home ground and returned home "pushing the concept hard," as he put it. "I argued that everybody except the U.S. was successful with this concept and we should get in on the ground floor with it."[43]

Euromarché, one of Carrefour's leading rivals, beat Walton to the punch. In 1984, the French company joined with Supervalu, the largest U.S. food wholesaler, to form Bigg's. In 1984, Bigg's built the first American hypermart, in Cincinnati. Bigg's had added half a dozen additional stores by the time that the first Hypermart USA store opened in a suburb of Dallas in 1987. Wal-Mart was still new to food, so Hypermart USA was set up as a joint venture with the Cullum Companies, whose Tom Thumb supermarkets dominated the Dallas market. Over the next three years, Wal-Mart built a second Hypermart USA in the Dallas area and also put stores in Kansas City and Topeka.

Walton was right in one respect: American shoppers were willing to exhaust themselves hunting bargains in bare-bones stores the size of five football fields, with cartons of merchandise towering twenty-two feet high. Hypermart USA never lacked for customers. To the contrary, the stores did such big volume right from the start that Wal-Mart never was able to manage them properly. In short, the Hypermart was just too hyper. The giant, labor-intensive hypermarts generated profits so puny that they were not worth Wal-Mart's time. "We over-built our Hypermarts and spent too much on them," recalled Donald Soderquist, a former Ben Franklin executive who joined Wal-Mart in 1980 and was promoted to chief operating officer in 1988. "We were able to generate more sales than we ever had in a Wal-Mart store, but we struggled to produce a profit because we had too much overhead."[44]

Even before Wal-Mart officially terminated Hypermart USA, it began experimenting with a scaled-down, 125,000-square-foot combination discount and grocery store known in the trade as a "superstore." This format had been pioneered in the 1960s by a couple of regional supermarket companies with coincidentally similar names: Meijer out of Grand Rapids, Michigan, and Fred Meyer of Portland, Oregon. Meijer had sixty superstores in the Upper Midwest and Fred Meyer close to 100 throughout the Pacific Northwest by the time that

Wal-Mart finally opened its first experimental "Supercenter" in 1988 in Washington, Missouri, an hour's drive west of St. Louis. Walton's comments during the grand opening of the Washington store were prophetic. "I have a different feeling about this store than I've ever had," Wal-Mart's founder told the store's 300 employees. "It's a Wal-Mart, but it's not a Wal-Mart. But it may be our future."[45]

As Wal-Mart began to come of age as a corporation, Walton had little choice but to fill most newly created senior management positions with experienced managers from other, established retail chains. However, the second generation of home-office executives—which came to the fore in the 1980s and 1990s—was almost entirely home-grown and thoroughly indoctrinated in the Wal-Mart Way. To climb the ladder in Bentonville to its upper rungs, it wasn't necessary to drive a beat-up old pickup truck to work, as Walton did (though it sure couldn't hurt), but you had better embrace the Protestant work ethic unreservedly, respect your marriage vows, and not flash your cash around town. "I just don't believe a big showy lifestyle is appropriate for anywhere, least of all here in Bentonville, where folks work hard for their money and where we all know that everyone puts on their trousers one leg at a time," Walton declared.[46]

The senior management cadre that formed an essential part of Walton's corporate legacy was as racially and ethnically homogeneous as the first generation of Wal-Mart clerks and cashiers had been. Many of its members were Ozarkers, but even those who were not tended to hail from small towns in the South or Midwest. And it was indeed trousers that they put on one leg at a time every morning. Wal-Mart's executive suite differed from the field in one glaring way: an utter absence of women. As late as 1989, there was not a single woman among the company's twenty-two highest-ranking execs and only two female vice presidents among its top eighty-eight officers.[47] And only about 3 percent of Wal-Mart's stores had a female manager.

It wasn't that Walton thought that a woman's place was in the home exactly. How could he, when he hired women by the thousands for his store? It's even possible that he thought women were perfectly capable of holding down a big job at the home office. The problem, in short, was that as a gentleman of the old school, Walton would much rather charm female workers in the stores than have to berate female executives in the home office. Despite all the warmth and encouragement that Walton ladled out as cheerleader-in-chief, he was a real taskmaster as executive-in-chief. He demanded results from his executives, and if he did not get them, he could be downright rough, much like a military commander dressing down a subordinate. "When it came to dealing with hourly associates, Mr. Sam could really give a soft hand," recalled Jon Lehman, a longtime Wal-Mart store manager who was born and raised in Harrison, Arkansas. "But if you were a manager, or one of his executives, he'd rip you up one side and down the other and fire you. I mean, he was sharp and tough."[48]

Wal-Mart's management hierarchy was unusually flat for a big corporation, with only three layers between store managers and executive vice presidents, who exercised companywide authority. Wal-Mart did have regional buying offices scattered around the country, but merchandising, marketing, logistics, information technology, personnel, and the other corporate functions all were centralized in Bentonville. However, Walton wasn't Wal-Mart's only travelin' man—far from it. By 1990, the company had fifteen airplanes (only two of which were jets) and "Air Wal-Mart" was almost always fully deployed. Regional vice presidents were real road warriors, flying out to inspect their territories every Monday morning and returning to Bentonville on Thursday evening. Every other senior executive was expected to spend at least one day a week in the stores, taking the retail pulse where it beat strongest.

Everyone had to be back in Bentonville by 7 A.M. on Friday at the latest for the weekly management meeting, which included all company officers and division heads and usually lasted all morning. At noon, the regional VPs met with all the merchandise buyers over sandwiches and iced tea. The focus in the morning was the stores; in the afternoon, it was all about product. But the two meetings were similar in tone: candid, often contentious, microscopically detailed sessions reflecting the "bias for action" that Walton had instilled in the company through his constant tinkering, his compulsion to make incremental improvements.[49]

Early Saturday, the whole executive group plus a few hundred other Wal-Marters piled into the auditorium at the home office for what was the pièce de résistance of Walton's inspirational oeuvre: the Saturday-morning meeting. Its trademark blend of business fundamentals, encounter-group psychodrama, and country corn pone had the few reporters who were allowed to attend over the years reaching for metaphors. To one, the meeting seemed "a corporatized version of *A Prairie Home Companion*."[50] To another, it was "Family Feud Meets Ernst & Young."[51] To Walton, it was simple: "The Saturday morning meeting is at the very heart of the Wal-Mart culture."[52]

Wal-Mart's competitors generally waited until Monday to review their weekly store figures and make adjustments in their merchandise purchasing plans. However, the rule in Bentonville was that corrections were to be made in all the stores by Saturday noon. Getting the jump on the meeting that gave Wal-Mart a jump on its rivals, Walton liked to be at his desk by 3 A.M. on Saturday to bone up on all the data before the meeting started at 7:30. "When I'm done I have as good a feel for what's going on in the company as anyone here— maybe better on some days," he boasted.[53]

The Saturday-morning meeting evolved into Wal-Mart's main venue for brainstorming ideas and for debating philosophical or strategic issues. Walton usually arrived with a few notes scribbled on a pad, but his agenda was private and subject to improvisation. He liked to go around the room lobbing questions at people, and he mixed a fair number of hand grenades in with the softballs. He might take a manager in need of humbling down a notch or two by suggesting that he "think before he talked" or making him get up and sing "Red River

Valley," as he did to a longtime exec named Al Miles. Walton might lead the group in song or in calisthenics, read from a favorite book, present an award to a "hero" associate flown in for the occasion, or turn the microphone over to Garth Brooks, Joe Montana, Jack Welch, or some other special guest. Anything could happen on Saturday morning, and that made these three-hour sessions both unnerving and more entertaining than a business meeting had any right to be.

For Walton, relinquishing power over Wal-Mart did not come easily. His first, absurdly premature attempt at succession took place in 1974, when he was just fifty-six years old. In what amounted to a belated midlife crisis, Walton caved to heavy pressure from his wife, who wanted him to retire while he was still young and healthy. He had hired a hyper-ambitious young hotshot named Ron Mayer away from a competing retail chain in 1968 and made him Wal-Mart's first vice president of finance. Rather than risk losing Mayer, Walton handed him the positions of chairman and CEO, keeping only his seat on the board (and control over a huge chunk of stock, of course). Wal-Mart soon cleaved into two warring camps: the technology-savvy outsiders that Mayer had gathered around him in Bentonville, and the old guard of merchants and store managers who were aggrieved that the new CEO hadn't come from their ranks. The company's performance began to suffer, alarming Walton, who was bored silly anyway. One weekend in 1976, Walton abruptly reclaimed the titles he'd willed to Mayer, who resigned in a huff, taking many promising young executives with him.

Walton had the good grace to blame himself for this fiasco, which shredded the company's executive ranks and damaged its standing on Wall Street. The bookish Glass, who had joined Wal-Mart a few weeks after Mayer departed, proved a far more patient heir apparent. Walton was diagnosed with hairy cell leukemia in 1982, but he opted for an aggressive treatment program that proved highly effective. With the leukemia in remission, Walton was able to carry on with barely diminished energy until 1988, when, not long after his sixty-sixth birthday, he relinquished the posts of chairman and CEO to Glass, who was fifty-three years old.

This time, succession was smoothly realized. In fact, its timing seemed downright providential when, less than a year later, Walton learned that he had contracted a disease far more lethal than leukemia: multiple myeloma, or malignant cancer of the bone marrow. By the end of 1991, he was too weak to continue visiting stores but continued to come into the office pretty regularly. He often felt cold while working at his desk, but refused to let his secretary, Becky Elliott, spend money on a space heater. While Walton was out, Elliott had heating strips installed at the top of one wall that were automatically activated when someone entered the office. After a few days of warmth, he asked Elliott about the popping sound he kept hearing. Walton smiled indulgently at Elliott's explanation until she told him she'd spent $500. "He didn't like that," Elliott recalled. "It was more than he would have okayed."[54]

Walton died on April 6, 1992, a week after President George H. W. Bush presented him with the Presidential Medal of Freedom. The Bentonville staff thronged a private memorial service at the home office; Arkansas governor Bill Clinton interrupted his presidential campaign to attend with his wife, Hillary Rodham Clinton. An evening memorial open to the public drew an even larger crowd of more than 1,000 people to the stadium of Bentonville High School, where Walton was eulogized by a procession of tearful friends and neighbors. "Arkansas, to other people, was just a hillbilly backwater, but Sam changed all that," said George Billingsley, the realtor who had been Walton's favorite tennis partner.[55]

True to form, Walton was laid to rest in a common, $200 corner plot in Bentonville's municipal cemetery, just a half-dozen blocks from the house where he had lived for five decades. His grave was adorned only by a small block of rose-gray marble with a single word chiseled in block letters: WALTON.

CHAPTER FOUR

SO HELP THEM, SAM

Whatever else might be said about Sam Walton's successors—CEO's David Glass and Lee Scott—they brilliantly realized his ambition to grow Wal-Mart to the sky. During Glass's twelve years as CEO, from 1988 through 1999, sales soared tenfold, to $165 billion from $16 billion, as Wal-Mart blew past Sears to become America's biggest retailer. The company began to aggressively expand abroad, moving first into Mexico, Puerto Rico, and Canada, and it also thrust its way into the grocery business at home through the new Supercenter format. Wal-Mart hit a rough patch in the mid-1990s, as runaway operating costs cut into profits. Glass succeeded in reasserting the rigorous financial discipline he had learned at Walton's knee and retired as a hero to Wall Street, though certainly not to many of Wal-Mart's own employees.

Glass was a tenacious, tough-minded technocrat who failed to maintain the loyal, highly motivated workforce that Walton had bequeathed him. By 1999, Glass's last year, store employees were quitting at the astronomical rate of 70 percent a year. "Our turnover, in my opinion, had absolutely spun out of control," recalled Coleman

Peterson, Wal-Mart's personnel chief at the time.[1] Scott gradually brought turnover down to about 50 percent after taking over in 2000, but a company that loses half its employees each year has not solved its morale problems. To the contrary, the conviction that Wal-Mart was a much better place to work when Walton was alive has become deeply embedded in the ethos of the company—or at least in its stores. "The main focus of Wal-Mart is no longer the satisfaction of its customers and the welfare of its associates, its focus is on the welfare of the company!" wrote an anonymous associate from the Wal-Mart in Monaca, Pennsylvania, in a recent tribute to Walton posted on the Find-A-Grave Web site. "I only wish you were here today to see it, Mr. Sam. Thank you anyway."

In Glass's own estimation, his approach to the business differed from Walton's only in its heavy emphasis on technology. "Sam wasn't sure about technology," recalled Glass, noting that Walton often took computerized reports and recopied the data by hand into a ledger book.[2] Glass, on the other hand, was a true believer, a digital zealot. "A long time ago, I had a strong belief that technology would ultimately drive this business to be the size that it is," he said a few years after he had stepped down as CEO. (Glass remains a director and a very active consultant to Scott.[3])

Forget that annoying smiley face: The truest symbol of the post-Walton Wal-Mart is a supercomputer whirring quietly away in a temperature-controlled room in the David Glass Technology Center in Bentonville. Built within a converted aluminum plant located two miles from the home office, the center is home to Wal-Mart's 1,000-person Information Systems Division. Unlike the headquarters, which buzzes with the constant comings and goings of manufacturers' representatives vying to get their products onto Wal-Mart's shelves, the Glass Center is strictly off-limits to outsiders. A small placard hanging on the wall in the lobby offers a discreet hint as to why security is so tight, as well as explaining the company's innate paranoia. "We must be inventing and implementing faster than the competition is stealing," it reads. The Glass Center houses what is easily the business world's largest computer database. The 460-terabyte capacity of its data warehouse dwarfs Amazon.com's thirteen terabytes, AT&T's twenty-six terabytes, and is equal to nearly half of the information archived on the Internet.[4]

Wal-Mart uses its great digital brain not only to figure out what to put on its shelves and to streamline the movement of merchandise through its distribution system, but also to closely monitor and evaluate its employees. "I could tell you last year on July thirteen during the hours of 7 and 8 P.M. how much sales a store did and how much of it was rung up by Sally Jo, the cashier with operator number 342 [within] that hour," says Bill Thomas, a longtime store manager who recently left Wal-Mart.[5]

Wal-Mart also relies on its centralized computer system to devise work schedules, with the aim of suppressing payroll costs by fully staffing a store only when it is busiest. To better match the supply of workers with the need for their labor, the computer generates hour-by-hour projections of customer traffic and future merchandise deliveries. It then matches them up with workers' pay levels, availability, and so on to produce a weekly schedule for each store. As a result, associates' schedules not only vary weekly, but are subject to change on short notice. In effect, store workers now are on call virtually round the clock, subject to the dictates of a mainframe in Bentonville. In creating a retailing machine that spun faster and ground finer than any other in business history, Wal-Mart progressively transformed its store workers into faceless, low-cost, and frequently replaced component parts.

Although Walton himself set this demoralizing process in motion, he humanized Wal-Mart by his presence, his human touch. He worked hard at inspiring employees, poring over information sheets in advance of store visits to better personalize the chitchat and praise that he lavished on associates. And in keeping his door open wide to one and all as an arbiter of grievances, Walton conferred upon the lowliest worker the right to assert her individuality to an extent that is rare in a large corporation. You're less likely to feel like a machine part when you can sit down with the boss and speak your mind.

To ward off the threat of unionization, Walton had entered into a kind of moral compact with his employees. You won't make top dollar working here, he'd told them in so many words, but if you work hard and stick around awhile you'll share in the profits just like management does and you will be treated with respect as a member of the extended Wal-Mart family. Or, as Walton put it in *Made in America,* "If you're good to people, and fair with them, and demanding of them, they will eventually decide you're on their side."[6] Walton's notion of fairness was skewed by Ozark traditionalism, but his patronizing attitude toward women did not prevent the New Deal that he offered workers from outgrowing its initially expedient aims and taking deep root within the company. Under Walton, Wal-Mart developed a reputation within retailing as a great place to work even as it continued to pay lower wages than did its competitors.

However, the special compact that bound Wal-Mart to its workers through the Walton era expired unceremoniously some time after Mr. Sam did, as Glass made brilliant use of new technology to systemize and standardize every aspect of Wal-Mart's operations. Even as Glass was hailed on Wall Street for "saving" Wal-Mart during the latter half of the 1990s, company workers were bailing out at record rates. Glass didn't seem to care. Why should he? Wal-Mart was producing record profits. One can only conclude that the continuing mass exodus of workers was part of the plan—or at least the tolerable by-product of an overriding emphasis on cost efficiency.

Walton's open door to employees clanged shut, leaving Wal-Mart workers in thrall to a colossal, ultraefficient machine that Glass and his handpicked successor Lee Scott—master retail technicians both— continued to hone as the digital age progressed. Although Walton's egalitarian concepts and rah-rah rituals still live on within the company, they now seem to exist mainly to camouflage the grim workaday realities of stores squeezed mercilessly to deliver the sales and profits the home office has programmed them to produce. "Wal-Mart workers, from store managers to hourly clerks, are frequently taxed to the limit, both physically and psychologically," concluded Ellen Rosen of Brandeis University in her 2004 study, *The Quality of Work at Wal-Mart.*[7]

There was no way—short of relocating Ozarkers en masse—that Wal-Mart could have maintained the homogeneity and docility of its workforce as its expansion carried it from its natural rural habitat into urban America. Walton conceded as much in his autobiography, which was completed just before he died. In cities, he acknowledged, "we have more trouble coming up with educated people who want to work in our industry, or with people of the right moral character and integrity. Folks in small towns in Iowa and Mississippi are more likely to want to work for what we can pay than folks in Houston or Dallas or St. Louis. And, yes, they're probably more likely to buy our philosophy in the country than they are in the city."[8]

An optimist to the end, Walton believed that the company could overcome the perceived inadequacies of the urban labor pool by indoctrinating new hires in the Wal-Mart Way. "A smart, motivational, good manager can work what some outsiders call Wal-Mart magic with folks anywhere," Walton continued. "It may take more time. You may have to sift through more people, and you may have to become more skilled with your hiring practices. But I truly believe that people anywhere will eventually respond to the same sort of motivational techniques we use."[9]

As Wal-Mart moved into more competitive urban markets, the company had to resort to one motivational technique that had always been a last resort for Walton: money. To attract applicants, the company boosted its starting wage significantly above the federal minimum wage, while keeping it lower than at other big retail chains, preserving its decisive labor cost advantage. In his Los Angeles speech in 2005, Scott made the incredible claim that "Wal-Mart has dramatically upgraded the nature of retail work in America." This is true only in the very limited sense that the company pays a bit more than many of the small, independent retailers that it drives out of business.

But when it came to working that old "Wal-Mart magic" on employees, neither Glass nor Scott filled Walton's shoes. As Wal-Mart's founder, he had epitomized the company in a way that no successor ever could. For all his Ozarker parochialism, Walton was simply inimitable as Wal-Mart's cheerleader-in-chief. He was succeeded in this role not by the shy and charm-challenged Glass, but by Don Soderquist, who was Wal-Mart's second-ranking executive when Walton died and would remain Glass's right-hand man throughout his tenure as CEO. An amiable, relentlessly positive Midwesterner, Soderquist was nearly as ebullient in his enthusiasm for all things Wal-Mart as Walton himself. More or less by acclamation, Soderquist became Wal-Mart's "Keeper of the Culture," eventually writing a quasi-autobiography called *The Wal*Mart Way* that doubled as a hardcover indoctrination manual for employees.

In their eagerness to draft behind Walton's inspirational powers, Soderquist and Glass stopped just short of stuffing their late mentor and propping him up behind his desk. Instructions went out to the stores to put up a framed photo of the founder near the employee time clock. Although Sam's Pledge was deemed too ghoulishly personal to preserve, most of the inspirational techniques Walton had devised— the company cheer, the revival-like Saturday-morning meetings in Bentonville, the Ten-Foot Rule, and so on—survived his passing and often were performed by Soderquist and other managers in explicit homage to Mr. Sam. "The greatest fear we had after Sam died was not whether we could open new stores, but would we be able to preserve the culture that he'd created," Soderquist recalled years later.[10]

Discontent in the ranks already was evident by the 1993 annual meeting, held in Fayetteville just a year after Walton's passing. In his remarks to some 17,000 shareholders, many of whom doubled as employees, Sam's brother, Bud, got up and bluntly criticized management's recent decision to trim payrolls in some stores to maintain profit margins. "Maybe the executives should take a pay cut instead," grumbled Bud, who, at age seventy-one, remained a director and a senior vice president (and a large stockholder).

The crowd roared its approval as Glass, Chairman Rob Walton, and their fellow directors sat stone-faced behind Bud onstage. "I want the people in operations to understand how these people feel." Glass patronizingly dismissed Walton's concerns. "Bud spends most of his time fishing these days," he told a reporter. The next year, Mr. Sam's only sibling again sat onstage but wasn't allowed to speak at what was his last annual meeting.[11] He died a year later on a Caribbean cruise.[12]

Like Glass before him, Lee Scott rose through the ranks by excelling at the mechanical aspects of retailing, playing an indispensable part in Wal-Mart's technology-induced rebound in the latter half of the 1990s. With his cherubic, sandy-haired good looks and cheery demeanor, Scott was much more approachable than Glass. But he, too, was an uninspiring communicator who was so uncomfortable with public speaking early in his career that he dreaded the Saturday-morning meetings. Whenever Walton called on him, Scott recalled, "I would shake and my voice would crack."[13]

As the third native Ozarker in a row to head the company, Scott assured it a large measure of continuity just by showing up for work each day. Born sixty miles north of Bentonville in Joplin, Missouri, Scott grew up just across the Kansas border in tiny Baxter Springs, where his father owned a gas station on Route 66 and his mother taught music at the elementary school. To pay his way through nearby Pittsburg State University, Scott worked the night shift for $2 an hour at a factory that made steel molds for tires. He married in college and lived with his wife and baby son in a ten-by-fifty-foot mobile home. After graduating with a degree in business, Scott went to work as a dispatcher with Yellow Freight Systems, a big trucking concern.

Scott was running Yellow Freight's terminal in Springdale, Arkansas, when he drove to nearby Bentonville in 1977 to try to collect from Wal-Mart on a disputed $7,000 bill. Glass, then Wal-Mart's chief financial officer, was unmoved by Scott's arguments, but was sufficiently impressed with the twenty-eight-year-old's moxie that he offered him a managerial job in the Bentonville distribution center. Scott declined and got off an exit line now enshrined in Wal-Mart lore. "I'm not the smartest guy that's ever been in your office," he told Glass, "but I'm not going to leave the fastest-growing trucking company in America to go to work for a company that can't pay a $7,000 bill."[14] Two years later, Scott did just that, signing on to run Wal-Mart's fledgling transportation department. (Tightfisted to a fault, Wal-Mart never did make good on that $7,000 bill.)

Despite his stage fright, Scott was an aggressive, even abrasive, manager. As a new recruit, he came on so strong in pushing warehouse managers to unload trucks faster that Soderquist took him aside after one meeting and told him to cool it. "He told me that if my intention was to irritate and annoy everyone in the room, I had succeeded," Scott recalled.[15] Every time a truck driver was drunk on the job or otherwise derelict in his duties, Scott sent out a memo scolding all of his drivers and threatening to fire anyone who flouted one of the countless rules he'd laid down. Infuriated by Scott's bullying, a delegation of truck drivers walked through the open door and asked Walton to fire him. Instead, Walton called the headstrong vice president of transport into his office. After enduring a long gripe session with the drivers, he made Scott shake each man's hand and thank him for coming forward. In time, Scott adapted to Wal-Mart's egalitarian ethos, but without quite being humbled. As CEO, he liked to recount in interviews how he had to fire one driver five times because Walton insisted on hiring the man back four times.

The quietly cocksure Scott made himself invaluable to Glass by building what is now the nation's largest trucking fleet while employing the latest in computer technology to continually squeeze more cost efficiencies out of transport. Promoted up and out of transportation into a series of senior logistics posts, Scott took the lead in upgrading and expanding the company's distinctive hub-and-spoke distribution network to equally beneficial effect. In 1995, Glass tested Scott by moving him out of logistics and putting him in charge of merchandising, an area in which he had no experience. Even so, the rising star helped Wal-Mart's return to form in the latter half of the 1990s by methodically cutting $2 billion of excess inventory, in part by convincing suppliers to ship smaller orders more frequently.

By the time Scott succeeded Glass in early 2000, he had mastered his nerves and was capable of delivering a respectable speech to any sort of audience. But if Walton had been the corporate equivalent of the Reverend Billy Graham, Scott came across like the boyish, mild-mannered director of the church choir. In other words, the new CEO needed his own Soderquist to excite and inspire the employee masses—and he got him in the outsized person of Thomas Martin Coughlin.

Like Soderquist, Coughlin was an Ozarker by calling, not birth. The son of a police detective, he had grown up in Cleveland and headed west to college, graduating from California State University in 1972. Coughlin followed in his father's footsteps in a sense, joining R. H. Macy's West Coast division as a store detective. Early one Saturday morning in 1978 he was sitting with his wife, Cynthia, in their car outside Wal-Mart headquarters awaiting a 5:30 A.M. job interview with Walton. Coughlin was explaining to his wife why he wanted to move to the hinterlands—Bentonville just that week had installed its first traffic light—to take a job as vice president of security for a company without a frisson of R. H. Macy's cachet, when a man in a khaki shirt emerged from the building and began chasing windblown newspapers around the parking lot. To Coughlin's amazement, the dutiful khaki-clad employee turned out to be Walton. "People here respond differently than what I'm used to," Coughlin later told his wife. "It's not a situation where it's someone else's job. If there is something to be done, you jump in and do it."[16]

At six feet four and a bruising 275 pounds, Coughlin was big and brash and altogether hard to miss as he swaggered around in his custom-made, lizard-skin cowboy boots. Much as the role of Wal-Mart's head bouncer seemed to suit Coughlin, "loss prevention," as Wal-Mart termed his domain, did not contain him for long. On his rise through the ranks at Wal-Mart, he worked in virtually every division of the company. As the first operations chief of Sam's Club, he spent much of the 1980s flying around the country with Walton, opening new warehouse stores and shotgunning the occasional game bird. Coughlin swallowed Walton's store-centric management philosophy whole, morphing from a gimlet-eyed store dick into a talented merchant very much in the populist, out-among-the-folks mold of his mentor.

While Soderquist had been a gracious, honey-tongued evangelist, Coughlin was the culture keeper as enforcer. He quoted General George Patton—"A good plan violently executed today is better than a great plan tomorrow"—almost as often as he did Walton and was famous within the company for padlocking the office of a store manager who did not spend enough time out on the floor mixing with customers and workers.[17] After Walton died, Coughlin refined the founder's rather long-winded ten rules of business into five Zen-like imperatives that he pounded into the brains of his colleagues at every opportunity. *Stock it. Price it right. Show the value. Take the money. Teach them.* Coughlin would forgive an honest mistake, but he was murder on subordinates who lied, cheated, or stole. "Anyone who is taking money from associates and shareholders ought to be shot," he said in 2000 (a comment that would come back to haunt him five years later, when documents came to light suggesting that he had subordinates create fake invoices to get Wal-Mart to pay for his personal expenses, from hunting vacations to a $1,359 pair of custom-made alligator boots, to a $2,590 dog pen for his Bentonville home).

Big Tom Coughlin was definitely not a man to cross. But he was also someone who would send you a card on your birthday or help you find the right doctor for your ailing spouse. He kissed so many babies as he made the rounds of the stores that shoppers easily could have mistaken him for a candidate for political office. Many employees looked on Coughlin as the one home-office executive they knew for certain was on their side. At Wal-Mart's annual meeting in 2003, a female department manager from New Mexico sat impassively through the raucous proceedings until Coughlin got his turn at the microphone. "For him, I stand," she told her companion.[18]

Picking up where Glass and Soderquist had left off, Scott and Coughlin got off to a rousing start by the measures that count most on Wall Street. From 2000 through 2004, Wal-Mart boosted its annual sales by $100 billion, to $256 billion in total, an impressive 64 percent gain. Net income more than kept pace—rising 68 percent, to $9 billion—showing that the new executive team was continuing to use Wal-Mart's technological prowess to pound cost efficiencies out of an increasingly far-flung empire of stores.

Scott and Coughlin managed to accelerate Wal-Mart's growth even as they brought the rate of employee turnover down from 70 percent to a bit under 50 percent by 2004. They achieved this not by loosening the company's purse strings and paying their employees better wages or giving them richer benefits, but rather by using a few of those terabytes of computer power in the Glass Center to more carefully screen job applicants. In essence, Wal-Mart consciously evaluated for a variety of pliant traits in job applicants that add up to the kind of servility Walton prized in his Ozarks population. By design, two-thirds of Wal-Mart's new hires now come from segments of the population not in their prime earning years: senior citizens, students, and second-income spouses. Virtually every job candidate— even the most outwardly docile grandparent—must undergo computerized aptitude and personality tests designed by Bentonville. To wear the blue smock, it helped to score high on multiple-choice questions like these:

A description of my childhood might be: A. Happy. B. Average. C. Unhappy.

Which one of the statements is true of you: A. I like a neat and tidy home. B. I don't mind a messy house as long as it's clean. C. I'm indifferent regarding neatness.

I sometimes have pretty wild daydreams. A. Agree. B. Undecided. C. Disagree.[19]

When journalist Barbara Ehrenreich was tested at a Wal-Mart in the Twin Cities, she was told that she had made a mistake. "Roberta takes [my survey] off to another room, where, she says, a computer will 'score' it. After about ten minutes, she's back with alarming news: I've gotten three answers wrong—well, not exactly wrong but in need of further discussion. . . . When presenting yourself as a potential employee, you can never be too much of a suck-up. Take the test proposition that 'rules have to be followed to the letter at all times': I had agreed with this only 'strongly' rather than 'very strongly' or 'totally,' and now, Roberta wants to know why." Ehrenreich was hired anyway, an error the company had cause to regret when her book *Nickel and Dimed: On (Not) Getting By in America*, an exposé of working poverty, became a bestseller in 2001.

Not long after Glass became CEO, the company began giving all new hires an employee handbook that perfectly, if unwittingly, revealed the dilemma of a company that mistrusted the very employees it nominally sought to empower. The manual was full of homespun advice of the sort that grandmas used to knit on samplers, like "Look for the good in others" and "Avoid idle gossip." At the same time, it set out all sorts of precise and rigid rules governing dress, comportment, and work routines. Hourly workers were not allowed to date one another unless each obtained the written permission of their store manager's boss, the district manager—the very sort of anti-fraternization rule that Walton had flouted years ago while working for J. C. Penney in Des Moines.

Even with the slowing of turnover under Scott, the typical Wal-Mart entry-level worker stays on the job less than a year—not nearly long enough to qualify for the profit sharing that helped cement the loyalty of earlier generations of employees. While many long-time associates still believe devoutly in the Wal-Mart Way and tend to break spontaneously into the company cheer at the annual meeting or other large company gathering, their numbers have dwindled sharply at a company that hires new workers at the unheard-of rate of nearly 800,000 a year. Today, the typical Wal-Mart associate lives not on a farm but in a suburb, thinks of Sam Walton as that old guy whose picture is on the wall, and doesn't know Lee Scott from weatherman Willard Scott.

She is someone like Jonnie Monroe, a twenty-two-year-old rock musician who went to a Wal-Mart store in Olympia, Washington, to buy a can of spray paint one day and applied for a job instead, intending to work only long enough to buy an amplifier for her band. She sailed through two interviews and a drug test and was hired in February 2004, as a full-time cashier making $7.91 an hour. Her training consisted of shadowing another cashier and watching a video that included scenes of a sinister-looking union organizer working a parking lot. "It was weird, like an after-school special," said Monroe, whose supervisor made her cover up the small tattoo on her arm after a customer complained.

Monroe soon made friends with a co-worker, but within a few weeks the Customer Service Managers, or CSMs, separated them, making sure they worked in different sections of the store and eventually on different shifts. Wal-Mart discourages associates from forming friendships with the people around them, apparently because it both fears such fraternization will result in lost productivity and because there is a greater chance such bonds will facilitate unionization. If Monroe made even the smallest computational error, she had to call a CSM to fix it while customers waited impatiently. "Customers scream at you and there's nothing you can do," she said. Monroe was told not to joke around with her fellow workers or to make political comments, even on her breaks. Monroe came to particularly dread the "opening ceremony," otherwise known as the Wal-Mart cheer: "You guys treat me like crap, you won't let me switch shifts, you won't let me dress like myself, won't let me act like myself, and now you want me to be, like, Yay, Wal-Mart?"[20] Monroe quit on the spot after eleven months when her boss refused to allow her time off to attend her brother's wedding in Chicago. On her way out, Monroe thought to herself, "I never want to come back here even to shop."

In her book, Ehrenreich quoted a co-worker named Marlene, who echoed many of Monroe's complaints: "'They talk about having spirit,' [Marlene] says, referring to management, 'but they don't give us any reason to have any spirit.' In her view, Wal-Mart would rather just keep hiring new people than treating the ones it has decently. You can see for yourself there's a dozen new people coming in for orientation every day. . . . Wal-Mart's appetite for human flesh is insatiable. We've even been urged to recruit any Kmart employees we may happen to know. They don't care that they've trained you or anything, Marlene goes on, they can always get someone else if you complain."[21]

Scott rarely mentions Wal-Mart's turnover rate when he steps forward to argue that the company is a great place to work. Instead, the CEO focuses attention on the application rate. "We had 500 job openings, we had 5,000 applications," said Scott of a new store opening in Phoenix. "Maybe it's different where you live, but where we live, people don't line up to get a new job that pays less and has less benefits. The world does not work that way." Actually, it does when better-paying jobs for the unskilled are scarce. As the writer John Dicker aptly put it, "Wal-Mart's claim that the number of applicants for its jobs reflects the quality of its jobs is like saying soup-kitchen lines are a referendum on soup."[22]

Wal-Mart's investments in technology have reduced its relative degree of reliance on workers, who tend to be more expensive to maintain and less readily programmable than their digital helpmates. Baggers disappeared from Wal-Mart stores years ago. Now the company, like other big-box chains, is eliminating as many cashier jobs as possible by adding self-service checkout counters in many stores. Wal-Mart cannot mechanize its stores to the same extent it has its distribution centers, because store work involves sorting and stocking merchandise and interacting with customers. "While we at Wal-Mart pride ourselves on our cutting-edge technology," Scott recently acknowledged, "retailing remains a very labor-intensive business."[23]

In Walton's day, department managers drew up weekly work schedules for the workers they supervised. Today, a computer in Bentonville makes these decisions, making it much harder even for sympathetic store managers to accommodate the scheduling needs of their workers, many of whom must work a second job elsewhere to make ends meet. Wal-Mart boasts that about 75 percent of its hourly store associates are full-time, compared to 20 percent to 40 percent at competing chains. This sounds like a significant difference—until you realize that Wal-Mart considers twenty-eight to thirty-five hours a week a full-time shift.

When Wal-Mart's sales for the first half of 2005 fell slightly below projections, headquarters promptly slapped new restrictions on store managers' ability to deviate from the staffing schedules generated in Bentonville that might add to their labor costs. At the same time, the company began shifting more of its employees to part-time status in an attempt to further reduce payroll and fine-tune its computerized matching of labor supply with customer traffic. "We didn't do as good a job as we should have in managing the wages in our stores," admitted Tom Schoewe, Wal-Mart's chief financial officer.[24]

Among the employees caught in the cost squeeze was sixty-one-year-old Reva Barrett. A recently divorced mother of six, she began working at Wal-Mart in 1990 as a sales associate in Pinellas Park, Florida. Since the late 1990s, Barrett had worked as the Supercenter's Community Relations Manager, a full-time, salaried position. In mid-2005, the store's new manager summoned her as soon as the teachers appreciation banquet she had organized ended and told her that her position had been eliminated. She was allowed to stay on as a cashier, but only if she took a pay cut and agreed to make herself available from 7 A.M. to 11 P.M. Barrett decided to stay, but she also hired a lawyer and filed a complaint alleging sex and age discrimination with the Equal Employment Opportunity Commission. "Wal-Mart used to be a pillar of this community, but it looks to me like they flushed the toilet on community involvement," Barrett said. "I'm that piece of toilet paper that sticks to the side and just won't get flushed down."[25]

At Wal-Mart, store managers are under enormous pressure from headquarters to continually reduce labor costs as a percentage of sales—to increase productivity, in other words. On a factory assembly line, making workers more productive often involves simplifying repetitive tasks so that they can be performed faster. Wal-Mart has done some of this in its stores, equipping clerks with handheld computers that automate inventory record keeping by scanning bar codes. For the most part, though, Bentonville has wrung productivity gains out of its labor force not by refining jobs, but by forcing employees to do more work in the same amount of time at the same pay. By most accounts, Wal-Mart deliberately understaffs its stores, making managers responsible for seeing that the work gets done one way or another—as long as it does not involve letting non-salaried workers rack up overtime. (Laws in most states require employers to pay time-and-a-half to workers after an eight-hour day or a forty-hour week.)

Dawn Douglas lasted six months as a Wal-Mart associate in Kingman, Arizona, quitting in May 2005, with a sore back strained by lifting too many oversized television sets into customers' cars. She had left a $6.25-an-hour job at a local Whataburger to join Wal-Mart as a full-time sales associate in electronics, starting at $7.10 an hour. After a few months, Douglas was raised to $7.40 an hour. She put in thirty to thirty-five hours a week, mostly working the night shift, which allowed her to help out at the pet-grooming business that her mother owns. "It was nice," said Douglas, who is twenty-four years old and single. "I liked the job and everything, dealing with the customers."[26]

Douglas's opinion changed radically after the discount store where she worked was converted into a Supercenter. The electronics section expanded from three aisles to five and added a music section, even as the staff shrunk. "For some reason, they started thinking it was over-manned," Douglas said. "I was the only person in the department. They started forcing me to lift 200- to 300-pound TVs by myself—twenty-seven- to thirty-two-inch TVs. Then they would get mad when I was out in the parking lot and wasn't there to guard the equipment. It was kind of a Catch-22." Reluctantly, Douglas was also pressed into service lifting heavy merchandise onto high shelves or risers. "There are supposed to be two people—one to make sure the ladder doesn't collapse—but sometimes I did it by myself," she said. "I'd let [the supervisors] know I needed help, but their attitude was 'Either do it, or get another job.'" She already had another job, and quit Wal-Mart to work full-time as a groomer at her mother's business, Pepi's Pet Haven.

Kate Moroney, who works the 10 P.M. to 7 A.M. overnight shift in a Florida Supercenter, is mainly responsible for stocking frozen foods in the deli department freezers. However, she is also required to answer the phone and assist customers. After the department managers leave, she often is left alone to cover other departments, including food, greeting cards, small appliances, and housewares. At management's request, Moroney recently trained as a cashier and is now frequently paged to the front of the store to run the cash register when the store is busy. If she cannot find the time to finish stocking the frozen-food section, the morning crew has to do the job, putting it behind schedule and in danger of rebuke from the day-shift supervisors.[27]

To honor the home office's overtime prohibitions, some managers allegedly flout the company's avowed policies—not to mention state and federal labor laws—by forcing workers to work through their breaks or past the end of a shift or by simply erasing hours already worked from electronic time cards. As a sixteen-year-old working in a Wal-Mart in a suburb of Denver, Leila Naijar claimed in a lawsuit that she was forced to miss breaks and put in more than eight hours per shift—in violation of a state law protecting minors. "The store closed at 11 and there were nights we had to stay to clean up until 12:30, 12:45," Naijar said. "It was a long day, and I was tired the next day at school. And sometimes, I'd have to work ten, eleven hours on a Saturday or Sunday."[28]

Included in the 2000 Wal-Mart audit that found massive violations of wage-and-hour rules in 128 stores were 1,371 instances of minor-age employees working excessive or inappropriate hours (as when school is in session). By its own admission, Wal-Mart ignored the audit, but soon had to pay a $205,000 fine imposed by the state of Maine for violations of child labor laws in each of its twenty stores in the state. Later, the U.S. Labor Department charged Wal-Mart with eighty-five additional violations, including the use of dangerous machinery such as chainsaws and cardboard balers, in three more states—Arkansas, Connecticut, and New Hampshire. In early 2005, Wal-Mart settled the federal charges by paying a meager fine of about $136,000. But the company stirred a political hornet's nest by negotiating a sweetheart deal with the Bush Administration Labor Department to give it fifteen days' notice before any future inspections for child labor infractions, as well as a ten-day grace period to bring a store into compliance if violations were found. The department's own inspector general found these "significant concessions" unwarranted, stating, "There was little commitment from the employer beyond what it was already doing or required to do by law."[29]

When a Wal-Mart store is verging on exceeding its monthly labor budget, managers have been known to send workers home and replace them with assistant managers, who, as salaried employees, are exempt from overtime regulations and thus can be pressed into service without financial consequence to the company. Assistant managers have filed class-action suits in at least four states, claiming that Wal-Mart should have paid them overtime when requiring them to fill in for hourly workers. One suit brought by night-shift assistant managers in Michigan asserts that they were nothing more than "glorified stockers who unload trucks, move products into the store, and stock shelves." Kim Comer, a Michigan plaintiff who spent thirteen years as an assistant manager in various stores, claimed that in addition to her managerial duties she often had to spend a full eight-hour shift working as a cashier, the position that she had first filled in joining Wal-Mart out of college.[30]

Shortly after Glass took over as CEO in the late 1980s, Bentonville began giving store managers the option of locking janitors and other night-shift workers into stores until morning—a practice to which none of the other national retail chains resorted. "Locking in workers, that's more of a nineteenth-century practice than a twentieth-century one," said Burt Flickinger, president of the consulting firm Retail Forward, after a *New York Times* article brought the Wal-Mart lock-ins to light in 2004. Imprisoning third-shift employees was one way to keep them from stealing merchandise or drinking beer in the parking lot while their managers were home asleep. However, Wal-Mart spokeswoman Mona Williams insisted that the lock-ins were just another way of putting employees first. "Doors are locked to protect associates and the store from intruders," she claimed.[31]

Michael Rodriguez was stocking shelves in the Sam's Club in Corpus Christi, Texas, about 3 A.M. one night when another worker, driving an electronic cart, ran into him and crushed his ankle. "I was yelling and running around like a hurt dog that had been hit by a car," Rodriguez recalled. As usual, the store was locked, and there was no manager to let Rodriguez out to go to the emergency room. Rodriguez would have gone through the fire exit had he not repeatedly been warned that using it for any reason but to escape a fire was grounds for dismissal. Finally, a co-worker succeeded in rousing a manager by telephone and the door was unlocked an hour later.

Although Wal-Mart still permitted overnight lock-ins as of 2004, the number of stores that engaged in the practice had dwindled to about 10 percent of the total. Did this reflect a new enlightened attitude on the part of the company? Not really. An increasing number of stores were open for business round the clock, which meant that managers could not lock employees in without also locking customers out. At least Bentonville no longer allowed managers to chain shut emergency doors—as some did when the lock-ins first began. Headquarters prohibited the practice after a stocker in Savannah, Georgia, collapsed and died inside a store while paramedics waited outside for the door to be unlocked.

On October 23, 2003, federal officials mounted one of the largest illegal-immigration crackdowns in years, raiding sixty-one Wal-Mart stores across twenty-one states and arresting 245 janitors from Mexico, Mongolia, Brazil, Uzbekistan, Poland, Russia, and other countries. Ten of the arrested janitors worked directly for Wal-Mart; the rest were employed by contractors that Bentonville had hired. Reporters, citing anonymous sources, wrote that prosecutors had recordings of Wal-Mart managers conspiring with contractors to hire illegals.

There seems little doubt that the Wal-Mart executives who approved the dubious contracts knew in a general sense that the janitorial industry was rife with undocumented workers. Over the last two decades, all sorts of companies have awarded their business to a new breed of fly-by-night cleaning contractors who specialize in hiring illegal immigrants at low rates. "These companies are pretending they're not the employer," scoffed Delia Bahan, a lawyer who successfully sued several California grocery chains for nonpayment of overtime to hundreds of janitors from Mexico. "The contractor is willing to work people seven days a week, not pay payroll taxes, not pay workers' comp taxes. The companies don't want to do that themselves, but they're willing to look the other way when their contractors do."[32]

The federal case against Wal-Mart began in Honesdale, Pennsylvania. This town of 5,000 is home to store No. 2480, one of 1,000 stores nationwide for which Wal-Mart had outsourced overnight floor cleaning to 100 contractors. In 1998 and 1999, two members of the Honesdale cleaning crew—a Russian and a Slovak—were arrested on charges unrelated to their jobs and found to have overstayed their visas. The Honesdale store manager told local police that he suspected that most of the janitors working the overnight shift lacked proper papers. Even so, Wal-Mart turned to its existing contractor for replacement janitors, who, it turned out, also were illegals.

The Federal Bureau of Immigration and Customs Enforcement in conjunction with other government agencies launched an investigation from Pennsylvania, and in 2001 agents arrested about eighty undocumented workers, mostly Eastern European, cleaning Wal-Marts in twenty-one stores. Most of the workers were deported, and thirteen contractors pleaded guilty to charges of knowingly employing illegal immigrants. However, no charges were brought against Wal-Mart, which agreed to cooperate with the ongoing Pennsylvania probe as well as a second federal investigation underway out of Chicago.

One of the guilty middlemen was Stanislaw Kostek of CMS Cleaning, which cleaned more than a dozen Wal-Marts in Pennsylvania, New York, and Virginia. Kostek was a subcontractor to a vendor who supplied about 100 Wal-Mart stores. Kostek said that Wal-Mart paid $10 an hour per worker to his contractor, who paid him $9. Kostek claimed to have paid his janitors $8 an hour, though it probably was closer to $7. He admitted to not paying taxes. "How do you pay workers' comp if you're making $1 an hour and you have to cover all expenses?" he demanded.[33]

Afterward, Wal-Mart began phasing out some contractors, reducing the number of stores cleaned by outside janitors to 700 from 1,000. The company told reporters that it had acted not out of concern for immigrant workers or even its legal liability, but because it calculated that cutting out middlemen would save about $66 million.[34]

Wal-Mart's promised cooperation most likely fell short, however, for the U.S. Attorney for central Pennsylvania authorized the big raid in the fall of 2003. The criminal case against Wal-Mart ended with a whimper a year later with a promise from Wal-Mart to tighten up its "contractor review process" and a payment to the feds of $11 million—not a fine, as the company hastened to point out, but a contribution to support the enforcement of immigration laws and curb exploitation of janitors. "We don't want these folks to be treated poorly," said spokeswoman Williams. "We're spending this money so that folks that do this can't get away with it."[35]

Wal-Mart still faced a civil racketeering suit in New Jersey by seventeen of the illegals arrested in the 2003 raids. The class-action suit accused Wal-Mart of conspiring with maintenance contractors to create a criminal enterprise in which janitors not only were underpaid and, in some cases, not paid at all, but also were "physically beat up, unlawfully imprisoned and coerced into continuing to work at Wal-Mart."[36] In late 2004, the judge in the case conditionally certified it as a class action and ordered Wal-Mart to supply the names and addresses of all janitors who had worked in its American stores since 2000.

At Wal-Mart, the pressure to dance to Bentonville's tune only intensifies as an employee moves up off the floor into store management. But at least managers are well compensated for the Darwinian rigors of their employment, giving the ambitious associates plenty of incentive to seek promotion. On average, male store managers in 2001 made $105,682; co-managers $59,535; and assistant managers $39,790. On the other hand, the average sales associate made only $16,526 and cashiers a mere $14,525. (The average for female employees was lower in each category.[37])

As Lee Scott tells it, Wal-Mart is the American dream of upward mobility realized. "Every year, thousands of hourly associates are promoted into management and most of these jobs do not require a college degree," he said.[38] Wal-Mart believes in promoting from within; 76 percent of its store management employees started out as hourly employees. However, the company has been slow to use its vaunted digital database to systemize the awarding of promotions based on merit. An analysis of the voluminous documentation that the company turned over to the plaintiffs in *Dukes v. Wal-Mart* revealed that promotions are still meted out as they were in Walton's day: employees—mostly men—simply "tapped on the shoulder" by their bosses and elevated, often over the heads of the women who trained them.[39]

Betty Dukes, the lead plaintiff in the huge sex-discrimination case, is an ordained Missionary Baptist minister who still works as a greeter at a Wal-Mart in Pittsburg, California. Dukes, a middle-aged African American woman, started at Wal-Mart in 1994 as a part-time cashier making $5 an hour. Three years later, she was promoted into a sales associate job, and there her career stalled. As positions came open, they were often filled by male workers of less seniority without having been posted. When Dukes complained that she was being discriminated against, her managers began to write her up for minor offenses such as returning late from breaks. After she was demoted back to cashier, she lodged a complaint with Wal-Mart's district office. Ignored again, she sought redress in court. "I have no fear in my spirit at all of Wal-Mart," Dukes said.[40]

Melissa Howard, a fellow plaintiff in the case, achieved what Dukes never did, rising all the way to store manager at the age of twenty-seven. Howard was running a Supercenter in Bluffton, Indiana, when she drove with her district manager and other store managers to Bentonville for a meeting in early 2000. Her colleagues, all of whom were men, stopped three times on the long trip to go to strip clubs. In a complaint later filed in court, Howard alleged that at one club her district manager offered a stripper $50 to join him and Howard in a "threesome out back." Howard was humiliated but chose not to report the incident to the home office. "I definitely feared retaliation," she said. "It seemed to me to be an accepted part of the culture." A few months later, a new district manager came in and demoted her to co-manager. "It honestly still makes me sick to my stomach to think about it," said Howard, who promptly resigned and filed suit.[41]

While admitting to no wrongdoing or even to shortcomings, Scott responded to the outpouring of criticism of Wal-Mart's treatment of workers by announcing a series of reform initiatives in 2003 designed to make the company "a corporate leader in employment practices." Wal-Mart established an Office of Diversity to administer programs to move more women, blacks, and Hispanics into management while equalizing rates of pay. The goal, Scott said, was "to make sure that the percentage of qualified minorities and women we promote is equal to the percentage who apply"—meaning, for example, that if 50 percent of the qualified applicants for assistant manager jobs are women, at least 50 percent of the promotions would go to women. If Wal-Mart fell short of its annual diversity goals, each officer all the way up to Scott would have his or her pay reduced by as much as 7.5 percent in 2004 and by 15 percent beginning in 2005.

To date, "no Executive Officer's incentive payment [has been] reduced as a result of the diversity goals," as Wal-Mart disclosed in its 2005 proxy statement.[42] Was this flawless performance real improvement in the company's treatment of women and minorities, or does it reflect the softness of its diversity goals? It is impossible to judge from the scant information that Wal-Mart has made public.

At Wal-Mart's annual meeting in 2004, Scott got up and effectively declared that Wal-Mart's computers weren't a contributing cause of the company's labor-relations problems, but rather they were a solution. The big brain in the Glass Center now would send an electronic alert to remind cashiers to take their meal breaks. "If the prompt isn't responded to," Scott said, "the cash register will shut down because that associate's lunch is the most important thing."[43] In addition, new scheduling software would factor in each state's unique work-hour restrictions. For example, in states that prohibited minors from working past 10:00 P.M., the system would not schedule them past 9:30. Scott announced a third reform, as well: Any time a store manager added to or subtracted from an employee's record of hours worked, the employee would be notified of the change and be asked to verify it. (Of course, if an employee is afraid of being fired or retaliated against for refusing to sign off on the officially clocked hours, this change would not help.)

In response to the question on the tip of every associate's tongue—"Will I get a raise?"—Scott put forth a new job classification and pay structure, one of such confounding complexity that it could only have been generated by computer. Hourly employees now would be slotted into seven categories, instead of the current four, and have their pay adjusted in the process. "No one's pay will be reduced as a result of implementing this new structure," Scott said, "but some associates will receive an increase." The deserving could look forward to annual raises of as much as 50 cents an hour, he said. "I think we all know how Sam Walton felt about the importance of treating people right."[44] Store workers in attendance might have turned cartwheels in the aisles if only they could have figured out what Scott was saying.

Confusion was perhaps the best Wal-Mart could hope for given the underlying reality that its tortuous new pay system betrayed, namely, that the company wanted to create the impression of being more generous to rank-and-file workers without doing anything to jeopardize the big labor-cost advantage that it held over competing retailers. The fact is, "Every Day Low Prices" and Every Day Low Wages and Benefits are flip sides of the same coin. In fact, this irreconcilable conflict between Wal-Mart's business model and the aspirations of its workers turned the company's unveiling of a new health benefits plan in the fall of 2005 into a public relations fiasco.

With only half of its workforce enrolled in the company health plan, because of its high cost relative to employee wages, Scott announced that the changes were designed to "bring insurance within reach of all Associates" by introducing a new "Value Plan." The monthly premiums of $25 for an individual, $37 for a single parent, and $65 for a family were 40 percent to 60 percent less than those for the current lowest-cost plan. Employees also now could set up a health savings account and make as many as three doctor visits a year with a $20 co-payment before the $1,000 deductible kicked in. Outside experts predicted that Wal-Mart's unwillingness to cut this $1,000 deductible would cause the company to fall well short of its avowed goal of universal coverage for its employees. "It provides some coverage for people who otherwise are probably not going to have any coverage," said Alwyn Cassil of the Center for Studying Health System Change. However, in health insurance "you get what you pay for," she added. "To keep a premium low means you're going to have less comprehensive benefits."[45]

A few days after Scott's announcement, the health plan Wal-Mart had touted as a helping hand extended to its lowest-income employees was exposed as yet another cost-control scheme in a *New York Times* article based on a leaked internal memo written by M. Susan Chambers, the company's executive vice president for benefits. "Growth in benefits costs is unacceptable," wrote Chambers, noting that from 2002 to 2005 the total cost to Wal-Mart of the employee benefits it provided had risen 15 percent a year, to $4.2 billion. "Unabated, benefits costs could consume an incremental 12 percent of our total profits in 2001, equal to $30 billion to $35 billion in market capitalization," warned Chambers in what was supposed to have been a confidential memo seen only by Wal-Mart's board members.[46] Chambers laid out various proposals, all intended to slow the increase in benefits outlays without further damage to Wal-Mart's reputation.

By Chambers' analysis, the biggest single problem was health-care costs, which were rising at 19 percent a year, mainly because Wal-Mart employees were sicker than the average American, "particularly with obesity-related diseases," and also tended to make excessive use of expensive hospital and emergency room visits. "Most troubling," she wrote, "the least healthy, least productive Associates are more satisfied with their benefits than other segments and are interested in longer careers with Wal-Mart." Among other things, Chambers proposed that Wal-Mart try to attract a healthier workforce by introducing an education benefit to appeal to students, giving employees a discount on healthy foods, and redesigning the jobs of all store workers to include the gathering of shopping carts or some other sort of physical activity. "It will be far easier to attract and retain a healthier workforce than it will be to change behavior in an existing one. These moves would also dissuade unhealthy people from coming to work at Wal-Mart," wrote Chambers, who estimated the potential savings to the company at $220 million to $670 million by 2011.

Rarely has the gap between image and reality—between what Wal-Mart wants the world to believe about it and what the company actually is—been illuminated as starkly as it was by Chambers' clinically candid memo. "I don't think the DNA of Wal-Mart has changed at all," said Mark Husson, an analyst at HSBC Securities. "It's like a religious cult—it has a low-cost gospel to bring to the country and sees it as a divine duty to do that and nothing is going to get in its way. It will do what it has to do and say what it needs to say to get there."[47]

AMERICA'S FIRST FAMILY OF DISCOUNTING

It was a great disappointment to Sam Walton that none of his four children—Rob, John, Jim, or Alice—was willing or able to succeed him as chief executive of Wal-Mart. In fact, Rob, who was named chairman of the company upon his father's death, was the only member of the next generation to make a career at Wal-Mart. As it has turned out, though, Walton couldn't have asked for more devoted heirs. Along with their mother, eighty-six-year-old Helen Walton, the four Walton siblings have managed to boost the family's controlling stockholding in Wal-Mart from 38 percent to over 40 percent by 2005, even as the company has grown enormously. By all appearances, the Waltons also have avoided the internecine disputes that have undermined many a corporate dynasty, and they have collaborated in using the family's influence to preserve Wal-Mart in their father's image.

Today, the Walton family's stake in Wal-Mart is worth about $80 billion,[1] which is more than the fortunes of Bill Gates and Warren Buffett *combined*, and more than the total annual economic output of Egypt, a nation of seventy-seven million people.[2] Their dividends alone amounted to $974 million in 2005,[3] or nearly $195 million for each family member. This works out to $533,000 per person per day. In other words, the members of Sam's immediate family collect more in dividends in each hour of every day—in excess of $22,000 per person—than the typical full-time Wal-Mart associate is paid for an entire year. Even adjusted for inflation, the Walton fortune is on a par with the greatest industrial fortunes in American history.

By all rights, Bentonville, Arkansas, should have been renamed Waltonville years ago. Wal-Mart remains the biggest employer in town by far, with its headquarters located on a road named for its founder, Sam Walton Boulevard. People who live in Bentonville are likely to work for the Walton family's company, shop at the Walton family's stores, have an account at the Walton family's bank, and read what until recently was the Walton family's newspaper. Many townsfolk attended Sam Walton Junior High School and send their sons and daughters to day care at the Helen R. Walton Children's Center. Residents often drive thirty miles south to Fayetteville, where they might take in a lecture at the Sam M. Walton School of Business at the University of Arkansas, take in a play or a concert at the Walton Art Center, or catch a basketball game at the Bud Walton Arena, named after Sam's brother. To get away from it all, the locals catch a flight at the local airport—after checking in at the Alice L. Walton Terminal Building, named for Sam's daughter.

However, Walton sightings are rarer than they once were in Bentonville. As chairman of Wal-Mart, Rob keeps an office at the company, but moved to Colorado some years ago. Alice lives on an enormous ranch in Texas. Helen, the matriarch of the Walton clan, still lives in Bentonville, in the same low-slung creekside house (designed by E. Fay Jones, an accomplished student of Frank Lloyd Wright) that she shared with her husband. Third-born Jim Walton also lives in town, where he runs Walton Enterprises, the private company that holds the family's stake in Wal-Mart, from a plain office on the third floor of an unremarkable brick building on Main Street. Jim also oversees the family's operating businesses, notably Arvest Bank Group and Community Publishers, a publishing chain that until mid-2005 included the two biggest regional newspapers, the *Benton County Daily Record* and the *Northwest Arkansas Times*.[4]

John Walton, a former Green Beret who won the Silver Star in Vietnam, died in June 2005 in the crash of an experimental ultra-light aircraft near Jackson, Wyoming, where he lived. He was fifty-eight years old and left a wife and a son. Walton, who had worked as a crop duster and a builder of yachts, was the family's most active philanthropist. His principal interest was the conservative cause of education reform through the use of school vouchers and other taxpayer-financed incentives to aid private school attendance. A longtime Wal-Mart director, John was replaced on the board by his brother Jim.

Even before John's death, the Walton family suffered its share of trial and tribulation. Jim is the only one of Sam's children not to be divorced; Rob is now separated from his second wife. Alice struck and killed a pedestrian with her car in 1989, and she was convicted of drunk driving in 1998 after crashing her Toyota 4Runner into a gas meter. Car accidents seem to run in the family: A year later, Helen Walton was badly injured when she drove her Chrysler into a dump truck, according to witnesses, after running a red light.[5] More recently, one of Bud Walton's granddaughters, Elizabeth Paige Laurie, was kicked out of the University of Southern California after it was learned that she had paid a classmate $20,000 over three years to do most of her work for her.

The wealth of Wal-Mart naturally has freed the Waltons from having to worry about making a living. Rob, despite being chairman of Wal-Mart, spends ample time racing bicycles, collecting and racing sports cars, and flying his corporate jet. Alice, who dabbled in finance and economic development when younger, now concentrates on raising horses on her ranch in Texas and on building an art museum in Bentonville. In recent years, Alice has emerged as a major buyer of American paintings at the New York auction houses of Sotheby's and Christie's, causing quite a stir in the spring of 2005 by paying more than $35 million for a single work by Asher B. Durand. The Walton museum, the Crystal Bridges Museum of American Art, is expected to open in 2009 in a $50-million building designed by the celebrated architect Moshe Safdie.

Although the Waltons keep their distance from Wal-Mart's day-to-day operations, they maintain close contact with one another, and they do not hesitate to exert control over Wal-Mart's direction and its culture. Sam Walton remains a venerated figure to his children, who gather at Helen's house three times a year to discuss his legacy—the family business. Their thoughts on the stores—about where to expand, what kinds of customers to target, when to invest more in growing the company, and how to treat employees—are relayed to the board of directors and to senior managers through Rob. Their thoughts about the other businesses, the banks, and the newspapers pass to Jim, who is directly in charge. Their thoughts on philanthropy, an increasingly important focus over the last decade, were communicated through John, who has yet to be replaced in this role.

All of the Waltons' decisions are guided by their religious beliefs as devout Presbyterians. Helen Walton was chairwoman of the Presbyterian Church (USA) Foundation and is still a trustee emeritus; she regularly attends services at First Presbyterian Church in Bentonville.[6] When John died, his local house of worship, the Presbyterian Church of Jackson Hole, held a memorial service. John and Jim both attended the College of Wooster, a small liberal arts school in Wooster, Ohio, because their mother approved of its

Presbyterian affiliation. (Jim left after two years and graduated from the University of Arkansas, closer to home.) The family, through its private charitable foundation, has given generously to Presbyterian charities, including $500,000 to the Dwight Presbyterian Mission, which ministers to Indians in Oklahoma, and $400,000 to Presbyterian Church USA.

The Walton Family Foundation is one of three bountifully endowed charities that the family influences or controls. In addition to the family foundation, which is funded by and directly controlled by the Waltons, there is the Wal-Mart Foundation, which is funded primarily by the company, and the Walton Family Charitable Support Foundation, which is funded by the family but includes outsiders on its board. Each has tens or hundreds of millions of dollars in assets, and doles out the money in grants as small as $500 (for example, to the Benton County Historical Society and the Oklahoma Safe Kids Coalition in 2004) or as large as $300 million (to the University of Arkansas in 2003, the biggest gift ever to a public university). In 2004, the Wal-Mart Foundation distributed $170 million to more than 100,000 groups, while the Walton Family Foundation gave away $107 million to more than 800 groups.

Much of the family's personal philanthropy, as expressed by the family-directed foundation, has been used to encourage the expansion of publicly funded but privately run charter schools and the use of school vouchers in fostering alternatives to traditional public education. In 2004 alone, according to documents on file with the Internal Revenue Service, the family foundation gave about $3 million just to one charter school group, the Knowledge is Power Program. Millions more were given to individual charter schools, including Aspire Public Schools in Oakland, California, and Harborside School in San Diego, as well as to groups promoting them, including the Colorado League of Charter Schools and the Charter School Resource Center. The Waltons' increasingly assertive sponsorship of a conservative educational reform agenda has antagonized many of the same critics who object to Wal-Mart's business practices. In their view, the Walton family is funding initiatives that are undermining public school systems across the country by shifting money to private schools while opening the door to public funding of religious schools.[7]

More broadly, critics complain that much of Wal-Mart's charitable giving—well-publicized grants of a few hundred to a few thousand dollars to local Girl Scout troops or libraries—has coincided with its efforts to open new stores, wrest zoning changes from cities, or press local governments to pay for sewers, roads, or other improvements to properties where it wants to build. "The Waltons' and Wal-Mart's philanthropy deserves more scrutiny than praise," said Jeff Krehely, deputy director of the National Committee for Responsible Philanthropy, a watchdog group in Washington.

It is not clear how such criticism affects the Waltons, because their reflexive secrecy makes them difficult to read. But like the second generations of other dynastic families, Sam's heirs face challenges different from any their father did. He started with virtually nothing and built the world's biggest publicly traded company; they inherited unimaginable wealth and must reconcile the company's red-in-tooth-and-claw culture with the broader social role that success has forced upon it.

Playing hardball with suppliers, squeezing employees, and scrapping with local governments is one thing for a small or mid-sized regional retailer in small rural towns happy for a low-cost shopping opportunity. It is something else entirely for a company whose decisions set the wage-and-benefit standards for an entire industry and result in turning venerable manufacturers into shell companies that merely import what they used to make in order to meet your price demands. Corporations with enough power to materially affect the world's largest economy need to think and act differently than a small-town five-and-dime just trying to make a living by saving a neighbor a nickel.

These are the challenges that have confronted the current generation of Waltons for more than a decade. But whether because of their loyalty to Sam's legacy, their steadfast paternalism, their Protestant work ethic, or naked self-interest, they have so far failed to rise to meet them.

CHAPTER FIVE

WAL-MART'S WAR
AGAINST THE UNIONS

After nine years of working at a Wal-Mart store in northern New Jersey, Donna DiIenno was totally fed up. It really wasn't so much the low pay and the lousy benefits that finally got to her, though naturally she could have used more money. DiIenno, who had just turned forty, was tired of getting pushed around by her bosses. In August 2003, DiIenno's job as a support manager at the Washington Township store was eliminated, and she was offered a choice of new positions at the same pay and hours. Angered by what she considered a lack of respect and appreciation, DiIenno made use of Wal-Mart's open-door policy to write a letter of protest to her store manager.

A few days after posting the letter, DiIenno was summoned without explanation to the office of her store manager's boss, the local Wal-Mart district manager. Twice she was told to sit down. Twice she refused. According to DiIenno, the rest of her truncated Wal-Mart "exit interview" went like this: "He said, 'Why are you being insubordinate?' I said, 'I'm not being insubordinate for refusing to sit down.' He pushed the door shut and said, 'You're not leaving until you sit down.'" DiIenno replied that she had to get back to her job and left. The district manager shouted after her, "You don't have a job."

Incensed by her firing, DiIenno called Local 1360 of the United Food and Commercial Workers union and volunteered her services in its drive to unionize area Wal-Mart stores. Soon, she was working a 7 P.M. to midnight shift for the union, sitting in her car in the parking lot in front of the store where she once worked. Periodically, managers would come out and tell her to shove off. Less frequently, a former co-worker would stop by to surreptitiously pick up a union authorization card. Said DiIenno, who was five months pregnant at the time: "Somebody needs to fight the fight."[1]

In Washington Township, as in most places, the UFCW got nowhere in its attempt to organize Wal-Mart. If every unhappy and demoralized worker in the store had signed a card, the UFCW would have easily reached the 30 percent threshold required to force a union representation vote, DiIenno said. The problem was that many of her former colleagues lived paycheck to paycheck and were scared silly that any pro-union display would get them demoted or fired. They had reason to be afraid. Every worker soon learns there are two unforgivable sins at Wal-Mart: stealing from the company and consorting with a union. "In my 35 years in labor relations, I've never seen a company that will go to the lengths that Wal-Mart goes to, to avoid a union," said Martin Levitt, a consultant who helped the company perfect its anti-union tactics before writing a memoir called *Confessions of a Union Buster*. "They have zero tolerance."[2]

What distinguishes Wal-Mart from the many other large American corporations that are "union-free" and determined to stay that way is not only the depth of its antagonism toward collective bargaining, but also the steadfastness of its refusal to admit to it. Like every other bedrock tenet of the Wal-Mart Way, the company's evasive brand of anti-unionism was Sam Walton's doing. "I have always believed strongly that we don't need unions at Wal-Mart. . . ." he wrote in *Made in America*. "Historically, as unions have developed in this country, they have mostly just been divisive. They have put management on one side of the fence, employees on the other, and themselves in the middle as almost a separate business, one that depends on the division between the other two camps. And divisiveness, by breaking down direct communication, makes it harder to take care of customers, to be competitive, and to gain market share." Wal-Mart's partnership with associates "works better for both sides than any situation I know of involving unions," added Walton, whose tightfisted, patriarchal benevolence was perfectly expressed by his "Mr. Sam" nickname.[3]

Many of Wal-Mart's corporate contemporaries—especially the southern ones—hired union-busting consultants in the mold of John Tate, who helped Wal-Mart ward off the half-hearted Retail Clerks organizing drives in two small Ozarks towns in the early 1970s. But Walton elevated Wal-Mart's anti-union efforts to the highest level of corporate priority by creating a full-time senior executive position for Tate and installing him on Wal-Mart's board of directors.

Walton had personally taken the lead in battling what remains to this day the drive that came closest to unionizing an entire Wal-Mart facility in the United States: a 1978 bid by the International Brotherhood of Teamsters to organize the Wal-Mart distribution center in Searcy, Arkansas—the same partially automated DC that was an important stepping-stone on David Glass's upward climb. Nearly 200 workers suffered injuries in the DC's first four months of operation, mainly because Wal-Mart had insisted on putting it into service well before construction was completed. Workers were even angrier when they learned that their counterparts at a newly opened DC in Texas were getting $1.50 more an hour than the $6.20 hourly wage at Searcy. After their complaints fell on deaf ears at the home office, angry workers called in the Teamsters.

In no time, 200 of the 415 workers at the Searcy DC signed cards asking the union to represent them. An election was promptly scheduled, as required under federal law, but a variety of stall tactics used by Wal-Mart succeeded in delaying a vote all the way until 1982. In the

interim, Walton had met repeatedly with the Searcy workers, alter-
nately charming, cajoling, and threatening them—first with the loss
of their profit sharing and then with the loss of their jobs. "He said
people could vote any way they wanted, but [if the union won] he'd
close her right up," recalled one worker. Walton also pointedly mentioned that Wal-Mart had 500 job applications on file for the DC,
implying that pro-union workers were dispensable. After the vote,
which was 215 to 67 against the Teamsters, many of the pro-union
employees were indeed fired.[4]

Since Walton's day, Wal-Mart has honed union suppression to a
fine art. Typically, the home office swings into action as soon as it
learns that employees have been asked to sign union representation
cards. The store's manager is tipped, usually by an employee who has
been relentlessly drilled by the company on the dangers of so much as
talking about unions. Someone from the store often starts watching
people suspected of harboring union sympathies—basically anyone
who has pushed for a raise or resisted extra work. Wal-Mart associates who have been through the process said they have spotted their
managers loitering in parking lots outside early organization meetings or have noticed that managers who rarely associated with them
suddenly started taking breaks with employees. Some Wal-Mart
workers have claimed that closed-circuit security cameras were
installed after an organizing drive began.

At the first whiff of a union, or very quickly thereafter, Wal-Mart
begins requiring employees to attend hour-long meetings at which
they are lectured about how the presence of a union would poison the
atmosphere inside the store by turning manager against associate
while also costing employees a sizable chunk of their paychecks in
dues. They are shown anti-union videos that hammer home that
message. Union-busting experts from the "People Division" in Bentonville typically are flown in on corporate jets to run the meetings
and to keep headquarters informed.

Then the real onslaught begins. The experts from Bentonville teach store managers to meet individually with every employee who might sympathize with the union and its pledges to improve wages, benefits, and work rules. The goal of these one-on-one sessions is to intimidate associates and condition them to be suspicious of outsiders. One associate who went through the process, Eric Jackson, a cashier at the Wal-Mart in Paris, Texas, said that in the early stages of an organizing drive at his store, a group of five managers summoned him into a back room and made him watch an anti-union video and participate in a role-playing exercise. "I was supposed to be a manager, and one of them was the associate who came to me with a question about a union," Jackson recalled. "So I quoted the video. I said, 'We do not believe we need a union at Wal-Mart,' and they were like, 'Good, good!' and then I said, 'We're not anti-union—we're pro-associate,' just like I'm supposed to say."[5]

If employees persist in trying to organize, Wal-Mart has been known to transfer, demote, or even fire associates suspected of pro-union sympathies. At other times, it has reclassified suspected sympathizers as managers, rendering them ineligible to vote. Wal-Mart often has been accused of "flooding the unit"—that is, adding many new employees shortly before a union vote, on the theory that new employees are more likely to vote with management. This tactic, though illegal, is easy for Wal-Mart to mask because of its high turnover rate: It naturally replaces half of its workforce every year as it is.

Wal-Mart's anti-union arsenal has proven extraordinarily effective. No entire store or distribution center in the United States has so much as held a union representation vote since the Teamsters went down to defeat in Searcy twenty-four years ago. The UFCW has managed a dozen times to petition for votes by employees of individual departments within stores, mostly butcher shops and Tire & Auto Lube Express shops. With the conspicuous exception of a meat-cutting department in Texas (discussed later in this chapter), Wal-Mart has prevailed in every such vote in the United States.

Remember Joshua Noble, the epileptic who led the 2005 drive to organize a Tire & Auto Lube in Loveland, Colorado? Noble persuaded eight of his sixteen colleagues to join him in signing UFCW cards. But by the time the election was held three months later, one pro-union worker had been fired and two others had gone off to college. Wal-Mart replaced them twice over, transferring in six new workers. The five other card signers backed away, leaving Noble as the last union man standing. The vote was 17 to 1. "It wasn't a fair fight. Every day they had two or three anti-union people from Bentonville in the garage full time, showing anti-union videos and telling people that unions are bad," complained Noble who, at last report, was still working at Wal-Mart.[6]

If you set out to translate *Don Quixote* into a modern setting, you could do worse than to cast its windmill-tilting protagonist as an American union organizer. When the union movement was at its peak a half-century ago, one in three workers carried union cards in their wallets; today, barely one in ten does. That organized labor, such as it is, has been reduced to irrelevance across a vast swath of the U.S. economy is not entirely, or even mostly, the fault of union leaders. Automation and the internationalization of markets have combined to vaporize millions of high-paying jobs in the manufacturing industries that long were the pride of unionism. Since the mid-1980s, union membership also has steadily eroded in many service industries as employers have bowed to intensifying economic pressure to cut payrolls and improve productivity.

The increasing prevalence of retaliatory firings and other illegal union-busting tactics reflects the weakness of the National Labor Relations Board, a federal agency established during the New Deal of the 1930s to safeguard workers' legal right to organize for collective bargaining. "Toothless" is the adjective favored by the NLRB's critics and even by some of its officials. "The [National Labor Relations Act] is not being obeyed," Leonard Page, the NLRB's general counsel, declared in a speech in 2001. "We have a sixty-five-year-old statute and there are a percentage of rogue employers that are able to take the low road during an organizing drive." The process of prosecuting companies resorting to unfair labor practices was too protracted and the penalties levied too weak to deter abuses, Page added. "If workers have to face this gauntlet and look at a remedy three or four years later, which amounts to posting a notice on the board for 60 days, what are we talking about? That certainly is not the rule of law."[7]

Given the prohibitive odds, why do Wal-Mart workers like Noble and DiIenno continue to try to organize the company after so many years of failure and frustration? Many are motivated by the same sense of the dignity of work that drew them to Wal-Mart to begin with, the idea of a fair day's pay for a fair day's work. It is the company's avowed philosophy, after all—at least on paper. Anger over the company's betrayal of its own ideals tends to drive the most passionate of Wal-Mart's pro-union employees.

There is no better example than Jon Lehman, a native Ozarker who spent twenty-four years working at Wal-Mart stores, starting as a part-timer during his high school years in Harrison, Arkansas, and ending as a store manager in Indiana making close to $200,000 a year. Lehman's long run at Wal-Mart began when Sam Walton was still going strong, spanned David Glass's entire tenure as CEO, and spilled over into Lee Scott's first few years as boss. Through most of it, he embraced the Wal-Mart Way wholeheartedly. "I was really into them," said Lehman, who not only enjoyed leading his associates in the company cheer but also tacked on the theme song from *The Beverly Hillbillies* or *Gilligan's Island* whenever he felt that morale was bumping bottom. "I'd say, 'All right everybody, stand up! We're going to sing a silly song.' And they'd look at me kind of funny," Lehman recalled. "'Mr. Sam told us to do that, people,' I'd say. 'Read Rule Number Six' [of "Sam's Rules for Building a Business"]."[8]

Yet by 2001, Lehman was so disillusioned with Wal-Mart that he defected to the UFCW and worked full-time in its campaign to organize his former employer, first in his hometown of Louisville, Kentucky, and later in Las Vegas. In Louisville, Lehman made such a nuisance of himself, parading through Supercenters that he used to run with a big sign reading "Union Yes," that Wal-Mart went to court and obtained two restraining orders against him. "I got to where I wouldn't drive by a Wal-Mart without going in there and raising some hell," said Lehman, a deceptively mild-mannered forty-four-year-old whose unflappable calm and good cheer mask kamikaze conviction.

Lehman seemed destined to work for Wal-Mart the way that some boys are stamped from an early age as future cops, pilots, or insurance adjusters. The eldest of four siblings, Lehman was "raised up" in Harrison, home to Wal-Mart No. 2. His father was a Baptist preacher subsisting off the donations of a small congregation, and his mother was the church organist. The Lehman family needed every one of the dollars it saved by shopping at the Wal-Mart that opened in 1964. Jon's favorite babysitter, Sue Cox, started as a fabric cutter at the Harrison store from the day it opened (and would not retire until 2004, with millions in her profit-sharing account).

As kids, Jon and his younger brother, Gary, got haircuts at a barbershop near the Wal-Mart and were supposed to wait in the snack bar there for their father to pick them up. "He'd give us a quarter, but we never went and drank a Coke," Jon recalled. "We went into sporting goods." The Lehman brothers especially liked the sporting goods department because it was connected to the rest of the store by a long concrete ramp perfect for testing the aerodynamic potential of shopping carts. One day when Jon was eight and Gary six, they flew sideways off the ramp and crashed into a table of towels. "This old woman picked us up by the collar and sort of hurled us into these folding chairs up in the manager's office," Jon said. "They were doctoring the cut on Gary's arm with a Band-Aid. The man I assumed was the manager got on the PA system and paged my dad, but he wasn't there yet. So we had to just sit there and wait while this guy kept staring at us."

The mishap did not prevent Jon from landing a part-time job at Wal-Mart during his high school years, nor did it prevent him from becoming a true believer in the Wal-Mart Way. Lehman spent at least as much time at the store as in school, starting as a janitor, cart pusher, and errand boy before moving up to sales jobs in shoes and then in menswear. "I worked my butt off at Wal-Mart," he recalled. "My grandpa told me if I worked hard at Wal-Mart, there was a chance I could get ahead in life."

After graduating from high school in 1979, Lehman was accepted into the Wal-Mart management training program and was assigned to Wal-Mart No. 265 in Terrell, Texas—known within the company as "Terrible Terrell" because it was home to a state prison. A year into his training, Lehman enrolled at Baylor University in Waco, where he had won a small music scholarship (he's proficient on the trumpet). He remained with Wal-Mart even so, transferring to a store near the Baylor campus. Through his church, he met Jill Brown, a granddaughter of country music star Judy Lynn, and married her in 1985. Frustrated by the slow pace of his advance through Baylor, Lehman dropped out in his junior year and devoted all of his energies to getting ahead as a Wal-Mart store manager.

Lehman no doubt would have gotten a store of his own in a few years had he and Jill not been set on living in Dallas. As it was, though, he spent seven years as an assistant manager cycling through Wal-Marts scattered along Dallas's exurban fringe. While working in the store in Grapevine, Lehman caught Tom Coughlin's act for the first time. Coughlin, who was then the company's vice president of operations and, more important, an old hunting buddy of Mr. Sam's, noticed that someone had divided the store's inventory of Red Ball rubber boots between two end-cap displays when, in Coughlin's view, one would have done nicely. Big Tom made his point by kicking one of the end caps to pieces, stopping only when he tore a hole in one of his eel-skin cowboy boots. "The funny thing was, by the time Tom got to the front to leave he calmed down and was complimenting us on how the store looked," Lehman said. "He looked at my name tag and said, 'Jon, you look good today, even if you are wearing a pink shirt.' I never wore a pink shirt to work again."

One sweltering July day in 1986, Lehman was working in Wal-Mart No. 426 in The Colony, a small town about twenty-five miles north of Dallas, when a call came in from Bentonville. Walton was en route to Dallas on a corporate jet with Glass, Jack Shewmaker, Don Soderquist, and a fourth executive, and they needed a ride from the airport in nearby Addison to an office downtown. Lehman was chosen because he was the only manager who had not driven a pickup truck to work and had room for five passengers. With a felt-tip marker, he copied out his store's vital statistics on his palm and took his beat-up Ford LTV to a car wash. He blew all his quarters on copies of the *Wall Street Journal* and a couple of other newspapers, and still got to Addison early.

Walton took the passenger seat, picked up one of the newspapers that Lehman had carefully feathered across the front seat, but gave it no more than a glance. "Jon, where are you from?" Walton asked.

"Well, I'm from Harrison," replied Lehman in his best Ozark drawl.

"Harrison? That was my second store."

"I know that, Mr. Walton."

"Don't call me Mr. Walton. Call me Sam."

They got to talking about Harrison, and Lehman went into the story of how he and his brother had crashed the shopping cart. "Mr. Sam just sort of locked on me," Lehman recalled. As he got to the part where the manager paged his dad, Walton's jaw dropped and he started shaking with laughter. "That wasn't the manager; that was me," Walton said. "I can even tell you what you boys were wearing that day. You had on matching white shirts with these little blue and white stripes."

As they talked, Lehman said he'd eventually like to get up to Louisville, where his wife had relatives. "Why don't you do that then, Jon?" Walton said. "Tell your district manager you want to go to Louisville and tell him Sam told you to tell him."

In his first year as a Wal-Mart store director, Lehman earned a $90,000 bonus on top of his $52,000 salary—a lot more money than he'd ever seen, nearly enough to put him in the top rank of store directors. Sam Walton had flown in for the grand opening in Clarksville, and he returned a few months later for a visit.

In 1990, Lehman was chosen to open a new store across the river in Louisville proper this time, and again Mr. Sam was there with bells on. Over the next decade, Lehman would change stores six times, usually moving because Wal-Mart offered him a bigger or a better store to run, but sometimes it was to get away from a district manager who disliked him or vice versa. As it was, Lehman was making more money and living larger as a Wal-Mart store director than he could ever have imagined while growing up poor in Harrison. Throughout the 1990s, he never made less than $140,000, and in 1996, his best year, he pulled down close to $220,000.

It was only after his experience as a union organizer that Lehman recognized how the cash and the comfortable life it bought had warped his moral code. Sure, it could have been worse; had he been more ruthless in suppressing labor costs he might have boosted his income into the $300,000 to $400,000 range that defined the top tier of Wal-Mart store managers. But even to reach the sales and profit numbers required to make his more-modest bonuses, Lehman routinely altered pay records to delete overtime and to make it look as if workers had taken breaks they in fact had forgone—and he admitted as much under oath in 2003, testifying in a class-action suit brought against Wal-Mart in Indiana. "At the time, I didn't think I was stealing time," Lehman said. "Now, I'm very ashamed of it. I believe what I did was appalling."[9]

Lehman also admitted to passing over deserving female associates for promotions without ever giving it much thought. "There are no policies at Wal-Mart that say, 'We discriminate against women,' of course, but it's one of those systemic things that's taught and passed down. I developed that mentality, too," Lehman told me. "It's just like growing up in Harrison. They called blacks niggers down there. When I first moved away from Harrison to a town that was half black, I had to make a conscious decision right there: Was I going to continue the mentality that blacks are the scum of the earth, or was I going to love them? I never consciously made a decision before that to be prejudiced against blacks, but I think that's what's happened at Wal-Mart against women. It's taught. It's kind of a rite of passage thing. You come up through the ranks, and the attitude is that women don't make good managers because they have babies and they don't want to move. That's just the way it is, so you go with it."

Lehman's path began to diverge from Wal-Mart's in 1997, when his wife fell severely and mysteriously ill. He resigned from his job and moved the family from Springfield back to Louisville, a renowned medical center, where Jill eventually underwent surgery to remove a brain tumor. After a half-year of unemployment, Lehman accepted an offer from Meijer, the Michigan-based chain that had pioneered the superstore, to run the store it was preparing to open in Louisville.

Meijer did not pay its store managers nearly as well as Wal-Mart, but the most difficult adjustment for Lehman was running a unionized shop. Like any true Wal-Marter, he mistrusted labor unions on principle. "I would preach against the union in my floor meetings, tell all my workers that it was like a cult, you know—it was evil and all they wanted was to take your money," he said. Meijer's contract with the UFCW provided the workplace with a well-defined matrix of job descriptions, grade levels, pay categories, and so on that existed only in rudimentary form at Wal-Mart. Much as Lehman chafed under these constraints at first, he came around to the view that a more regimented, less frantically improvisatory workplace was better for all concerned. "I'm not saying it was a perfect system, but, man, it was a whole lot easier than trying to pull rabbits out of a hat all the time," he said.

Lehman found, to his surprise, that union officials did not come equipped with horns and pointy tails. "I got to know my union reps and they would tell me about stuff that was getting ready to happen with the workers that I didn't know anything about. 'Hey, did you know these people over here are upset?'" Lehman said. "It was a big help, and I started to really enjoy that relationship. I even started to think that I might want to go to work for the UFCW one day and to bring the truth back to Wal-Mart associates and let them know how good the union really is."

In 1999, Wal-Mart's district manager for the Louisville area enticed Lehman back to the company by making him manager of a Supercenter slated for Louisville's affluent Hillview district. Although the Hillview store was a considerable success, for Lehman the thrill he'd once felt working for Wal-Mart was pretty much gone. It was just a job now, a job he would have quit soon enough.

Then one day a flyer turned up in the men's room.

It wasn't much, just a printout from someone's home computer bearing a simple message: We need a union. Lehman dutifully telephoned Bentonville's union hotline and faxed the flyer to the home office. The next day, three labor relations specialists flew in from Bentonville and began meeting individually with the store's salaried staffers, pressing them to identify the troublemakers among the hourly workers. "I wouldn't say they were mean-spirited, but they were very probing," Lehman recalled. "They asked me how I felt about unions, and that's when I stuck my foot way down deep in my throat. I said, 'You know, I think they have their place.' I was trying to give a candid answer, but I saw in their faces that I'd made a mistake. I added real quick, 'But we don't have a need for a union here.' They kind of relaxed a bit, but I walked out of there kicking myself all the way down the back hallway."

The United Food and Commercial Workers have remained more militant than most unions through organized labor's long decline in the United States. It was formed in the 1979 merger of the Amalgamated Meat Cutters and the Retail Clerks, the very union that had chased

Walton into the arms of the union-busting lawyer Tate. The UFCW absorbed other unions representing beauticians, barbers, shoemakers, and members of a few other trades to become the largest of the more than fifty unions in the AFL–CIO, with 1.4 million members currently.

The UFCW was quick to recognize Wal-Mart as a threat to the retail and grocery stores that employed two-thirds of its members, but slow to take on the Herculean task of trying to organize the company. Throughout the 1990s, the UFCW essentially fought a publicity war against the company instead. Union researchers dug up all sorts of documented dirt about the company, ranging from its suppliers' use of child labor abroad to the devious tactics it used to induce communities into subsidizing construction of stores and distribution centers at home. The UFCW scored a bull's-eye hit on the Waltons by unearthing a slew of sweetheart deals between various family members and Wal-Mart. The union succeeded in taking a bit of the shine off Wal-Mart's reputation and slowed its expansion into union strongholds like California, but accomplished little else beyond infuriating Bentonville, even as the threat posed to the UFCW membership grew exponentially with the Supercenter's coming of age.

The Supercenter taught the supermarket industry a lesson in brute capitalism. The typical chain supermarket could not slash its prices to match the Supercenter opening across the street and still turn a profit, largely because it was locked into UFCW contracts paying workers 25 percent to 30 percent more than Wal-Mart's non-union staffers made. The result was that every time a new Supercenter opened in America, two big supermarkets went out of business, taking some 400 high-paying UFCW jobs with them. In the late 1990s, Bentonville began stepping up Supercenter openings, from 113 in 1998 to 157 in 1999 to 167 in 2000. The UFCW was left with two basic choices: negotiate supermarket industry wages and benefits down to Wal-Mart levels, or take on the task of trying to force Bentonville to pay its employees up to union standards.

In September 1999, the UFCW organized a Supercenter "blitz," sending representatives into 300 stores to pass out pamphlets and chat up employees. Over the years, the union had picketed hundreds of Wal-Mart stores and had even organized a march on Bentonville without getting much of a rise out of the company. During one Mother's Day protest over Wal-Mart's treatment of female employees, associates in some stores even brought cookies and soft drinks outside to demonstrators. This time, though, the home office went ballistic, going to court to obtain a restraining order banning UFCW reps from all of its stores nationwide.[10] "In taking such harsh action against us, Wal-Mart was telling us where their vulnerabilities lie," recalled Allen Zack, a senior UFCW organizer who was the union's ranking Wal-Mart strategist at the time. "The difference was, this time we were going into stores and talking to associates. They didn't want us anywhere near their workers."[11]

One of those associates, a forty-five-year-old butcher named Maurice Miller, angered by his manager's failure to come through with a promised promotion, turned to the UFCW for help in organizing the meat-cutting department of Wal-Mart No. 180 in Jacksonville, Texas. To unionize a workplace, at least 30 percent of its workers must sign cards calling for an election that is administered by the NLRB. If the union prevails, the employer is required by law to meet with it and bargain in good faith over a contract. (What sounds simple in theory is fraught with complications in practice.) Wal-Mart employed only twelve butchers in Jacksonville, but it took Miller months of heavy persuasion to convince a majority of them to back the union. In February 2000, the butchers voted in the UFCW by a 7-to-3 margin, establishing the Jacksonville meat counter as the first unionized Wal-Mart unit in the United States.

This breakthrough emboldened hundreds of Wal-Mart employees around the country to sign union cards. The NLRB authorized elections for the meat departments of four more Supercenters, including one in Florida and another in Illinois. Just two weeks after the vote in Jacksonville, however, Wal-Mart offered its draconian response. It disclosed plans to eliminate meat-cutting in all Supercenters in Texas, Arkansas, Missouri, Louisiana, Oklahoma, and Kansas—180 stores in total—and switch to pre-cut, cellophane-packaged meat. Undoubtedly Wal-Mart would have gone to pre-cut meat in all its Supercenters eventually, even if there had never been a pro-union vote; the cost savings were hugely compelling. But it's equally likely that Bentonville accelerated the move in an attempt to stop the UFCW's organizing momentum.

Wal-Mart turned over boxes of records to the NLRB that established that it had begun experimenting with case-ready meat on a small scale in Arkansas for the better part of a year. However, the agency found no mention whatsoever of a plan to extend the program to Jacksonville. "I was very, very suspicious of that, but in the end all I had were suspicions," recalled Page, the NLRB's chief prosecutor.[12]

Enter Michael Leonard, on a Harley-Davidson. Leonard was a talented field organizer who somehow managed to rise to the third-highest position in the UFCW without ever acquiring the slick, blow-dried patina of the professional union executive. He loved big bikes and he looked the part, even in a tie and jacket. Leonard, a native of Louisville, was a second-generation employee of Kroger Co., now America's largest grocery chain. His dad drove a truck for Kroger, and Michael worked as a clerk in Louisville before and after a tour of combat duty in Vietnam in the mid-1960s. "The grocery industry I grew up knowing was one where if you worked full-time, you could own a home and be part of the middle class," Leonard recalled. "It was a good job."[13]

Leonard was the regional director for Kentucky and Ohio when UFCW President Douglas Dority brought him to Washington just a few weeks after the Jacksonville vote and put him in charge of "strategic programs." Leonard quickly concluded that nothing else that the UFCW might do to advance its strategic interests compared to battling Wal-Mart. He easily convinced Dority to let him focus exclusively on Wal-Mart, but the issue of how best to take the fight to Bentonville proved contentious among the union's leaders. Leonard, the consummate field organizer, wanted to enlist the union's 600 locals in an all-out drive to force Wal-Mart to the bargaining table. "You can't run from your basic mission as a labor union, which is to organize and represent workers," Leonard recalled. On the other hand, the locals answered to their members every week and were loath to commit money to organizing unless it offered a quick and certain payoff.

Leonard won the argument and the union's executive committee agreed to a full frontal assault on Wal-Mart. He and Zack laid the organizational groundwork for a national campaign, one that could strike wherever the company seemed most vulnerable. At the same time, they wanted to heighten the drama of the UFCW's showdown with Bentonville by creating a central battleground. They chose Las Vegas, which was a show unto itself, of course, but also happened to be the most heavily unionized major city in America. Wal-Mart usually shied away from union strongholds, but Las Vegas's sizzling growth pace and large working-class population made it irresistible. Wal-Mart had just opened its first Supercenter in Las Vegas and was planning to add five more in 2001. The supermarket contracts the UFCW had negotiated in Las Vegas ranked among the most generous in the country. The members of UFCW Local 711 had a lot to lose, and rallied to the union's calls to arms.

The UFCW went noisily into Las Vegas in the fall of 2000, as if merely attracting the attention of Wal-Mart's associates was half the battle in unionizing the company. There were indeed lots of disgruntled associates amid the blue-smocked ranks of true believers in Las Vegas, but they were more like cult members in need of deprogramming than wage slaves with a grievance. "Wal-Mart is ruthless in controlling its employees, and I don't just mean the sophisticated surveillance it puts them under. It really gets into their minds," Leonard stated. "I can't believe how many times I heard people say, 'That's not the Wal-Mart Way.' It was almost biblical or something."

Las Vegas's overriding identity as a city of tourists and transients worked against the UFCW's Wal-Mart campaign. In Vegas, the employee roster of a retail establishment tended to turn over nearly as fast as the clientele of a craps table. In fact, many of the city's clerks and cashiers were just biding their time to meet the year-long residency requirement of casino employment. Tenured Wal-Mart employees (that is, anyone who'd put in at least a year) might have been strait-jacketed into the Wal-Mart Culture, but a great many other workers cared so little about their jobs that they would gladly sign a union card today only to vanish tomorrow.

It took the union nearly a year to persuade a majority of the 200 workers at Sam's Club 6382 on the outskirts of Las Vegas to sign union authorization cards. On September 18, a week after the terror-ist attacks on the World Trade Center, the union filed with the NLRB, which scheduled an election for November 29.

Greg Roberts, the manager of the Sam's Club, had given no quarter in his battle with the union. He had confiscated the ballpoint pens the union had passed out after the company started charging workers for the pens they used on the job, and even ordered workers to remove the UFCW-provided American flag stickers they'd affixed to their name tags after 9/11.[14] But it was only after the vote was scheduled that Ben-tonville pulled out all the stops. "Loss prevention" managers—security experts who catch shoplifters and employee thieves—from around the country were flown in to patrol the store and the parking lot and keep union organizers off the premises. Several "people managers" were brought in from California to keep watch on union supporters, many of whom were transferred into jobs reducing their contact with other workers and some of whom were fired. Anti-union workers were promised raises and promotions at some unspecified future date. Meanwhile, the labor relations operatives from Bentonville stepped up the frequency of their anti-union seminars, segregating committed union supporters in separate sessions to keep them from influencing the other workers. Three large glass cases filled with anti-union mes-sages were installed in the break room, covering an entire twenty-foot section of wall. Roberts added a new punch line to the Sam's Club cheer that all workers had to perform at the start of every shift. "What are we going to do?" he'd ask. Mandatory answer: "Vote no!"

Leonard could have let Wal-Mart get away with what he believed were rampantly unfair labor practices and hope that his majority would hold through the election. Or, if it looked like the union was going to lose, he could file allegations against the company and stampede the NLRB into postponing the election. A few days before the scheduled vote, Leonard flew out to Las Vegas and effectively conceded defeat at Sam's Club 6382 by filing a massive complaint with the NLRB. By the time the board finished adjudicating the complaints, almost all of the workers who signed UFCW cards were gone from Wal-Mart. The board ultimately upheld many of the unfair labor practice allegations made by Leonard, handing the UFCW yet another Pyrrhic victory.

As the Battle of Las Vegas raged, Jon Lehman's disillusionment with Wal-Mart reached the flash point. In the summer of 2001, he approached the UFCW for a job as word of the union's national organizing drive spread through the loosely organized underground of disaffected Wal-Marters around the country. Leonard was skeptical. "There were a lot of people out there who'd worked for Wal-Mart, but I only wanted the sort of bona fide folks that any organization wants as employees and weren't just looking to settle a score or something."

Lehman persisted, telephoning Leonard over the next month or two to talk about Wal-Mart, impressing the UFCW leader with his knowledge of the company and his character. "Jon just seemed to me to be a very decent, honest guy," said Leonard, who cautioned that he could not offer Lehman anything close to the $160,000 a year he was making as a store manager in Louisville. Lehman's willingness to take a big pay cut cinched it for Leonard, who finally extended an offer of full-time employment at $80,000 a year in November, just as the tussle over Sam's Club 6382 was climaxing.

The warm relationship Lehman had enjoyed with his district manager had frosted over since he'd begun talking with the union. "Suddenly, I couldn't do anything right," he said. Lehman had been invited to a resort near Bentonville for a week-long leadership seminar, but was taken aback to find that one of his roommates worked for the home office and had just returned from Las Vegas. Lehman returned to his room one night to find that someone had gone through his briefcase, which contained printouts of his e-mail correspondence with Leonard and Zack.

He became even more alarmed after a childhood buddy who worked at the home office gave him a private tour. "He took me into a room that was wall-to-wall computers and these little people sitting there with headsets," Lehman recalled. "He told me this was where they monitored Intranet and telephone traffic at the stores. I was thirty or forty feet down the hallway before it hit me: Oh, shit! I hope they haven't been listening to all my phone calls to Washington." (Wal-Mart says that it only monitors phone calls in stores at risk of bomb threats.)

Lehman left Wal-Mart without telling his colleagues that he was taking a job with the union, and thus was able during his first few months with the UFCW to function as a kind of covert advance scout. He spent long hours kibitzing with managers and associates in dozens of Wal-Marts throughout Kentucky, Indiana, and Ohio, gathering intelligence to help the union brain trust in Washington focus on the most promising organizing opportunities in the region. Leonard decided that the place to start was the hometown that he and Lehman shared—Louisville. Leonard parachuted in one of the union's best organizers, Harold Embry, to run the campaign, which began in March 2002.

Lehman was one of two dozen organizers working the campaign. But none of the others could electrify a store the way he could just by walking into it and moseying around. He was not just another union guy in a UFCW windbreaker: He was a dissident, a defector. He'd hired many of the workers he now was trying to persuade to sign union cards—as well as many of the managers bent on stopping him. And Lehman's style was deliberately provocative. His theory was that the best way to expose Wal-Mart as a bullying, self-interested employer was to set off Bentonville's union trip wire. "You suddenly take a store from union threat level of zero up to three or four and look, here comes the Citation jet!" Lehman said. "Workers who had no inclination to even think about unions soon are complaining, 'Why are they making us go to all these meetings and showing us these videos that make the union look like crooks?' . . . And then my phone starts to ring. It's like, 'I want to sign a card, by God. I'm tired of this bullshit.'"

Lehman made a big hand-lettered placard saying "Union Yes," like the one that the plucky minimum-wage worker played by Sally Field holds aloft in the movie *Norma Rae* while standing defiantly atop a table. Lehman carried his sign as he threaded his way through the checkout lanes at a dozen Wal-Mart stores throughout Louisville. This was provocation squared. Even customers reacted, making thumbs-up or thumbs-down gestures as they waited in line. Lehman would usually get in a good fifteen to twenty minutes of sign time before a posse of managers succeeded in herding him out an exit. (Under the law, they could not lay hands on him.)

Most of Lehman's buddies in Wal-Mart management treated him like he was radioactive. The manager of a Supercenter in Louisville told him, "Do you know what the labor relations guys call you now?" Lehman shook his head. "The Antichrist," his friend said. One evening in June 2002, a sheriff appeared at his door with a summons. Wal-Mart obtained two temporary restraining orders against Lehman, one for each of the counties that encompassed most of the Louisville metro area. One of the orders was rescinded. However, the "temporary" restraining order for Jefferson County still stands, nearly four years after it was issued.

Lehman's freelance shenanigans annoyed Zack, who believed that the UFCW's best hope against Wal-Mart was a subtle, legalistic strategy that he and the union had been teasing out for years. Its object was to lessen the playing field's tilt in Wal-Mart's favor by persuading the NLRB to impose an "extraordinary nationwide remedy" against the company. In 99.9 percent of unfair labor practice complaints issued by the board, the sanctions applied are narrowly local. But if an employer is caught using the same illegal tactics in various places, the NLRB can impose nationwide penalties. Even in such cases, the typical remedy is the decidedly un-extraordinary bulletin board posting in which an employer admits to breaking the rules and swears never to break them again. On the other hand, violating a nationwide remedy puts a company on a slippery legal slope that can send it careering out of NLRB hearing rooms into Federal courts where judges could impose large fines and other draconian penalties on repeat offenders.

In the wake of the UFCW's blitz of 300 Wal-Mart Supercenters in 1999, the UFCW had barraged the NLRB with allegations of unfair labor practices against the company. By 2001, the board had found that Wal-Mart had indeed broken the law in a half-dozen different locales. Furthermore, it found that the cases had common elements, suggesting a nationwide anti-union strategy directed out of Bentonville. Page, the NLRB's general counsel, told Wal-Mart's chief labor lawyer that he was going to file a national complaint but wanted to give the company a chance to come in and argue its case first. This was just two months after George W. Bush had been sworn in as president. As a Clinton appointee, Page expected to be replaced. If the customary pattern of presidential appointments held, his time in office would expire in the fall. But in April, just a week before Wal-Mart's lawyers were due in, Page got a call from the White House giving him thirty-six hours to clear out his office. Page's successor decided against bringing a national complaint against Wal-Mart.

For lack of a better alternative, Al Zack clung to the hope that the union somehow could maneuver the Bush Administration NLRB into seeking an extraordinary nationwide remedy against Wal-Mart. "Even after Page left, we did see indications at times that the board was considering extraordinary remedies; they'd dance up to it and then dance back," Zack said. "Especially with a Republican in the White House, we needed to be consistent in our behavior in the field so that there would be similar violations all around the country and Wal-Mart couldn't blame violations on a rogue manager." And consistent Lehman was not. "Jon would go off and do things on his own that we told organizers not to do because it could hurt us with the NLRB," Zack said.

In the end, Lehman and his fellow organizers in Louisville collected hundreds of signed union authorization cards. In several locations, including the Hillview Supercenter that Lehman had opened in 1999, the union attained the 30 percent minimum threshold needed to petition for an election. But Leonard didn't ask for a vote, because he wanted to be certain of victory. Ultimately, the union was unable to get 50 percent support in any store.

In early 2003, Michael Leonard finally conceded defeat in Louisville, and transferred Embry and Lehman to Las Vegas. In Vegas, Lehman worked alongside a half dozen other former Wal-Mart employees. One, Stan Fortune, forty-seven, was an ex-cop who'd spent seventeen years working at Wal-Marts throughout the Southwest, moving up through the store security ranks to become co-manager (the second-ranking position) at a Texas Supercenter. When Fortune refused to fire a pro-union worker, Wal-Mart fired him. Another disillusioned Wal-Mart employee was Gretchen Adams, fifty-seven, who worked for Wal-Mart for ten years in five states, starting as a deli manager and ending as a co-manager of a Supercenter in Florida.

One day Lehman let *Fortune* reporter Cora Daniels accompany him as he tried to infiltrate a Wal-Mart. "Lehman gets out just a few hellos to workers before declaring, 'We are being stalked,'" Daniels wrote. "Since his head never seems to look anywhere but straight down the empty aisle, I'm convinced he's paranoid. But out of nowhere, one of the store's managers appears. The two exchange pleasantries the way co-workers do: Lehman compliments the manager on losing a little weight; the manager says politely, 'Thank you for noticing.' Then the manager asks Lehman to leave. It is back to the car. Lehman hasn't talked to a single new face today about the union."[15]

Lehman gravitated toward working the Supercenters' third shift, which began about 10:30 P.M. and ended at 8:00 A.M. He found that he had a lot more room to maneuver and improvise in the wee hours. Managers were scarcer and less inclined to care about union interlopers and the late-night workers tended to be rougher around the edges and more outspoken than their colleagues.

In October 2003, 70,000 UFCW members went on strike against the three largest grocery chains in southern California: Safeway, Albertson's, and Kroger. The supermarket companies justified the hard line they took in negotiations over health and retirement benefits with an argument that can be summed up with the cry: *Wal-Mart is coming! Wal-Mart is coming!* Bentonville had announced plans to gingerly enter the California grocery market by opening forty Supercenters over three years. Of course, if the usual pattern held, Wal-Mart would follow this toe dipped in water with a headlong dive into the pool. Safeway and the others were trying to hold the line on wages and benefits in anticipation of full-on competition with Wal-Mart. The resulting impasse lasted 139 days, the longest strike in the history of the U.S. supermarket industry.

The California grocery strike was a great convulsive trauma that drained the UFCW's treasury and monopolized its attention, shoving the Wal-Mart campaign so far down on the union agenda that it effectively disappeared. When, in March 2004, the UFCW's members ratified a contract that closely resembled the one its negotiators had rejected at the outset, not even Leonard wanted to continue battling a chain like Wal-Mart that was larger than Safeway, Albertson's, and Kroger combined. As soon as the strike ended, UFCW President Doug Dority stepped down and Leonard, a longtime Dority ally, retired with him. Leonard had planned to leave a year earlier, when he turned fifty-five, but had gotten caught up in the Wal-Mart campaign. Zack also called it quits. "I thought it was time to give someone else a chance to beat their head against the stone walls of Bentonville," said Zack, who was about to turn sixty. All of this happened so quickly that Lehman and the other Las Vegas campaigners were left hanging. "We were all calling Mike's secretary, saying, 'Where's Mike?'" Lehman recalled.

The Vegas campaign puttered along ineffectually for another few months until June 8, when Lehman, Adams, and Fortune were summoned to UFCW headquarters in Washington. (Miller had left to take a job with a local in Texas.) Lehman was expecting to sit down with representatives of the AFL-CIO to discuss tactical changes in the Wal-Mart campaign. Instead, he and his colleagues were gently but firmly let go. The UFCW's new president, Joe Hansen, had ordered the dismantling of Leonard's strategic issues department, effectively ending the Wal-Mart campaign in its fifth year. Lehman, Adams, and Fortune shared a cab to Reagan Airport, where they drowned their sorrows at a T.G.I. Friday's while awaiting flights home. Leonard felt bad for his protégés but did not take issue with Hansen's decision. "We'd taken it as far as we could and had to make a change," he said. "Wal-Mart is just too much for one union."

Judged on its own terms, Leonard's organizing campaign had failed: There still was not a single union member in Bentonville's employ. However, the UFCW had awakened other unions to the threat Wal-Mart posed to organized labor generally and had galvanized liberal activist groups like the National Organization for Women into picking up the cudgels against Bentonville. Zack never did get the extraordinary nationwide remedy he coveted, but the NLRB upheld dozens of unfair labor practice allegations against Wal-Mart all across the country, begging the question of whether there was anything that Bentonville wouldn't do to remain union-free and exposing the utter falsity of Wal-Mart's mantra that it is "pro-associate, not anti-union."

In the Jacksonville case, the NLRB had ruled in the end that Wal-Mart had broken federal law by refusing to bargain with the meat cutters after they'd voted in the union. The agency ordered Wal-Mart to reestablish the meat-cutting department while it bargained with the UFCW.[16] Wal-Mart ignored the ruling, and the NLRB let the matter slide. The NLRB also charged Wal-Mart with illegally firing four of the Jacksonville meat cutters in retaliation for their pro-union vote. One of the four, seventy-one-year-old Sidney Smith, was accused of stealing the banana that he ate while waiting in line to pay for it. Wal-Mart paid Smith $7,000 and settled out of court with the other three.[17]

Back home in Louisville, Lehman is still banned from the Wal-Marts of Jefferson County. Every now and then, a Wal-Mart associate calls to arrange a clandestine meeting in a parking lot or a coffeehouse and hand over a packet of signed authorization cards. "The workers are getting them signed now, not me," says Lehman. "I don't think having a union is going to create any perfect working environment, but a collective bargaining agreement would really help those workers at Wal-Mart. . . . I think a lot of this bull-riding kind of cowboy mentality among the store managers would go away and they wouldn't ride roughshod over the workers as much as they do. Sam's gone, you know. The workers have to look out for themselves now."

WITH JON LEHMAN,
INSIDE A WAL-MART SUPERCENTER

It's about 3 o'clock on a Friday afternoon when Jon Lehman and I walk into Wal-Mart No. 1 in Rogers, Arkansas, a few hundred yards from where Sam Walton opened his first discount outlet in 1962. We speed past the elderly greeter stationed just inside the door, leaving him no chance to do more than give us a friendly little wave. "Come on, let's find cereal," Lehman says.

We find the cereal section, which is vast and quite amply stocked. "I'm impressed," he says. "For a Friday afternoon, that's pretty full. Cereal is the hardest counter in the store to keep full, especially on a Saturday."

Having established the essentiality of cereal as a measure of the quality of store management, we move on. "What would you guess is the highest profit category in groceries?" Lehman asks.

"I really have no idea," I answer. "Peanut butter?"

Lehman glances at me with what I hope is mock disdain. "I mean category, not product," he says. "Peanut butter is classified as dry grocery, OK?"

We turn a corner and the temperature plunges. Both sides of the aisle are lined with refrigerated glass cases for as far as the eye can see. "Here it is: frozen food," he says. "On some of this stuff they're making 30 percent. I used to walk the frozen-food section two or three times a day to look for things that were out, like that," he says, pointing to a nearly empty shelf that should have been heaped with barbecue-chicken-and-potato dinners. "That's bad, but there's a reason for it. There's a reason that's out of stock. Either they've flown out of it—it's a great seller—or they are having a problem getting it."

Next, Lehman asks me to name the most profitable department in general merchandise but doesn't give me a chance to answer. "Obviously, it wouldn't be toys, though toys is pretty good," he says. "It's fabric. Actually it goes back and forth. Stationery is either number one or number two, or fabrics is number one or number two. It depends on the price of paper at the time."

"Which would you rather run—a discount store or a Supercenter?" I ask, knowing he had run both in his day.

"Supercenter," he replies.

"Because they do more business?" I ask. Wal-Mart store managers are paid a salary, plus a bonus pegged to their store's profits.

"Because you get more people to get the job done," Lehman says. "And, yeah, you can make a little more money in a Supercenter because they do tend to put up bigger numbers. I'd guess this guy is making a quarter-of-a-million a year anyway."

We're walking down an aisle lined with bags of sugar. "Look at that presentation," says Lehman, coming to a stop. "It's almost all Great Value. It's private label—Wal-Mart's own brand—but it's made by the same company that makes Domino sugar. They squeeze the national brands and expand the private label."

"I don't see any Domino," I say, scanning the shelves as we walk on.

"Me either," Lehman says. "Here's another example: Great Value flour. You're supposed to have four facings of Great Value and two facings of Gold Medal, because you are making about 22 percent more on private label."

We check the price of a five-pound bag: $1.84 for Gold Medal versus 89 cents for Great Value. "But you know what?" Lehman asks. "They're making more profit on the private label even so, because their cost is so much lower."

Here's the fresh-meat section, a potent symbol of Wal-Mart's anti-union resolve.

"A lot of this stuff comes from Iowa and Texas. Ironically, some of it comes from union processing plants," says Lehman, hoisting a T-bone and peering at it intently. "What I look at is what they call the bloom—how red the meat is. It's supposed to make your mouth water when you look at it, but this is pretty nasty."

"It doesn't look so bad to me," I say.

"It's bloody," he replies, picking up another package. "It's supposed to have a little pad under there to absorb all the blood."

I ask Lehman how much latitude he had as a store manager to set prices.

"I could mark items down, but I could not mark items up from Wal-Mart book retail. I could mark down at any time to meet the competition, but you had to answer to people sometimes. In the end, my district manager might say, 'Why did you go to two for a dollar on that or why did you charge $30 for that, it's supposed to be $34.95?' 'Well, Target had it for $33 and I had to beat 'em.'"

"Could you add things to your product line on your own?"

"You're only supposed to add items that are from approved vendors, but I don't know of a store that hasn't experimented with local items," he says. "I had a little Amish guy in the area whose family made Amish candy, cookies, and cakes. My customers loved them. I couldn't keep them on the shelves because it was good-quality stuff. It wasn't authorized by the home office, but I brought it in and 70-type it."

He picks up a bag of Doritos and points to the Universal Product Code stamped on it. "You have a UPC code, but you're not an approved vendor, so I go into the computer and assign you a Wal-Mart item number that starts with 70," he says. "The home office tracks that stuff, so they know I'm doing it, but the nice thing is they don't know exactly what it is. All my local vendors—Pepsi, Coke, Little Debbie, Frito-Lay—all that stuff is 70-type, too, even though it's been approved by the home office. That's because it's delivered by the supplier instead of coming from a Wal-Mart DC."

We come across a bunch of Felida-brand mops jumbled together in a jerry-built wooden rack sitting too high off the floor to offer easy access. "Now that's creative," Lehman says sarcastically.

On the other hand, Lehman is impressed with the faux wood floors we come across in the ladies' apparel section. "It's plastic and can't really pass for wood, but it does give you the feel of a little better quality," he says, kneeling down to rap on the floor with a knuckle. "It's a great idea, because instead of having to vacuum the carpet, now they can just run a floor machine over this."

Who can resist pawing through a bin of DVDs selling for $1 apiece? "These are the cheapest DVDs I've ever seen," I say.

"There you go," Lehman says. "But I'd bet you they'd sell 20 percent more of these DVDs if they priced 'em at 99 cents instead of a buck."

A female clerk who doesn't look a day over sixteen is restocking a circular rack of men's shirts. Lehman pulls a hanger out from the side of the rack opposite where she is working. He asks me to guess where the shirt was made: China, Bangladesh, Honduras, or Guatemala.

"China."

"Ding, ding, ding, ding," Lehman says. "You win."

"I've been reading a lot in the newspapers about Wal-Mart workers trying to get together and organize and get a union going," he says to the clerk. "Is that true?"

The clerk giggles nervously. "I have no idea," she says.

"Well," Lehman continues. "If it's going to happen, it probably wouldn't happen here."

"No, not in Rogers, Arkansas," she says with a slight edge. "This is store number one, you know."

"How long you been here?"

"About a month now. But my fiancé, his six months is coming up in June. He's only eighteen, but he'll probably be here the rest of his life in, you know, LP—Loss Prevention. I hope he does, 'cause he's got his heart set on it."

"It depends on who you know," Lehman says quietly. "Good luck."

As we're heading for the exit, I ask Lehman whether this is a typical Supercenter.

"Yeah. I guess. But I have seen a lot of workers [here] today. I wonder if just because this is store number one they give it a little bit sweeter numbers—more payroll, more bodies to get the job done. But I wouldn't want to run a store right by the home office no matter what. Even when you're far away, they're always looking over your shoulder."

CHAPTER SIX

WHEN WAL-MART COMES TO TOWN

It was around the improbable figure of Kenneth Stone that national resistance to Wal-Mart's inexorable expansion first began to coalesce in the late 1980s. Stone, a lanky, agreeably mild-mannered professor of economics at Iowa State University, single-handedly moved the simmering debate over Wal-Mart's impact on Main Street beyond anecdote to econometric analysis with his 1988 study "The Effect of Wal-Mart Stores on Businesses in Host Towns and Surrounding Towns in Iowa." Despite its less-than-scintillating title and dry prose, Stone's forty-page study struck a resounding chord in towns and cities across the United States. Soon, "the Wal-Mart Man," as Stone was dubbed, was flying here and there making speeches to local government and business groups while dodging the occasional lightning bolt hurled from Bentonville.

Ken Stone made Wal-Mart his life's work, issuing a series of reports over the next fifteen years that confirmed what Main Street merchants in Decorah, Independence, Muscatine, and scores of other Iowa towns had come to understand all too well since the Arkansas interloper first entered Iowa in 1982: Wal-Mart kills. By Stone's count, nearly 2,200 of Iowa's retail stores had closed from 1983 to 1993, including 43 percent of its men's and boy's apparel stores, 42 percent of its variety stores, 37 percent of its grocery stores, 33 percent of its hardware stores, and 30 percent of its shoe stores. In Stone's view, what was true of Iowa likely was true of other slow-growth, rural economies across the country. "There is strong evidence that rural communities in the United States have been more adversely impacted by the discount mass merchandisers—sometimes referred to as the Wal-Mart phenomenon—than by any other factor," Stone concluded.[1]

Stone birthed a growth industry in its own right, for the issue of Wal-Mart's impact on the communities it enters has never been more contentious than it is today. Sam Walton fought many a "site fight" in his day, but he picked his spots. "If some community, for whatever reason, doesn't want us in there, we aren't interested in going in and creating a fuss," Walton wrote in his 1992 autobiography. "Wal-Mart wants to go where it's wanted."[2] Today, the magnitude of Wal-Mart's ambitions does not permit Lee Scott the luxury of geographic selectivity. To meet Wal-Mart's growth promises to shareholders, he must open 250 to 300 new U.S. stores a year every year ad infinitum. Wal-Mart now wants to go where it *needs* to go, which basically is everywhere there are Americans with two quarters to rub together.

Wherever it goes, Wal-Mart's main calling card is "Every Day Low Prices." Emek Basker, a University of Missouri professor, who analyzed Wal-Mart's effect on the prices of ten staples in 165 cities from 1982 to 2002, found that the retailer's entry into a new market tends to knock prices down by "an economically large and statistically significant" 7 percent to 13 percent for such products as aspirin, toothpaste, shampoo, and detergent.[3] "Wal-Mart's effect is strongest for products traditionally sold in drugstores, and weakest, or absent, for cigarettes and Coke (sold in many outlets, including convenience stores) and clothing," wrote Basker, who found that prices fell farthest in smaller cities, where competition tends to be less intense.[4]

Other geographically narrower price surveys have shown that Wal-

Mart can also have a dramatic effect in large cities. In 2002, the investment bank UBS Warburg collected price data on 100 grocery and non-grocery items from a sampling of stores in Sacramento, which Wal-Mart had yet to enter, and compared them to prices in three Wal-Mart strongholds—Las Vegas, Houston, and Tampa. This study found that prices were 13 percent lower on average in the Wal-Mart cities than in Sacramento. UBS Warburg also documented Wal-Mart's remarkable competitive tenacity. Competing stores in Las Vegas, Houston, and Tampa cut their prices by 13 percent on average, but hadn't come close to matching Wal-Mart's prices, which remained 17 percent to 39 percent lower.[5]

These percentages all translate into big money saved for consumers—and a big advantage for Wal-Mart going into any site fight. When the company comes to town, it's as if everyone gets an $800 or $900 tax cut. What politician wouldn't want to run on the slogan "Delivering Low Prices Every Day"?

However, the economic case in favor of Wal-Mart pretty much begins and ends with the undeniable boon of its bargain prices to consumers. The company invariably promotes a new store as a high-powered engine of job creation and sales-tax generation. The available evidence suggests that such claims are vastly overstated. Basker studied Wal-Mart's effect on local employment in a separate study that posed the question: "Has Wal-Mart created more jobs than it destroyed?" Her short answer: Barely.

After sifting through a mountain of data spanning 1,750 U.S. counties from the years 1977 to 1998, Basker found that retail employment within a county typically rose by just 100 jobs when Wal-Mart opened, even though the typical Wal-Mart employed 150 to 350 people. This suggests that other retailers already had cut back or even shut down in anticipation of its entry into the market. What is more, half of this 100-job gain melted away over the next five years as competing stores failed. Their demise in turn caused the loss of twenty jobs at local wholesale supply firms. The net gain: a mere

thirty jobs. Basker also found that a new Wal-Mart brought no mea-
surable spillover of added business to restaurants, gas stations, and
other businesses that did not compete with it directly. "The small
magnitude of the estimated effect of Wal-Mart on retail employment
is striking in light of the level of public discussion on this topic,"
Basker concluded.[6]

Small as it was, the positive job-creation effect documented by
Basker disappeared altogether in an even broader subsequent study of
Wal-Mart's effect on local employment nationwide by David Neumark, a senior fellow at the Public Policy Institute of California, a
think tank. Working from more precise information about dates of
store openings supplied by Wal-Mart itself, and adjusting for the
company's preference for locating stores in faster-growing counties,
Neumark found that retail employment in a county actually declines
by 2 percent to 4 percent after a new Wal-Mart opens, even as overall
employment rises slightly.[7]

Viewed through either Basker's or Neumark's wide-angle lens,
Wal-Mart's expansion is essentially a zero-sum game in which a new
store wrests away almost all of the business it does from smaller and
less-efficient competitors. This is progress of a sort, though the negli-
gible net increases in employment and sales-tax receipts that result
barely register on the economic Richter scale. But in looking at a particular city, county, or state, Wal-Mart's impact can be downright cat-
aclysmic, as documented in Ken Stone's Iowa studies.

As Stone found in analyzing a decade's worth of sales-tax records
from thirty-five Iowa counties, a Wal-Mart store can be a high-
powered retail magnet indeed. "Host" towns saw huge increases in
general merchandise sales, with a 54 percent gain in the initial year,
tapering off to 44 percent after three years, and holding firm for the
next two years.[8] Wal-Mart itself accounted for most of the gain, but
the town's restaurants, bars, and gas stations rang up more business
than before, as did stores that specialized in merchandise Wal-Mart
didn't carry (yet, anyway)—notably furniture, consumer electronics,

major appliances, and upscale apparel. Didn't this contradict Basker's findings? No, because Stone also found that a new Wal-Mart took a ruinous volume of business away from competing merchants in town and also sucked cash out of the surrounding countryside for miles around. "The impact that Wal-Mart was having just amazed me," Stone recalled.[9]

In the end, Stone, too, charted a zero-sum outcome. The impressive growth of Wal-Mart and the handful of other mass discounters that had moved into Iowa was counterbalanced by the utter collapse of Mom and Pop retailing throughout the state. "Wal-Mart has taken the place of Main Street," lamented a newspaper publisher in Independence, Iowa, a county seat of 6,100 where Wal-Mart opened in 1983.[10] Independence lost its quaint old downtown shopping district, and most of the smaller communities around it were reduced to commercial ghost towns. During the ten-year period that Stone studied, Iowa towns of 5,000 or less lost half their retail sales—$2.46 billion in total.[11]

Although Professor Stone's work won him no friends in Bentonville, he did not style himself as a Wal-Mart opponent.[12] He was no anti-business rabble-rouser, but rather a conservative sort of business economist who believed in a survival-of-the-fittest brand of capitalism epitomized by Wal-Mart. "In no way is this an attempt to berate the Wal-Mart company," he wrote in the preface to his first study in 1988. "Its stellar national reputation speaks for itself."[13] Even as Stone's work served to stiffen the spine of many a Wal-Mart opponent around the country, the professor carefully steered clear of site fights, considering them both misguided and futile.

Stone shed no tears over the fate of small-town merchants run out of business by Wal-Mart, figuring that most of them had it coming. "Before the mass discounters came along, many small-town merchants had forgotten that their first obligation was to customers," Stone recalled. "They closed at 5 o'clock, had bad return policies, and kept their prices too high."[14] As Iowa State's extension economist, he did make a concerted effort to try to help Main Street shopkeepers adapt to the new retail order, appending a detailed and surprisingly upbeat primer on how to take on Wal-Mart to most of his research studies. "In general, it is best to take a positive attitude toward the opening of a new mass merchandise store in your area . . ." he advised. "Try to figure out ways to capitalize on the increased volume of traffic in town."[15]

Stone, who recently retired from Iowa State, concluded that Wal-Mart's overall impact on America is "slightly positive. The main factor in its favor is its impact on prices, its suppressing of price inflation." However, he added, too many cities and towns have tilted the balance to the negative by subsidizing its construction of stores and distribution centers. "That's always been a pet peeve of mine," he said.[16]

Walton skillfully played a sly sort of game, feigning interest in potential store sites in towns adjacent to the one where he actually wanted to build. "Whenever he thought he could get away with it— which was often—he would politely but firmly demand concessions: a break on property taxes, use of tax-exempt bonds to finance construction, infrastructure subsidies, a rezoning, even a change of town boundaries so he could get city services at his site," wrote biographer Bob Ortega.[17] Although Walton might already have decided on a site, Wal-Mart was financed on a shoestring well into the 1970s, and every little bit helped. However, Bentonville's persistence, long after it needed the money, in hitting up small-town America for contributions most towns could ill afford amounted to an unseemly racket for a company that so loudly professes to have the best interest of everyday people at heart.

According to a study published in 2004 by Good Jobs First, an advocacy group based in Washington, the construction of eighty-four of Wal-Mart's ninety-one distribution centers in the United States was subsidized by state and local governments to the tune of $624 million.[18] Public officials across the negotiating table from Wal-Mart claim the company has come to regard DC subsidies not as a concession but as its due. "They expect it," says Gary Smith of the

Delaware Economic Development office.[18] In only one location—Apple Valley, California—did Wal-Mart turn down a subsidy, for fear that accepting it would trigger a legal requirement obligating the company to pay the prevailing market wage to construction workers. Distribution center projects rarely prompt site fights. However, one deal that would have lavished $45 million in tax credits on Wal-Mart to build a $60 million DC in Killingly, Connecticut, created such a public outcry in 2003 that Bentonville had to back away.

Although cities and states subsidize Wal-Mart stores, it is much easier for these governments to rationalize underwriting the cost of a DC because it brings a lot more higher-paying jobs than a Wal-Mart store and does not compete with local businesses. Good Jobs First's researchers uncovered 160 store subsidy deals totaling $383 million (an average of $2.4 million per deal). They concluded that about 1,000 of Wal-Mart's stores had gotten some kind of financial break. Apply that $2.4 million average to all of these outlets and a rough estimate of the total store subsidies paid to Bentonville soars to $2.4 billion.

A city's willingness to subsidize Wal-Mart correlates mainly to the degree of leverage that the company applies. Independence, Iowa, is a classic case in point. When Wal-Mart came to town in 1983, Iowa's farm economy was reeling. Independence is the seat of Buchanan County, which was devastated during the 1980s by the failure of 200 farms and the loss of 10 percent of its population. Nevertheless, Independence floated a $1.3 million tax-exempt bond issue that covered most of Wal-Mart's construction costs and extended its water and sewer lines to Wal-Mart's building site, which lay outside the city limits. "Wal-Mart threatened us," explained Frank Brimmer, the mayor of Independence. "They told us if they didn't build here, they'd build in a nearby town, and that would have been equally hard on Main Street. You simply cannot beat Wal-Mart, so we joined them."[20]

"Infrastructure assistance" of the sort that Independence supplied is the most common form of subsidy given Wal-Mart. Its prevalence goes a long way toward explaining why the company is synonymous with urban sprawl in much of America—and why it was satirized as "Sprawl*Mart" on *The Simpsons*. (For example, in an episode called "On a Clear Day I Can't See My Sister," Homer replaces Grampa as the people greeter. The store manager likes Homer's work but demands that he work overtime without pay. Homer agrees after the manager threatens to deport him to Mexico on the suspicion that he is an illegal immigrant. Homer eventually removes the obedience chip Sprawl*Mart had implanted in his brain and tries to rally his co-workers to help him shut down the store in protest of its mistreatment of workers. Homer's associates refuse to follow him because they have learned to accept the things they can't change—and to steal what isn't nailed down. Homer recognizes a superior form of protest when he hears it and rides triumphantly off into the night on a stolen forklift bearing a load of big-screen plasma TVs.)

Wal-Mart undoubtedly has despoiled more prime country acreage than any other retailer, not only because of its size but also because of the development strategy that Walton established. Many of Walton's first stores were located on town squares or main streets. But as Wal-Mart began to expand into larger markets in the mid-1970s, it typically located as far outside the city limits as practicable to minimize land costs. "We never planned on actually going into the cities," Walton recalled in the early 1990s. "What we did instead was build our stores in a ring around a city—pretty far out—and wait for the growth to come to us. . . . We're still more or less following this same strategy, although today we've moved into some cities outright. But I think our main real estate effort should be directed at getting out in front of expansion and letting the population build out to us."[21]

Wal-Mart was not nearly as passive as Walton makes it sound, of course. In inducing public officials to extend city limits and make costly new investments in roads, water systems, and the like, Bentonville went beyond merely anticipating a city's growth to shaping and stimulating that growth to its own, purely commercial ends. A heavily patronized new Wal-Mart sitting by itself in an erstwhile cow pasture exerted an almost gravitational force, pulling a town toward it and accelerating development of the acreage in between. It is impossible to quantify the cost to taxpayers of the sprawl Wal-Mart induces; neither Basker nor Stone even raise the issue. It's fair to say, though, that the development tab that Wal-Mart sticks government with offsets a sizable portion of the cost savings that shoppers pocket at the cash register.

When Wal-Mart abandons a town, its departure can be just as contentious and traumatic as its entry. Almost always, the company shuts a store because it has built a larger outlet within what it considers the same market area. In Wal-Mart lingo, these are "consolidations" or "conversions," not closures. It is not uncommon for a new store to be located within walking distance of the store it is replacing. However, in the rural areas where Wal-Mart concentrated its first stores, the new and old locations easily could be separated by fifteen to twenty miles or more. In these instances, the town abandoned by Wal-Mart in favor of the new Supercenter often takes a punishing hit to its economy.

Consider Hearne, Texas, "the town that Wal-Mart killed twice." Before Wal-Mart opened a 46,000-square-foot store on its outskirts in 1982, Hearne, a central Texas community of 5,200, had a small but bustling downtown dominated by long-standing locally owned businesses. Over the next five years, the downtown was hollowed out by the failure of ten retailers in the typical pattern documented by Ken Stone. In 1989, Wal-Mart announced that it was pulling out of Hearne because its store was unprofitable. After it closed, there was no place left in town to buy a pair of dress socks or a spool of thread. Residents had to drive twenty-two miles to Bryan to do most of their shopping. "No matter what else Wal-Mart may say for itself in marketing, it cannot say that it really cares about the communities it goes to, especially the small ones," declared Steve Bishop, a local minister who had grown up in Hearne. "Its service came at a very high price."[22]

A few years later, Wal-Mart abruptly pulled out of two small Oklahoma towns—Nowata and Pawhuska—closing discount stores of the same vintage as the one in Hearne. "They came in and ravaged all the small businesses. And when it came to the point where they were not satisfied, they left," complained the president of the First National Bank of Nowata, who had enthusiastically supported Wal-Mart's entry. The loss of income from the city's 3 percent tax on Wal-Mart's sales left a gaping hole in the municipal budget, pushing the town into a budget deficit. Nowata had to boost its water and sewer taxes by 32 percent and impose a new $5-a-month tax on homeowners to pay for fire protection. What particularly galled locals was that Wal-Mart left shortly after it had erected signs in front of both the Nowata and Pawhuska stores vowing eternal loyalty. "The rumors are false: Wal-Mart will be here always," proclaimed the one in Nowata, where resentment of Wal-Mart inspired a derisive new schoolyard chant: "Wal-Mart Fall-Apart."[23]

Wal-Mart did not abandon Nowata and Pawhuska (which is just an hour's drive from Claremore, Helen Walton's hometown) and scores of other communities of similar size because it soured on small towns per se. Rather, the mid-1990s emergence of the Supercenter as the company's preferred growth vehicle effectively doomed the classic discount store that Walton had pioneered. Three to four times bigger than early discount stores, Supercenters were designed to draw customers from a larger market area. The Nowata and Pawhuska stores were among the first of at least 900 stores that Wal-Mart has shut down to make room for new Supercenters. The number of closings has steadily risen in tandem with Supercenter openings, reaching 160 in 2004.

In Bardstown, Kentucky, a city of 10,000 with no less than 300 buildings in the National Register of Historic Places, Wal-Mart built progressively larger stores in three different locations over a fifteen-year span, shifting the town's economic center each time. The first store was abandoned in 1991; the larger Wal-Mart across town that replaced it closed in 2004 when a giant Supercenter opened just outside the city. "How did this happen? How are we on our third Wal-Mart, in a town riddled with preservationists?" asks Julia Christensen, a Bardstown native who was inspired by Wal-Mart's molting to make reusing the abandoned stores an artistic and academic specialty.[24]

Wal-Mart Realty, a 500-employee division based in Bentonville, tries to extract as much value as it can from the hundreds of discarded stores scattered across America's rural and suburban landscape like unburied corpses. As of September 2005, it listed 370 properties for sale or lease across thirty-five states. Texas topped the list with thirty-seven stores, followed by Georgia, Illinois, North Carolina, Tennessee, and Ohio. The 44,752-square-foot store that Wal-Mart strong-armed the town of Independence, Iowa, into subsidizing long ago will come available in April 2006, about the time a new Supercenter is scheduled to open a mile across town.

California outdoes all other states both in expansion potential for Wal-Mart and in the intensity of resistance to Wal-Mart. The company's slow rate of progress to date toward the modest goal it announced in 2002 of opening forty Supercenters in California by 2008 is a serious, nagging problem for Lee Scott, who simply cannot afford to fail in the Golden State and keep his job. Against this backdrop of mounting pressure and frustration, Wal-Mart waged a site fight in the South-Central Los Angeles community of Inglewood that damaged its image worldwide by revealing the sneer beneath the smiley face it presents to the public. Inglewood looms large in the recent history of Wal-Mart as the place where Bentonville plumbed the depths of its disrespect for local government—and lost for a change.

Inglewood is about as far removed culturally from Wal-Mart's Ozarks comfort zone as it is possible to be without leaving the United States altogether. People of color predominate in every sense in this city enfolded within America's second-largest metropolis. But what

Wal-Mart seemed to find most daunting about Los Angeles as a whole is that it is a union stronghold where, as one veteran observer of the city put it, "politicians rarely go far without big labor's endorsement."[25] As is often the case with the worst of Wal-Mart's behavior, its blunders in Inglewood were rooted in part in a visceral hatred of labor unions, a hatred that caused it to overreact to the provocations of its archenemy, the United Food and Commercial Workers.

In 1999, less than a year after Wal-Mart had slipped quietly into California by opening a few relatively small stores, the UFCW pushed legislation through the state assembly that effectively would have banned the sale of groceries at all big-box stores statewide had not Governor Gray Davis vetoed the measure. The union then redirected its anti–Wal-Mart lobbying to the local level, succeeding in getting big-box ordinances on the agendas of city councils in a number of cities, including Los Angeles, the great cloverleafed jewel of California's vast retail market.

Wal-Mart countered with lobbying of its own, but made no immediate attempt to enter L.A. The company had scattered ten stores throughout the Gateway Cities and other exurbs of eastern Los Angeles County before venturing into L.A. proper in 2003 to open what it described as "one of its first truly urban stores." It was located on Crenshaw Boulevard in Baldwin Hills, a mostly middle-class black district notorious in the 1980s for cocaine-related gang violence. Breaching the L.A. city limits by moving first into Baldwin Hills was so politically astute a maneuver that not even the UFCW dared protest too loudly. Although Wal-Mart much prefers to construct its own stores, on Crenshaw it took over a historic department store building left vacant for five years. Much to the annoyance of local political leaders, all sorts of supermarkets and major retailers had passed on this site, which had been a commercial hub of black Los Angeles for two decades. Bernard Parks, the councilman for the district, supported Wal-Mart's entry so avidly that his photo was pinned to the store bulletin board next to a head shot of Rob Walton.[26]

Inglewood is four miles down Crenshaw Boulevard and a world apart from Baldwin Hills. Inglewood is considerably more affluent than more notorious sections of South-Central L.A., with a median household income of about $35,000. To the out-of-towner flashing by on Interstate 405, the town looks like just another undifferentiated stretch of south L.A. However, Inglewood long was a city unto itself until it was swallowed by the metro area's gargantuan sprawl, and many of its residents retain a pronounced, even prickly identity as Inglewooders first and Angelenos second. Actually, L.A. might rank third in the loyalties of the many residents who originally hailed from rural Texas, Louisiana, and other Deep South states. "Inglewood is a country town in the city," said Daniel Tabor, a longtime city council member who himself moved to "the Wood" from Texas in 1967 as a boy of fourteen.[27]

Sports fans around the country know Inglewood as the home of the Hollywood Park Racetrack, founded in 1938 by a consortium of movie stars and studio bigwigs, including Jack Warner, Walt Disney, Bing Crosby, and Irene Dunne, and also as the site of the Forum, where the Los Angeles Lakers held court from 1967 until 1999, when they broke Inglewood's heart by decamping for the neon dazzle of the Staples Center in downtown L.A. The racetrack and the Forum sit on either side of a great expanse of asphalt parking lot just a dozen blocks from Market Street, Inglewood's well-tended but sleepy downtown shopping district. In its heyday, Market Street resembled a thousand other small-town downtowns across America, except for its two ornate movie palaces, each of which was owned by a Hollywood studio that continued to stage swanky movie premieres in Inglewood well into the 1960s.[28]

Like many communities within greater L.A., Inglewood has a history as a racial kaleidoscope of sorts. In 1960, the federal census counted only twenty-nine "Negroes" among its 63,000 residents. Not a single black child was enrolled at any of its schools and Realtors routinely refused to show homes to black families. The Watts Riots of 1965 triggered a white exodus that put blacks in the majority by the time the 1980 census was taken. Thanks to a massive influx of Mexicans and other Latin Americans over the last two decades, Inglewood now is about 47 percent black and 46 percent Hispanic. However, the Latinos tend to be poorer and less active in civic affairs than black residents, who completely dominate government. Koreans and other Asians also figure importantly in the mix, not as residents but as owners of a great many of Inglewood's small businesses.

Over the last decade, Inglewood has started to attract some significant investment from national retail chains. Costco, Target, Home Depot, and Kmart all built stores along Century Boulevard near the Hollywood Park racetrack and adjacent casino (though the Kmart didn't last long). When the company that owns Hollywood Park put sixty acres of parking lot between the racetrack and the Forum on the market in 2002, the L.A. developer Stanley Rothbart pounced. Rothbart, who'd already built a dozen stores for Wal-Mart throughout California, took an option on the property and drew up plans for a $100 million shopping center called The HomeStretch at Hollywood Park. Wal-Mart was so enamored of the project and its prime location that it cut a deal to put two giant stores—a Supercenter and a Sam's Club—into the center, potentially filling more than 60 percent of the 650,000 square feet Rothbart was looking to build.

Wal-Mart's bid to enter Inglewood did not sit well with its city council, which was pro-union in its sympathies. In September 2002, the council approved an "emergency" ordinance effectively banning stores of the size the company was planning from selling groceries. This was the very same law that the UFCW had been urging on many California cities. "Wal-Mart's plans to enter the retail grocery business in Inglewood are dead!" crowed Ricardo Icaza, president of UFCW Local 770.[29]

Icaza soon had to eat his words. Wal-Mart's local operatives gathered 9,000 signatures on a petition to put the issue on the ballot, more than twice as many as needed to force a referendum. The company also threatened the city with a lawsuit for alleged procedural violations. On the advice of the city attorney, who doubted that the big-box ordinance would survive a court challenge, the City Council voted to rescind its ban. Icaza was irate, and his mood darkened a few months later when Lorraine Johnson, an investment banker who sat on the city council, reversed herself and came out in favor of Wal-Mart as her term was expiring. "She went south on us," Icaza recalled.[30] The UFCW drafted one of its business agents, Ralph Franklin, to run against Johnson. Franklin, a Boy Scout leader and longtime Inglewooder, ran on an anti–Wal-Mart platform and won handily.

Now it was Wal-Mart's turn to seethe. Even allowing for the fact that many Inglewood residents belonged to one labor union or another, one could argue that the UFCW had gained inordinate influence over Inglewood's government. While it did not necessarily follow that the union's success in imposing its agenda was bad for the city, Wal-Mart clearly was suffering for it. "Wal-Mart and our customers are tired of being bullied by the unions," complained Peter Kanelos, the Wal-Mart community affairs manager responsible for L.A. "If the union and the local politicians they put in office want to attack Wal-Mart, they can rest assured that we'll fight back.[31]

It is one thing for a corporation to complain about the undue political influence of an opponent. But it is quite another to hold itself out as representing the popular will, as Wal-Mart has done frequently in site fights across the country. From Scott on down, the company's executives seem to regard the act of spending money at Wal-Mart as an implicit endorsement of the company's expansion imperative. Or, as Kanelos put it in Inglewood: "People support and want Wal-Mart Supercenters. We're going to do everything in our power to make certain that Wal-Mart customers are heard."[32]

To this point, the city council had not taken any formal action on the HomeStretch proposal. Wal-Mart was not without influence at City Hall. Inglewood Mayor Roosevelt Dorn was officially neutral but clearly favored the shopping center and eventually would come out foursquare for it. Rothbart's staff had been working harmoniously with Inglewood's city planners, some of whom favored the project, to prepare the development plan for formal consideration by the council. However, Wal-Mart now overplayed its hand. It decided that trying to deal with Inglewood in the customary way was not worth the company's while. As Kanelos put it, "Why spend hundreds of thousands of dollars just to be denied?"[33]

In August 2003, Wal-Mart helped organize a group called the Citizens Committee to Welcome Wal-Mart to Inglewood, which quickly gathered signatures requiring the city to put HomeStretch to a popular vote through Measure 4-A. Instead of the usual page or two of prose laying out the particulars, it consisted of seventy-one pages of abstruse plannerese that no layman could possibly understand. A vote in favor would not merely indicate support for building a Supercenter in Inglewood but would exempt Wal-Mart and its developer from Inglewood's land-use regulations. It would also approve HomeStretch as designed, without city review or public hearing. "Under the guise of 'direct democracy,' Wal-Mart would shut out government and public oversight," the Los Angeles Times noted in "A Big-Box Ballot Bully," an editorial denouncing 4-A. "Love Wal-Mart or loathe it, the ballot box is simply not the place to decide how many parking spaces this mega-center should have, how many new traffic signals would be needed to prevent gridlock or whether local sewer lines can handle an extra 50,000 gallons of waste a day."[34]

Many of Inglewood's elected officials reacted as if they had been slapped in the face. "This initiative is quite unfair to the voting public and extremely insulting," said Eloy Morales Jr., the only Latino among the city council's five members. "It's even more insulting that its sponsors claim it is the purest form of democracy. That's just false. They know what they're doing and they wouldn't do it in Beverly Hills."[35]

The Vote No On 4-A campaign drew the support of almost all of Inglewood's federal, state, and local officials and the great majority of its African American ministers. Although Wal-Mart had to make do with the Chamber of Commerce and some black business leaders, it did enjoy the inestimable political advantage of unlimited funds. The company spent heavily on TV and radio advertising, while its opponents concentrated their comparatively meager financial resources on door-to-door canvassing. Wal-Mart kept it simple, emphasizing the standard economic arguments: The new shopping center will add jobs (1,200 overall, including 300 at Wal-Mart) and boost sales-tax receipts (by as much as $5 million a year). Meanwhile, opponents emphasized Wal-Mart's disrespect for representative government, but also let fly every accusation and complaint contained in the We-Hate-Wal-Mart manifesto: It tramples small business, underpays and overworks its employees, discriminates against blacks and women, fights dirty against unions, and rapes the environment.

Cox Menswear is an ideal place to take the street pulse of Inglewood while adding to your wardrobe. It's on the corner of Market and Manchester, right in the barely thumping heart of what once was Inglewood's busy downtown shopping district. Cox's is a compact little store, so there is no missing Darian Jackson, better known as "DJ," haberdasher to the 'hood and man in the know. DJ is a short, husky black man in his mid-thirties with a little hoop in his left ear, a shaved pate, and an amiable been-there, done-that attitude.

Like most stores on Market Street, Cox Menswear has a poster in its front window that reads, "Save our Community from Wal-Mart. No on 4-A." The special election is just four days away—April 6, 2004. "I'll vote, but not everybody will, know what I'm saying?" DJ says. "They feel it don't do no good—they're going to put a Wal-Mart here anyway, so why bother? But this is *my* neighborhood," he continues, putting a little steel in his voice. "I'm from here. As I got older, I realized you got to pay attention."[36]

DJ and I stand just inside the store's front door and talk. Only five customers—all of them black men—enter during the next hour, and DJ is on hand-slapping terms with each one of them. Periodically, he glances at the Korean woman behind the cash register. She and her husband, Yoon Lee, have owned Cox Menswear for twenty-eight years and have employed DJ for four of them. When DJ alludes to the budding tension in Inglewood between black customers and Korean owners, he leans toward me and speaks sotto voce. Halfway through the interview, Mrs. Lee tells him that he's gone on long enough. He ignores her completely and keeps on talking. I ask DJ if he is the store manager. He gives me a sly look. "You could say that," he says.

DJ seems blissfully unaware of the political machinations behind the ballot measure. The main reason he is voting no on 4-A is that he thinks a Wal-Mart would cripple Inglewood's small businesses, black- and Korean-owned alike. "They put all the little businesses out of business," he says. "Not us, though, 'cause we carry different kinds of stuff than Wal-Mart carries. I guess I could see it if Wal-Mart was going to hire people from the community, but they won't."

Jobs are in short supply in Inglewood, but DJ has two of them. On the weekends, he works down the street as a security guard at the "swap meet," a kind of indoor flea market constructed from the ground-floor ruins of what long had been a J. C. Penney store. (Market Street also used to have a Sears and an elegant Boston Store branch, now a boarded-over discount jewelry mart.) Much of the merchandise sold at the swap meet and on Market generally is a step or two downscale from today's Wal-Mart. A general merchandise store called Crazy 5 is touting a year-end clearance sale (in April!) with a banner proclaiming, "$4.99 and up or down."

The fortunes of Crazy 5 no doubt would decline if a Supercenter were to open a half mile away, but amid the discount jewelry shops, sporting goods stores, and beauty salons on Market Street are a handful of businesses that already have done what Ken Stone and everyone else urges local merchants to do when Wal-Mart comes to town: specialize in what Wal-Mart doesn't carry. There are two large stores (Michael's School Uniforms and Cambridge Uniforms) that sell nothing but school uniforms, and a third (Lynton Uniform) exclusively offering nurses' outfits. A Wal-Mart might well stock uniforms, but not in the number and variety on display in these establishments, which draw their customers from all over Los Angeles, where public schools require both boys and girls to wear uniforms. The Korean-owned World Hat & Boot Mart Two, Market Street's largest store, is buoyed by a national mail-order business and also caters to the local demographic by offering a big, multihued selection of Kangol caps along with its row after row of cowboy hats and Western-style boots.

Market Street also is home to a number of black-owned, black-themed businesses heavily dependent on an Inglewood clientele. Would a new Wal-Mart stock dashikis, Masai shawls, African drums, hip-hop sportswear, and high-end cosmetics for "exotic skin tones" or put crawfish étoufée and catfish po'boys on its fast-food menu? Hardly. But most of the half dozen establishments that traffic in such fare on Market seem to be barely hanging on as it is. "You see how dead it is today?" says Derekshawn Brown, a makeup artist who runs the Four Seasons Cosmetics Beauty N Barber Studio for his brother, owner Jerry Smith. "We sit here waiting. Where are the customers?"[37]

Four Seasons got its start down the block in 1991 as a booth in the swap meet officially known as the Inglewood Market. Unlike most of the many beauty salons in Inglewood, Four Seasons has its own proprietary line of cosmetics. "We're a specialty store," says Brown, an even-tempered, rail-thin man of about thirty who is dressed way down in a gray T-shirt and gray sweats. Brown not only put a "No On 4-A" poster in his front window but convinced his landlord, a Korean woman who occupies the building next door, to put a sign in her window, too. "A lot of people in Inglewood are frightened of Wal-Mart," says Brown. "It's the power."[38] Brown, too, is intimidated by Wal-Mart, but opposes the HomeStretch development for an entirely counterintuitive reason: It would be too *far* from Market Street to bring spillover traffic to his struggling beauty parlor. "Why put it over there by Hollywood Park when you got Target, Home Depot, and other big-box stores already?" Brown says. "Put it here."

The question of Market Street's fate is freighted with significance far beyond its rather paltry economic contribution to the city. For many black residents, it is a symbol, at once infuriating and embarrassing, of Inglewood's failure to realize its potential as a model of African American self-determination. "Fleshing out any dream seemed so possible here . . . because blacks lived here in great numbers, not in the usual cordoned-off inner city or redlined enclave, but in a real town a few miles from the Pacific," recalls Erin Aubry Kaplan, a writer who grew up in Inglewood in the 1970s and returned to live here in 2001 after a long time away. Today, she continues, Inglewood is "the promising underachiever who fucked up and could least afford to because everybody was counting so heavily on his success. *What happened to you?* I want to shout out the car window at the offending landscape. *Where did you go?*"[39]

When white residents fled en masse in the 1960s and 1970s, they sold their houses to black families and their businesses to Asians. City Hall has yet to rise to the challenge of nurturing a black-owned economy in a black-run city. In fact, this is a city that has not had an economic development plan worthy of the name in decades. Its most ambitious undertaking was Market Street Renaissance. Launched by Mayor Dorn with great fanfare in 2000, the project has amounted to nothing more than a $4 million face-lift. Fixing up Market Street with streetlamps, wrought-iron benches, planters, and other accoutrements of upscale shopping has failed utterly to entice folks downtown.

With the new stores opened in recent years by Home Depot, Target, Staples, Bally's, and the like, Inglewood's center of retail gravity has shifted sharply eastward, toward the new, privately developed shopping centers along Century Boulevard near Hollywood Park. That these and other national chains were able to set up shop in Inglewood without anything like the outcry that Wal-Mart provoked only goes to show that a majority of Inglewooders—black and Hispanic alike—have nothing against big-box stores in particular or economic development in general. Chain stores may not recycle dollars locally to the extent that locally owned businesses do, but the jobs these stores created gave work to hundreds of youths who might otherwise be on the street.

In treating Inglewood the way it did, Wal-Mart antagonized a black population that had come to measure its failure in large part by its failure to determine its own economic destiny. *We've been exploited by absentee business ownership for years and now America's biggest company wants us to turn over sixty acres, no questions asked? No way.* If Wal-Mart accomplished nothing else, it unwittingly roused Inglewood from the lethargy induced by chronic underachievement. The Coalition for a Better Inglewood, a civic group formed in opposition to Wal-Mart, "encouraged a brand of activism in the city that it hasn't seen in a very long time. . . ." notes Aubry. "The fact that Inglewood was a black and Latino city that Wal-Mart assumed would be a path of least resistance made the victory that much sweeter."[40]

It might well have hurt Wal-Mart on balance that Mayor Dorn stopped feigning neutrality about a week before the election and came out "one thousand percent" for the HomeStretch development. Dorn, who has been mayor since 1997, is increasingly unpopular, particularly among the Market Street merchants. In their view, he literally led them down the garden path with the Renaissance project and now is selling them out to Bentonville. "I thought he would be a cool mayor 'cause he's from the 'hood," DJ says. "But he never comes around. I saw him more when I was a juvenile." (Dorn, a lawyer by trade, served as a juvenile court judge in Inglewood for eighteen years before becoming mayor.)

Sunday, April 4, is the thirty-sixth anniversary of Martin Luther King's assassination, and the Vote No On 4-A campaign makes the most of it, putting up posters and passing out pamphlets carrying King's image and invoking his moral authority in support of the cause. In one, the Southern Christian Leadership Conference, which Dr. King founded, comes out against the "deceptive" 4-A and also takes a direct swipe at Wal-Mart. "Of course, Dr. Martin Luther King, Jr., never shopped at a Wal-Mart," declares Rev. Norman John, the organization's L.A. director. "But he consistently urged us not to support stores that do not support the right of workers to organize."[41]

Meanwhile, the ministers in most of Inglewood's two dozen black churches take to the pulpit to urge their congregants to smite Wal-Mart at the ballot box. About 10,000 worshipers throng the Forum for a service led by Bishop Kenneth C. Ulmer, pastor of the Faithful Central Bible Church, which bought the Forum for $23 million in 2001. Bishop Ulmer eases into his Wal-Mart sermon after leading the huge choir massed behind him onstage in a couple of thunderous hymns. "An organization has come into this community, across the street, and structured a ballot issue that, if it passes—let me explain it to you," Ulmer says. "You will have to get more permission to build a doghouse. You will have to go through more approval by the city to add a carport to your home than this organization will have to go through if they come into this city. It is structured so there is absolutely no governmental or community accountability or input. I see it as an insult to us for them to come into our backyard and tell us what we can do." Ulmer pauses briefly as an outburst of applause ricochets around the Forum. "Wrong is wrong," he concludes, "no matter who does it."[42]

The next morning, Reverend Jesse Jackson brings the campaign against Wal-Mart and 4-A to its symbolic climax at a crowded press conference in the parking lot of the Bourbon Street Fish Restaurant, directly across Prairie Avenue from the Wal-Mart site. Eight speakers precede Jackson to the stage, including a fiery representative of Lewis Farrakhan's Nation of Islam, who denounces Wal-Mart as "a modern-day plantation" and as "this slick, slimy, sleazy, deceptive corporate giant." Jackson takes the rhetorical high road, exalting the fight against Wal-Mart as an extension of the civil rights movement. "We must not disconnect the struggle in Inglewood from the global struggle for economic justice," says Jackson, who was standing next to King when he was gunned down on a motel balcony in Memphis. "When Dr. King went to Birmingham, people said, 'Dr. King, you are from Atlanta, why are you in Birmingham?' This is one nation, one flag, and one set of rules. 'Why are you in Selma?' Because unless people can go into Selma, they cannot be empowered in Los Angeles and New York. One nation, one flag . . .

"There is in Inglewood today a legitimate fear, a fear of being wiped out by a Confederate economic Trojan Horse," Jackson continues. "It looks attractive on the outside, but like cyanide it's sweet at first taste—and then there is no more."[43]

After the press conference, Jackson and Maxine Waters, Inglewood's representative in the U.S. House of Representatives, tour a nursing home and then take a stroll down Market Street with a small entourage. Waters gamely attempts to converse with the Korean shop owners, none of whom seem to speak English and who smile and nod excitedly as the congresswoman speaks to them with the exaggerated simplicity of an overbearing grade school teacher. "If Wal-Mart come here, lose money. Do you agree?" she asks a couple behind the counter at a booth in the swap meet. "Yes, yes," they respond in unison. "I'm going to introduce you to Jesse Jackson then," she says.

Jackson hits the street with a big smile on his face, clearly amused by Waters' pluck. "Maxine's taking no prisoners today," says Jackson, who holds hands with Waters as they cross Market Street, headed for Cox Menswear. DJ is waiting for them outside the store, looking sharp in a black-and-white sweater and black gabardine pants. Waters greets DJ effusively and introduces him to Jackson.

"DJ, you the man," Jackson says. DJ smiles demurely, loving the attention, but unable to summon any words. "OK, you *one* of the men," says Jackson, who puts an arm around DJ and squeezes him so hard that he nearly falls over.

Standing in the doorway of the shop, Waters addresses the small crowd that's gathered before Cox's. "DJ is what is special about this store," she says. "He's taken me to places that most people have never been." She turns to Yoon Lee, DJ's boss, who's standing stoically at her side. "And Mr. Lee is very special, too, because he lets DJ leave work to help me. Give him a big round of applause."

"Plus, he's got a sign in his window," Jackson says. "No on 4-A."

As DJ shakes hands all around, and Waters talks into a television camera amid much milling about, Jackson stands off to the side, enjoying the chaotic scene. "Maximum Maxine," he murmurs to no one in particular. "Maximum."

The next day's turnout of 11,624 substantially exceeds expectations, and the outcome shocks both sides. Instead of prevailing by the five to seven percentage points that most experts had projected, Wal-Mart and its ballot measure go down to crushing defeat, 60.6 percent to 39.4 percent. Robert McAdam, Wal-Mart's vice president for state and local government relations, puts out a statement blaming "outside special interests" for leading Inglewood voters astray. The next day, given a second chance to rise to the occasion, McAdam reverts to the familiar union-bashing mode of Wal-Mart mouthpieces everywhere. "We are not going to get pushed around or bullied by unions," he vows. "We are here to state our case, and we are not going to go away quietly."[44]

Back in Bentonville, cooler heads eventually realized that the Inglewood misadventure was a full-fledged public relations disaster. For the last few years, Wal-Mart had made a concerted national effort to curry favor among African Americans, advertising heavily on black-themed television programs while passing out millions in donations to such national organizations as the NAACP and other African American advocacy groups. During the Inglewood battle, "the silence from mainstream black organizations—such as the NAACP and Urban League—that have been recipients of Wal-Mart largesse was deafening," noted the commentator and author Earl Ofari Hutchinson.[45] Even so, Jackson, Waters, Bishop Ulmer, and their many African American comrades in arms had succeeded in turning 4-A into a racial cause célèbre that put Wal-Mart in a place where no major consumer company can afford to be—on the wrong side of the legacy of Martin Luther King, the martyred saint of the civil rights movement.

At the same time, the copious coverage the Inglewood site fight generated placed an exclamation point on all the bad press Wal-Mart was getting in general. Long accustomed to receiving the benefit of the doubt from reporters as "America's Most Admired Company," Wal-Mart belatedly was coming under the sort of intensive journalistic scrutiny usually reserved for unpopular presidents and misbehaving celebrities. The multimedia onslaught of skeptical headlines aimed in Wal-Mart's direction in 2003 and 2004 included "Is Wal-Mart Good for America?" (*New York Times*, PBS/Frontline, and National Public Radio), "Is Wal-Mart Too Powerful?" (*BusinessWeek*), and "Should We Admire Wal-Mart?" (*Fortune*). The *Los Angeles Times* won a Pulitzer Prize for a three-part dissection entitled "The Wal-Mart Effect."

Wal-Mart took such a PR pounding that by the fall of 2004, about five months after the Inglewood vote, it dropped its traditional posture of disdain for and indifference to Big Media and started swinging back. The press-reclusive Lee Scott suddenly was everywhere, giving interviews and making speeches in an attempt to put some of the shine back on Wal-Mart's image. The company also ran full-page ads in the form of an argumentative "open letter" in more than 100 newspapers across the country. Essentially, the company had decided to be as aggressive in its public relations as it was in every other aspect of its business. Or, as Rob Walton put it in his 2005 letter to Wal-Mart shareholders, "It was time to set the record straight." At the same time, though, Scott promoted the idea of a kinder, gentler, more flexible Wal-Mart as he made his media rounds. He came hat in hand, in the sense that he refrained from directly criticizing past coverage, and mouthed conciliatory words not previously part of Wal-Mart's lexicon. "Where appropriate," he said, "we will compromise"—a comment that prompted a Southern Methodist University retailing expert to proclaim a "sea change" in attitude in Bentonville.[46] "What we're trying to do now is reach out," the CEO said. "Where we're wrong, we change, so our detractors don't have a foothold in attacking us."[47]

However, the only real error that the CEO tumbled to was the ill-fated ballot measure in Inglewood, where, Scott acknowledged, "I

think we came across as a bully who would get their way regardless."[48]
Coming from a Wal-Mart executive, this qualified as startling candor,
though a close reading suggests an attempt at what was known in the
Nixon era as a "modified limited hangout." *OK, we occasionally do stu-
pid things, but not out of arrogance (or greed, intolerance, or any other
moral defect). We're just a bit clumsy. What giant isn't?*

Two weeks after meeting with the *Post*, Scott underscored California's importance to Wal-Mart by flying out to Los Angeles to deliver
the corporate equivalent of a political convention's keynote address at
the Town Hall in Los Angeles. In his speech, Scott again used Inglewood as a token example of Wal-Mart's fallibility. "One of our mistakes
recently was the way we went about trying to open our store in Inglewood, not far from here," he said. "We learned from that experience,
and we're engaging with communities in a better way as a result." Scott
maintained a statesmanlike tone throughout his address, only to flash
his sharp teeth afterward in an interview with the *Los Angeles Times*.
Wal-Mart's opponents "need to bring their lunch, because we're not
going to lay down," he vowed. "We've got nothing to apologize for."[49]

Its spin campaign notwithstanding, Wal-Mart was as aggressive as ever
in pushing its building plans forward after the Inglewood fiasco. In California and elsewhere, a few dozen site fights were in progress during the
Inglewood battle, including one in Flagstaff, Arizona, that would result
in a public relations gaffe so horrendous that this time Wal-Mart's management would be shamed into apologizing directly and unequivocally.

Flagstaff is a scenic city of about 50,000 in northern Arizona with
an ecologically progressive city council and a mayor who once managed a local Safeway supermarket. In the fall of 2004, the city council
enacted an ordinance that prohibited the construction of any store
larger than 125,000 square feet and imposed an 8 percent limit on the
amount of floor space a large-scale retailer can devote to groceries.
Flagstaff's big-box ordinance grew out of a regional plan that had

been approved by a wide margin at the polls in 2000. "The goal was to have a mix of retailers that included national chains and locally owned business, but where no one store dominated," said Becky Daggett, executive director of Friends of Flagstaff's Future, a citizens' group that favored the big-box ordinance.[50]

More specifically, the intent was to prevent Wal-Mart from ever converting the discount store it owned in Flagstaff into a Supercenter. Wal-Mart had put forth no such plan, but wanted to keep its options open. Following its usual modus operandi, Wal-Mart bankrolled an aggressive campaign to put the new law to a popular vote via ballot measure. So much for Scott's post-Inglewood vow to "never again try to go over the heads of local politicians," though the Wal-Mart spokeswoman on the case blithely denied it. "This has nothing to do with the local government," she said. "It's about an ordinance that is anti-competition, anti-choice and anti-consumer."[51]

Proposition 100 split Flagstaff's electorate right down the middle, though not along clean, simple fault lines. Predictably, low-income residents of a city with one of the highest costs of living in the state tended to be against Prop 100 while Northern Arizona University, which happens to offer a master's program in Visions of Good and Sustainable Societies, was no less predictably a hotbed of support. Although small-business owners were generally in favor, the head of the Chamber of Commerce lined up with Bentonville and brought a large minority of members with her. The many affluent retirees who had fled the big city for bucolic Flagstaff avidly embraced Prop 100, but there also was a sizable group of well-off, older residents who opposed the ballot measure because they considered the big-box ordinance an affront to free-market principles.

Emotions were running high even before Wal-Mart bought its ad in the *Arizona Daily Sun* equating Proposition 100 supporters with Nazi book burners. Afterward, people were screaming at each other on the street. Frank Dickens, who headed the pro–Wal-Mart group Protect Flagstaff's Future, received death threats over the telephone and had to replace the windshield of his truck after a vandal shattered it. "It was the most hateful and divisive campaign I ever saw," said Dickens, a local real estate agent.[52]

Wal-Mart's Nazi ad quickly became a national news story, and the Phoenix office of the Anti-Defamation League was deluged by complaints from all over the country. "It trivializes the Nazis and what they did," said Bill Strauss, the ADL's Arizona director. "And to try to attach that imagery to a municipal election goes beyond distasteful."[53] In the blogosphere, spluttering outrage was the order of the day. "Wait. Let me get this straight," wrote DavidNYC on DailyKoz.com. "Some kind of ordinance making life tough for big-box retailers is EQUIVALENT TO THE NAZI REGIME. . . . Are these people out of THEIR FUCKING MINDS? . . . How dare they?"

The ad had been produced by a Flagstaff agency under contract to Wal-Mart and had been approved first by Peter Kanelos, the company's community affairs manager for Arizona as well as southern California, and then by his boss in Bentonville. Jay Allen, a senior vice president and Scott's chief PR adviser, immediately sent a formal letter of apology to Strauss. "While we did not know of the photo's historical context until after the fact, there is still no excuse for associating this photo with the upcoming election on the proposed retail ordinance in Flagstaff," Allen wrote.[54] The company also ran an open letter in the *Daily Sun* apologizing to the people of Flagstaff: "Any attempt to compare this issue with events that took place in Nazi Germany is thoroughly inappropriate and clearly false."

Wal-Mart's contrition had its limits; it stopped well short of disavowing the drive to overturn Flagstaff's big-box law. An eleventh-hour ad blitz pushed Wal-Mart's total spending above $280,000—a record for a political campaign in the city and six times as much as the UFCW contributed to the opposition. More than 60 percent of Flagstaff's registered voters cast a ballot, a much better turnout than in Inglewood. Wal-Mart prevailed in a squeaker, by a margin of 51 percent to 49 percent.

Flagstaff was a victory, Inglewood a loss. But it was Flagstaff that cost Kanelos his job. A few weeks after the vote, Kanelos left Wal-Mart on what he described as "mutually agreeable terms." At Wal-Mart's annual meeting in June, a question from the floor forced Rob Walton to comment on the Nazi photo fiasco. "We're just a bunch of humans trying to run this company," Walton said. "We make mistakes."[55] Walton's characteristically laconic statement was a variation on Scott's big-and-dumb defense and completely inadequate as an explanation of so egregious a blunder.

Even if one gives Bentonville the benefit of the doubt and acknowledges that Wal-Mart's senior management is not so culturally clueless as to knowingly approve the use of Nazi imagery to make a point, the ad is only slightly less repellent if the photo was indeed the "generic book-burning" image Wal-Mart and its ad agency thought it was. In equating a law passed by a city's elected representatives with the violent suppression of free speech, and in elevating discount shopping to parity with the freedoms affirmed by the Bill of Rights, Bentonville disrespected not only its local opponents but all Americans. Wal-Mart's belief in its own manifest destiny is so extreme that it often behaves as if it were a populist government in exile, rather than a particularly assertive—and dangerous—"special interest" of the sort that it is always denouncing.

CHAPTER SEVEN

WAL-MART'S CHINA PRICE

In western Ohio, a few miles from the Indiana border, the city of Celina sits at the edge of Grand Lake St. Marys. The seat of Mercer County, Celina is home to about 10,000 people. The surrounding countryside's particularly rich loamy soil is used to grow corn, soybeans, and wheat. Celina itself long has been a factory town. In the 1920s, its biggest employer at the time, the Mersman Brothers Corp., claimed that it produced one of every ten tables in America. More recently, Celina was home to the world's largest bicycle factory—822,000 square feet of assembly space, offices, and warehouses sprawling over a fifty-acre site. It was owned by the Huffy Corp.

Horace Huffman founded Huffy's predecessor, the Huffman Manufacturing Co., in 1925 to make steel bicycle wheel rims. Horace was building atop a foundation laid by his father, the sewing-machine magnate George P. Huffman, who had gone into the bicycle business in 1892 in Dayton, about seventy miles to the south. (The elder Huffman retooled his sewing-machine factory to make bicycles about a decade before two other Dayton bicycle manufacturers, Wilbur and Orville Wright, branched out into aviation.) Over the years, Huffman produced some of the most memorable bicycles made in America: the Huffman Dayton Streamliner in the 1930s, the Huffy Radio Bicycle in the 1950s, and the Huffy Dragster with a distinctive banana-shaped seat in the 1960s. The company made fast-selling drop-handlebar racing bicycles in the 1970s and did much to popularize mountain bikes in the 1980s.

However, by the mid-1990s, Huffy was in deep trouble. The U.S. bicycle industry had consolidated, sharply reducing the number of channels for selling bikes. "High-volume retailers," as Huffy called them, had claimed three-fourths of the U.S. market, gaining tremendous leverage over bicycle makers. Wal-Mart in particular was pressing Huffy: It ordered 900,000 bicycles at one time, but insisted that Huffy lower its prices significantly. To remain a major player in the bicycle market, the Ohio company had little choice but to agree. "Wal-Mart is really the only show in town as to mass market," said Matt Wiebe of *Bicycle Retailer*, a trade magazine.[1]

Huffy supplemented its production in Celina with a second factory in Farmington, Missouri, staffed with low-paid, non-unionized workers. This helped Huffy meet demand, but the company soon found that it simply could not make a profit selling bicycles at the prices that its biggest customer, Wal-Mart, was willing to pay. After losing $10 million in 1995, the company asked the union representing the workers in Celina—the United Steelworkers of America Local 5369—for a 20 percent across-the-board pay cut. The union quickly agreed to it, taking the average wage down to $12 to $13 an hour.

Huffy returned to profitability in 1996 and 1997 only to again crumple under the pricing pressure applied by Wal-Mart.[2] The following year, management informed the union that the company had to lower its costs by another 35 percent. The city of Celina, desperate to keep its biggest employer, offered a $14 million package of incentives, but it was not nearly sufficient to alter the calculus of Huffy's doom. Management insisted that the lion's share of the 35 percent reduction would have to come out of the one cost that was not fixed: employee pay. This time, the union balked.

When Huffy's Celina employees arrived for work a few days later, on May 28, 1998, their managers called them together in the plant's warehouse for what they said would be an important announcement. As Huffy executives informed workers that the company was closing the factory and laying off all 935 of them, a rumble of surprise and anger swept the warehouse. Several workers burst into tears. "I really thought I would retire from here," said Joann Jones, who had worked at the Huffy plant for twenty-two years.[3]

After closing the Celina plant, Huffy shifted production to its factory in Missouri and also opened another non-union plant in Southaven, Mississippi. Workers in these facilities earned $8 to $10 an hour—still more than Huffy could afford to pay, as it turned out. The bike maker abruptly closed both factories little more than a year later, firing another 900 employees. The company subcontracted all of its work to China, where bicycle-plant workers earned just 25 cents to 41 cents an hour.[4]

Even moving production to China was not enough to save Huffy. It did gain market share, but remained unable to operate at a profit. In late 2004, the venerable bicycle maker tumbled into bankruptcy court, listing assets of $138.7 million and liabilities of $161.2 million. Its biggest creditor was the company it contracted with to build the bikes it could no longer afford to make itself: the Shenzhen Bo-An Bike Co. Ltd. of Shenzhen, China. In federal bankruptcy court in Dayton, Ohio, Huffy's assets were turned over to its creditors, chief among them the China Export and Credit Insurance Corporation, or the Sinosure Group, an agency of the Chinese government that provides export credit insurance to Chinese exporters—like the Shenzhen Bo-An Bike Co. After years of struggling against the cut-rate Chinese bicycles that set the price target guiding Wal-Mart, Huffy essentially had become a Chinese-owned company.

Back in Celina, meanwhile, a developer turned Huffy's old factory site—once a landmark of American industrial prowess—into a symbol of the nation's future as a low-wage, service-based economy: He built a Wal-Mart Supercenter. The city fathers of Celina went to great lengths to accommodate a company that—indirectly, at least—had killed the town's biggest employer, enacting zoning concessions and absorbing the cost of widening a road and of improving water and sewer service at the store site. "We simply couldn't afford to lose Wal-Mart," Mayor Paul Arnold said.[5] When the Supercenter opened in May 2005 amid the usual hoopla, Senator Byron L. Dorgan of North Dakota marked the occasion by noting sourly, "Workers who got laid off from the Huffy plant can go and purchase a Chinese-made Huffy bike."[6]

Long before "the China price" became the key measure of competitiveness in consumer products manufacturing, Wal-Mart succeeded in using its access to cheap foreign-made goods to gain pricing leverage over its domestic suppliers, including many that were a lot bigger than Huffy ever was. By the mid-1980s, nearly half of the merchandise on Wal-Mart's shelves was imported, and many U.S. consumer goods makers had grudgingly come to accept Bentonville's everyday low price business model. To accommodate the demands of Wal-Mart, Kmart, Target, and other burgeoning big-box retailers, U.S. manufacturers of clothing, toys, shoes, and many other products shifted an increasing portion of their production to low-wage factories in Third World countries. By 1985, more than 40 percent of the apparel sold in America was imported.[7]

Sam Walton returned from a swing through Central America in 1984 worried that the outsourcing trend had gotten out of hand. He was still pondering what to do about it when he got a call from Bill Clinton, then the governor of Arkansas, requesting Wal-Mart's help in rescuing Farris Fashions, a flannel shirt maker struggling to remain solvent after losing one of its biggest customers to a factory in China. Clinton's distress call inspired Walton to come up with Wal-Mart's famous "Buy America" program (officially dubbed "Bring It Home to the U.S.A."), which was launched in 1985 by giving a $612,000 contract to Farris Fashions for 240,000 Arkansas-made flannel shirts.

With his customary flair, Walton extracted full promotional value from the Buy America initiative. In every Wal-Mart store, red, white, and blue banners proclaiming, "Keep America Working and Strong" were hung, along with dozens of smaller signs that read: "This item, formerly imported, is now being purchased by Wal-Mart in the U.S.A. and is creating—or retaining—jobs for Americans!" Wal-Mart featured the Buy America theme in national television commercials, and plainspoken testimonials from grateful American factory workers became a highlight of its annual meetings.

Buy America was the greatest PR triumph in Wal-Mart history (and would not be eclipsed until the company's star turn during Hurricane Katrina in 2005), but it was much more than a publicity campaign. After analyzing the economics of its foreign sourcing much more thoroughly than it ever had before, Wal-Mart management concluded that it had overlooked a host of hidden costs, including far longer lead times for placing orders and more onerous inventory financing requirements. "We had fallen into a pattern of knee-jerk import buying without really examining possible alternatives," Walton admitted. "In the past, we would just take our best-selling U.S.-made items, send them to the Orient, and say, 'See if you can make something like this.'"[8]

Under the Buy America program, Wal-Mart made this pledge to its domestic suppliers: If a "true apple-to-apple cost comparison," as Walton described it, puts you no more than 5 percent above the import price, then Wal-Mart will accept the smaller markup and go with the American product. From 1985 through 1991, Wal-Mart placed $5 billion worth of orders under its Buy America program with dozens of U.S. vendors large and small. The merchandise it purchased included candles, ladies' sweaters, men's knit shirts, beach towels, film, furniture, toys, and, last but not least, bicycles—made in Celine, Ohio, by Huffy Manufacturing.

But just because American companies got new Wal-Mart orders didn't mean that they made any money filling them. The fact was, the great majority of its U.S. vendors could not come within 5 percent of Wal-Mart's import price and have a prayer of turning a profit without making significant cuts in their operating costs. Buy America wasn't a scam exactly; in redirecting $5 billion worth of business, Wal-Mart did put a dent in the U.S. trade deficit. And the company often went beyond merely placing an order with an ailing American manufacturer and helped it obtain raw materials on favorable terms and participated in product design and distribution. In the end, though, Buy America in essence was a star-spangled Trojan horse that the company used to inveigle its U.S. and overseas suppliers alike into making further price concessions.

Consider the sorry fate of Frazier Engineering, a Morristown, Indiana, furniture manufacturer that Walton touted as a particularly worthy beneficiary of Buy America. Wal-Mart pulled a contract it had placed with a Chinese factory to make wire patio chairs for $4.98 apiece after Frazier agreed to supply the same chair at just $3.50. "The folks in the Orient heard about it . . . and you know what happened? They lowered their price. So it works both ways," Walton said triumphantly, hastening to add that Wal-Mart was sticking with Frazier Engineering nonetheless.[9] But not for long, it turned out. The Indiana company lost so much money selling cut-rate chairs to Wal-Mart that it went bankrupt within a year of landing the Buy America contract.

In its stores, Wal-Mart proudly posted a running tally of the value of contracts awarded and U.S. jobs saved under Buy America, but the company was not nearly as forthcoming with import data. The statistics it did make available strongly suggested that imports continued to account for a rising percentage of Wal-Mart's sales throughout the 1980s. For a company that remained as obsessive as ever about providing customers the lowest possible price at the highest possible profit to itself, the economics of Third World production were just too favorable to resist, "hidden cost factors" or no.

In late 1992, not long after Walton's death, David Glass was humiliated on camera in a *Dateline NBC* interview that tarnished Wal-Mart's Buy America patina beyond repair. In Wal-Mart stores in Georgia and Florida, *Dateline* had discovered rack after rack of clothes that were advertised as "Made in the USA" but in reality had been imported from Bangladesh, Korea, and China. As Glass squirmed on his hot seat, the program rolled footage of correspondent Brian Ross's visit to a notorious factory in Bangladesh where children as young as nine were locked in overnight to crank out apparel for Wal-Mart. After Ross handed Glass some photographs of twenty-five children who had perished in a fire at the factory not long before Wal-Mart had placed its first order, the CEO cut the interview short and stormed from the studio.

Within a day or two of the disastrous interview, Bentonville issued an urgent communiqué to all store managers. "We had to . . . pull every 'Buy America' sign, every 'Made in the U.S.A.' sign, everything that was red, white, and blue that was hanging on the walls. We even had permanent signs that were liquid-nailed to the cement walls, concrete walls, that we had to rip down," recalled Jon Lehman, who then was running a Supercenter in Indiana. All of this had to be done on a tight deadline. "If you didn't do it, your job was on the line," Lehman added. "It was an emergency situation."[10]

Even so, Wal-Mart never officially terminated Buy America. As recently as 1994, it still was touting it as "both a commitment and a partnership" in promotional material. As a practical matter, though, Buy America quietly expired in the mid-1990s and was buried under an avalanche of low-cost, high-profit imports from China and elsewhere.

The leverage that Wal-Mart exercises over its suppliers is grounded as much in its masterful use of technology as its brandishing of the club of foreign sourcing. From the introduction of bar codes and scanning devices to the innovations of electronic data interchange and Radio

Frequency Identification (RFID) tagging, Wal-Mart has blazed the way in using the power of information technology to remake the entire consumer products supply chain over the last three decades. Tens of billions of dollars of capital investment by Wal-Mart and by other big retail chains has enthroned "just-in-time" or "lean retailing" as the regulator of the U.S. consumer economy.

When manufacturers held dominion over the economy, they would adjust their production runs based on their own, often imprecise assessment of market demand and then offload merchandise onto retailers on their own terms and at their convenience. Led by Wal-Mart, the big-box chains gradually reversed this power dynamic by using the latest computer technology to obtain a far-more-detailed and up-to-date reading of consumer preferences than even the most sophisticated manufacturers could manage on their own. As a result, it is now the retailer that calls the shots. That is, "The retailer tracks consumer behavior with meticulous care and then transmits consumer preferences down the supply chain. Replenishment is put in motion almost immediately, with the supplier required to make more frequent deliveries of smaller lots."[11]

The triumph of lean retailing combined with Wal-Mart's cherished insularity to turn Bentonville into "Vendorville." Virtually all 500 of Wal-Mart's largest suppliers have chosen to open an office in northwest Arkansas. Most are staffed by no more than ten to fifteen people and are clustered together in nondescript office parks near a highway interchange within a few miles of the home office. Although Wal-Mart does not require its vendors to rent space locally, it does demand a high level of attentiveness from them that simply cannot be provided by telephone or e-mail. The consensus among suppliers is that living just down the street is a better way than racking up frequent-flyer miles to keep their largest customer happy.

The largest of Vendorville's corporate embassies is home to the 400 members of the Procter & Gamble Co.'s "Wal-Mart team." Cincinnati-based Procter & Gamble, the world's largest consumer product manufacturer, owns many of America's most famous and durable brands—Tide, Folgers, Crest, and Charmin among them. It was essential to its pioneering of lean retailing that Wal-Mart not only gain the upper hand over P & G, a notorious corporate bully in its own right, but that it do so by transforming what long had been an adversarial relationship into a close, collaborative one.

The breakthrough came in 1987, when Walton was persuaded to join his tennis-playing buddy George Billingsley on an Ozarks canoe trip with Lou Pritchett, a longtime friend of Billingsley's who was a vice president of P & G. On the waters of the Spring River, Walton and Pritchett worked through the mutual animosity that kept their companies apart to reach agreement over the root problem. Both companies were "focused on the end-user—the customer—but each did it independently of the other," Pritchett recalled later. "No sharing of information, no planning together, no systems coordination. We were simply two giant entities going our separate ways, oblivious to the excess costs created by this obsolete system."[12]

Soon after, P & G CEO John Smale called Walton and invited him to Cincinnati for a summit conference of sorts. Walton was annoyed that no officer of P & G had ever called on Wal-Mart in its history, but he swallowed his pride and agreed to fly to Cincinnati at the head of a small entourage that included David Glass and Don Soderquist. A few days before the meeting, Walton called Smale and said he couldn't come after all because the hotel rooms that P & G had booked for him and his colleagues were more than $100 a night. Walton did not commit to the meeting until Smale called back and said that he talked the hotel into knocking its price down to $59. "In truth," Soderquist recalled, "P & G had picked up the other half of the bill."[13]

Over the next few months, Wal-Mart and P & G established the protocols—both human and technological—of a broader, more interactive relationship. For years, the only point of contact between the companies had been Wal-Mart buyers and P & G salespeople. Now "cross-functional" teams were created that paired the logistics, technology, and finance specialists from one side to their counterparts on the other. This, in turn, led to the fashioning of intercompany computer links that largely eliminated the costly and contentious human factor from order-taking and order-filling. The result was a highly automated system of "continuous replenishment" that resulted in huge cost savings for both companies by reducing the amount of inventory each had to carry and the number of Wal-Mart buyers and P & G salespeople needed to interact with one another. Or, as Pritchett put it, "We broke new ground by using information technology to manage our business together, instead of just to audit it."[14]

Wal-Mart's relationship with P & G became the template around which it recast and computerized its dealings with all its major suppliers. Walton was enthralled with the bottom-line benefits, but was as reluctant as ever to invest as heavily in new technology as his operations people wanted. Glass, a digital true believer, succeeded Walton as CEO in 1988 but shrewdly waited until illness had forced his predecessor to the sidelines in 1991 to launch what was one of the boldest and, at a total cost of $4 billion, unquestionably the priciest technology project in Wal-Mart history: Retail Link.

Eight times a day, the details of every sale in every Wal-Mart store are fed through the Retail Link computer system into a vast data warehouse in the David Glass Technology Center in Bentonville. Through their own computers, Wal-Mart's vendors can tap into Retail Link and retrieve information pertinent to their products. P & G can keep close tabs on how each of its products carried by Wal-Mart—all 1,200 of them—has sold in a particular store, city, county, state, region, or the whole country for any period of time from the current day back through the last two years. This information is continuously computer-massaged to match supply and demand as precisely as possible, with the aim of reducing the likelihood that any Wal-Mart store will run short of items or, conversely, that it will be stuck with excess inventories.

Retail Link orchestrates this intricate merchandise ballet with minimal human input. According to Soderquist, the computer "determines the anticipated demand on discretionary items for each store based on that store's sales history, checks the inventory of the item in that store daily, and then automatically creates an order and immediately transmits it to the nearest distribution center."[15] The computer also monitors inventory levels at each distribution center, automatically transmitting purchase orders to suppliers when the time is right. From their perch in the Glass Center, Information Systems technicians monitor the computer-to-computer interplay using software that enables them to anticipate glitches, or "exceptions," as they're known in digitese, and intervene to prevent them from occurring. "We are pretty near real time. We can tell people that they need to go do something and we are within hours, depending on the event," said Linda Dillman, who, as Wal-Mart's chief information officer, runs the Glass Center.[16]

During a tour of Wal-Mart's Bentonville distribution center in 2003, I was amazed by how fast the merchandise moves through the cloverleaf of conveyor belts that snake through the cavernous building. Craig Ridgeway, the DC's general manager, said that the goods were hurtling past us at about the same rate that this mix of stuff was selling in the 127 stores supplied by the DC. In other words, Wal-Mart's distribution system had achieved a perfect equilibrium between input and output—or something close to it, anyway. For Wal-Mart as a whole, turnover is so rapid that 70 percent of its merchandise is rung up at the registers before the company has paid for it, saving the company huge sums for financing and storing inventory.

Wal-Mart has amassed more data about what it sells and about the buying habits of its customers than any other retailer. The company also takes an encyclopedic interest in the geographic market served by each of its stores, collecting information across some 10,000 categories ranging from racial and ethnic demographics to local sports team preferences and weather patterns. Information Systems staffers combine this data with the point-of-sale information gathered by Retail Link to project sales trends for each Wal-Mart store and localize their product mix.

This is called micro-merchandising, and Hurricane Frances provided a particularly dramatic, if trivial, example of its effectiveness in
August 2004. Just a month earlier, Hurricane Charley had roared
through the same swath of central Florida now menaced by Frances.
Analysts safely ensconced in the Glass Center "mined" the pre-
hurricane sales data from the Wal-Mart stores in Charley's path and
used it to predict what would happen as Frances made land. Soon,
Wal-Mart trucks were racing down I-94 with extra supplies, including thousands of cases of beer and strawberry Pop-Tarts, sales of
which had jumped sevenfold pre-Charley.[17]

Wal-Mart and its vendors also collaborate to create new products to
satisfy demand they try to predict by crunching Retail Link data. In
hopes of selling food to the many hunters who frequented the sporting
goods sections of its stores, Wal-Mart asked Hormel Foods, the maker
of Spam, to invent a snack that it could mix in with the rifles and fishing rods. Within weeks, "Spamoflage"—Spam in camouflage cans—
was selling like crazy in most of the 760 rural Wal-Marts that carried
it. Meanwhile, Pennzoil tapped into Retail Link to guide the creation
of forty-five new display variations of its motor oil.[18]

For suppliers, doing business with Bentonville is a Faustian bargain.
Plugging into the world's highest-powered consumer selling machine
allows manufacturers to move vast quantities of merchandise with
minimal advertising and promotional outlays. If all goes well, a vendor
can add handsomely to its market share and more than make up in
volume what it likely loses in profit margin to Wal-Mart's "Every Day
Low Prices." But what Bentonville demands in return is little short of
vassalage. The company not only determines the price at which it will
sell an item but also the price it pays for it—and under its "Plus One"
principle mandates that its suppliers must either lower the price or
improve the quality of every single product every year. Manufacturers
who fail to tailor a product to Wal-Mart's specifications or who fail to
deliver the specified amount of merchandise to a distribution center at
precisely the right time face draconian penalties. "Everyone from the

forklift driver on up to me, the CEO, knew we had to deliver on time. Not ten minutes later. And not forty-five minutes early, either," said Robin Prever, the longtime CEO of Saratoga Beverage Group. "The message came through clearly: You have this thirty-second delivery window. Either you're there, or you're out."[19]

Yes, Wal-Mart reconceived its relationship with suppliers as a partnership, but it was hardly a partnership of equals. None of Wal-Mart's 61,000 vendors is nearly as important to the company as Wal-Mart is to its major vendors. Procter & Gamble is Wal-Mart's largest supplier, but its products generate only 2 percent of the retailer's sales. By contrast, Wal-Mart, Procter's largest customer, accounts for 18 percent of P & G's revenues. Wal-Mart would hate to antagonize shoppers by pulling Tide or any of P & G's other staples from its shelves. But the fact is that Bentonville could replace P & G products a lot easier than Cincinnati could replace the loss of Wal-Mart's patronage.

Wal-Mart had the whip hand, and there could be no doubting its willingness to use it after the company's mid-1990s showdown with Rubbermaid. An old-line manufacturer of garbage cans, plastic pails, and containers of all kinds that was transformed in the 1980s into a growth company, Rubbermaid rose on the strength of inspired product innovation and rigorous attention to quality to become the most admired corporation in America as judged by its peers and affirmed by *Fortune* magazine in 1994. Based in the bucolic town of Wooster, Ohio, Rubbermaid was a great American success story with an abrupt, unhappy ending.

Rubbermaid's renaissance was largely the handiwork of Stanley Gault, a Wooster boy who went off to work for General Electric and returned in 1980 to run the hometown giant. A daring, egotistical sort of executive, Gault whipped Rubbermaid into fighting trim through sheer force of will. A reporter once told him that his subordinates thought him a tyrant. "Yes," Gault replied, "but I'm a sincere tyrant."[20]

Before Gault joined Rubbermaid, it did not deign to do business with Wal-Mart. Gault changed that in a hurry, positioning Rubbermaid on the right side of the coming big-box revolution. Rubbermaid supplied all the big discount chains, but found its greatest retail ally in Wal-Mart, which quickly became its single biggest customer. But even as Wal-Mart helped Rubbermaid post forty consecutive quarters of earnings gains, misgivings were growing among Gault's lieutenants. "On the positive side, at first the big retailers created a great deal of efficiency," recalled Fred Grunewald, who ran Rubbermaid's home products division. "But they squeezed too hard. . . . We couldn't recoup our product-development costs before they'd slash prices."[21]

Gault was safely retired by 1994, when the price of resin started to soar, putting Rubbermaid's back up against the wall. Every increase of a penny per pound cost the company $10 million, or about $250 million in total in 1995. Wolfgang Schmitt, the new CEO, flew to Bentonville to explain Rubbermaid's desperate need to offset its exploding raw materials costs by raising the prices of many of its products. In one of the little meeting rooms off the lobby of Wal-Mart's home office, Schmitt sat down with Bill Fields, a senior executive then considered a potential successor to Glass.

Fields listened politely to Schmitt's spiel and refused to pay a penny more for Rubbermaid wares. Schmitt, an imposing executive known for his forbidding manner, soon grew so frustrated that he stood up for emphasis. "You need to understand something," he more or less shouted at Fields, "we have to do this."

"No, no, no," replied Fields as he, too, rose from the table and, at six-foot-six, towered over Schmitt. "It's you, Wolf, who needs to understand something." Charge more for a product, Fields said, and we will stop carrying it.

Other, less confrontational meetings followed, but the end result was that Rubbermaid did raise prices and Wal-Mart did pull many of its products. Bentonville also imposed strict new delivery demands, often requiring a turnaround of just forty-eight hours. When Rubbermaid missed a deadline, as it did about 20 percent of the time,

Wal-Mart fined it for every dollar of lost sales. What most bothered executives of the Ohio company was that Bentonville dictated to Rubbermaid, an acclaimed innovator, on product design issues. "You'd have this meeting with Wal-Mart, and some twenty-five-year-old buyer would come in and pretty much tear apart something that professional, gifted designers had spent months developing," complained one marketing executive.[22]

There is no question that Rubbermaid was complicit in its own collapse. In *Good to Great*, Jim Collins argued that the company was such a one-man show under Gault that it never developed the depth of management needed to sustain its success. "Gault did not leave behind a company that would be great without *him*," Collins concluded.[23] Clearly, though, Wal-Mart's bullying hurt the company badly. Wal-Mart elected Gault to its board of directors in 1996, but it was too late for Rubbermaid to repair its ruptured relationship with America's largest retailer or, for that matter, to maintain its independence.

In 1999, Rubbermaid was acquired by Newell Co., an up-and-coming consumer products manufacturer almost slavishly eager to please Wal-Mart. The design of Newell Rubbermaid's office in Bentonville was guided by the principle that imitation is not just the highest form of flattery but also of customer service. The budget carpeting and no-frills cubicles are Wal-Martesque. The first floor contains what the company bills as "an exact replica of a Wal-Mart store," showing the placement of Newell Glassware, Sharpie pens, Levelor blinds, Graco strollers, Little Tikes toys, and other staples of the expanded Newell product line. On a wall upstairs hangs a photograph of Sam Walton, alongside his "Rules for Building a Business." Said Steven Scheyer, who runs Newell's Wal-Mart Division: "We live and breathe with these guys."[24]

Huffy bicycles are not the only iconic American product now made exclusively in China. There are many others: Levi jeans, Black &

Decker home appliances, Stanley tools, Fedders air conditioners, Sunbeam mixers, Radio Flyer wagons, and Etch-A-Sketch toys. Even many of the American flag lapel pins worn by members of Congress are stamped, plated, and enameled in a factory in Shenzhen, a boomtown of 10 million people that now rivals nearby Hong Kong as a hub of untrammeled capitalism.

Shenzhen also is home to a factory owned by the Lakewood Engineering and Manufacturing Co., a Chicago-based company that makes room fans, space heaters, and humidifiers. When the time came in 2000 to expand to fill growing orders, the company saw no way to add the needed capacity and meet Wal-Mart's price without moving some production to China. The price of one of its box fans already had fallen by half over the previous decade, and Lakewood had run out of options to cut costs further in America. It already had automated its factories on the west side of Chicago, reducing the number of people required to assemble an appliance to seven from as many as twenty-two. But those seven Americans still needed an American wage of about $13 an hour. Chinese workers in Shenzhen are paid about 25 cents an hour.[25]

No U.S. industry has been hit harder by China's explosive emergence as a manufacturing powerhouse than textiles, which has lost more than 500,000 jobs—or half of its total employment—over the last three decades. One of the biggest recent failures in the textile business came in 2003, when the Pillowtex Corp., maker of Cannon and Fieldcrest towels, fired its last 6,450 employees. Pillowtex, which had emerged from bankruptcy protection a year earlier, struggled to find a way to make towels profitably at a price that its biggest customer, Wal-Mart, would be willing to pay. In the end, it could not. Entire families were thrown out of work, whole towns devastated. "That mill *was* the city of Kannapolis," said Leann Harrington, a waitress at the Towel City Junction Cafe & Grill, a diner frequented by mill workers in the North Carolina city of 37,000. "We live in a ghost town now."[26]

The truly scary thing for Wal-Mart's American vendors and their

employees is that Wal-Mart has just begun to concentrate on developing China as a source of merchandise for its U.S. stores. Wal-Mart has
been buying Chinese goods since the early 1970s, first through American and Japanese importers and later through its own offices in Hong
Kong (opened in 1981) and Taipei (1983). But it was not until 2002
that Wal-Mart moved onto the mainland by opening a buying office
in Shenzhen. Within a year, Wal-Mart made the Shenzhen office its
global purchasing headquarters, an emphatic declaration of China's
central importance to the company. Today, about 80 percent of the 6,000
foreign factories in Wal-Mart's supplier database are located in China.

Wal-Mart's Shenzhen quarters occupies three floors of a nondescript
glass office tower. In the lobby, the only indication of its presence is a
sign no bigger than a sheet of paper, reading "Wal-Mart Global Procurement." An arrow points to an escalator. In China, as in the United
States, Wal-Mart does not need to seek out suppliers because suppliers
seek it out. Despite the low profile it keeps, the Shenzhen procurement
office is swarmed daily by hundreds of entrepreneurs and sales agents
hoping to get their wares onto Wal-Mart's shelves in the United
States and elsewhere. In 2003, the company opened a second office in
the North China port of Tiajin, the first of what likely will be a score
or more of regional procurement outposts throughout the country.

Already, China is Wal-Mart's single largest source of merchandise
outside the United States. In 2005, the company bought about $22
billion worth of Chinese-made goods, up from $18 billion the previ-
ous year and $12 billion in 2002. By itself, Wal-Mart now accounts
for 30 percent of total foreign buying in China and 10 percent of U.S.
imports from the country. Yet China represents only 11 percent of
Wal-Mart's overall purchase budget, quite a bit less than for many
other big U.S. retailers. Because Wal-Mart "has been buying relatively
little from Chinese suppliers . . . this amount is likely to increase substantially in the future," predicted Misha Petrovic and Gary Hamilton, two University of Washington scholars who recently co-authored
a study of Wal-Mart and its suppliers.[27] At a meeting with analysts in

Shenzhen in early 2005, Wal-Mart executives said it was possible that the value of the company's purchases in China would double by 2010.[28]

China's low wages have created a "cost standard" for manufacturers around the world, the consulting firm Deloitte Touche Tohmatsu has concluded,[29] and Wal-Mart's single-minded embrace of the standard makes it difficult for other employers to resist. *BusinessWeek* called this "the China price," and few other places, even formerly booming low-wage manufacturing countries like Mexico, can match it. Often, these lower production costs result in the same problems that Wal-Mart is criticized for in the United States: penurious wages and benefits, cruelly long hours, and poor working conditions. "Wal-Mart has really been at the forefront in driving down wages and working conditions," said Kent Wong, the director of the UCLA Labor Center. "They're not only exporting the Wal-Mart name and the corporation and the identity. They're also exporting that way of doing business."[30]

Like most major U.S. consumer goods importers, Wal-Mart espouses the principles of "ethical sourcing." Ever since 1992, the company has imposed a code of conduct on foreign suppliers that is intended to improve working conditions in factories making goods for its stores. Wal-Mart claims to have the world's largest overseas monitoring program, employing some 200 full-time inspectors who visit 30 factories a day, or about 5,000 a year. "In 1996, I personally saw how important ethical sourcing would be to our company when I went to Bangladesh to investigate allegations of poor conditions at factories where garments were being produced for Wal-Mart . . ." Lee Scott wrote in the spring of 2005 in his introduction to the latest of the reports that the company compiles annually on its enforcement of supplier standards. "The Ethical Standards program is a vital part of our business."[31]

Scott's assertion drew heavy fire a few months later in a lawsuit accusing Wal-Mart of failing to effectively enforce its code of conduct not only in China, but in Bangladesh, Indonesia, Nicaragua, and Swaziland. The suit was brought by the International Labor Rights

Fund in the United States because the sixteen workers who are party to it would have faced reprisal, perhaps even death, in their home countries. Their stories, as contained in the complaint, paint a picture of almost Dickensian deprivation: employees paid pennies an hour and regularly forced to work ten or twelve hours a day for six or seven days a week for weeks on end. To keep wages low and workers handy, companies have employees sleep in corporate dormitories and eat in factory-run canteens. Men who worked for Wal-Mart contractors in Shenzhen said in the lawsuit that management withheld the first three months' pay of every new worker and threatened to withhold the money if they quit, a practice that effectively made them indentured servants. One woman said that because she was unable to meet her quota her boss slapped her face so hard that her nose began bleeding.[32]

Bentonville reacted scornfully to the International Labor Rights Fund's lawsuit, saying that the group had "a history of presenting opinions as facts" and had brought the suit at the behest of the company's sworn enemy, the United Food and Commercial Workers. "We are a global leader in monitoring supplier factory conditions," Wal-Mart declared in a public statement, "and if we find that any of our suppliers' factories are unwilling to correct problems, we end our relationship with them."[33]

Accusations of worker abuse have long dogged Wal-Mart's suppliers in China. Five years earlier, *BusinessWeek* documented similar abuses at Chun Si Enterprise Handbag Factory in Zhongshan, another industrial metropolis in the Pearl River Delta.[34] Chun Si's 900 workers were locked in the walled factory compound for all but sixty minutes a day for meals, the magazine said. Guards regularly punched and hit workers for talking back to managers or even for walking too fast, and also fined them up to $1 for infractions such as taking too long in the bathroom.

One worker, Chun Sei, said that the company, which made Kathie Lee Gifford handbags for Wal-Mart, paid him $22 a month and then deducted $15 a month for food and lodging. The man, a farmer from the countryside who had come to Zhongshan in response to a Chun

Si ad promising good work and fair pay, said he was afraid to just quit because the company made him surrender his identification card before he started work. In place of his ID, the company issued him an expired temporary-residence permit, a worthless document that effectively made him a captive of the factory complex. After three months of ninety-hour workweeks, he finally screwed up the courage to leave—with just $6 of savings in his pocket. "Workers there face a life of fines and beating," he said.

Long hours, low pay, and abysmal working conditions are commonplace at Wal-Mart's Chinese contractors. At He Yi Electronics & Plastics Products in Dongguan, people who make small toy cars for Wal-Mart are paid as little as 16.5 cents an hour and are routinely required to work more than twelve hours a day, seven days a week, according to the National Labor Committee, an anti-sweatshop group in New York. "Conditions at this factory are as bad as you find anywhere in the world," said Charles Kernaghan, executive director of the N.L.C. "They are illegal under Chinese law, and Americans would find them appalling."[35]

In 2004, Wal-Mart suspended purchases from 1,200 contractors for at least ninety days for having failed to fix serious violations after being warned. It permanently banned more than 100 other factories, chiefly for breaking child-labor laws. Even so, Terry Collingsworth of the International Labor Rights Fund, an advocacy group based in Washington, dismissed Wal-Mart's monitoring system, saying that more than 90 percent of its inspections were scheduled in advance, giving company managers time to conceal records, warn employees not to complain to inspectors, and fire anyone they think might tell the truth.

Wal-Mart's history of policing sweatshops is less than stellar. When the problems at Chun Si, the handbag maker, were first made public in 1997, Wal-Mart angrily shot back that allegations of worker abuse were "lies" and denied it had any relationship with Chun Si. But when *BusinessWeek* confronted it with damning business records that workers had smuggled out of the factory, Wal-Mart conceded that it had lied about using Chun Si. It continued to buy handbags from the company until 1999.

Workers in Shenzhen and other industrial centers are beginning to discover that the Wal-Mart Way ultimately could make them as expendable as the Americans, Mexicans, and others whom they have replaced. Gladpeer Garment Factory, a sizable maker of underwear, pajamas, and children's clothing, started in Hong Kong, but bowed to price pressure applied by Wal-Mart and moved 100 miles up the Pearl River Delta to Dongguan, where seamstresses were willing to work nine-hour days, five or six days a week, for about $55 a month. To cut costs further, the firm's managing director, Simon Lee, soon began preparing to move Gladpeer much farther inland, to remote Guangxi Province. Lee said electricity, housing, taxes—and, of course, labor costs—are much cheaper there. "Competition is intense, and our biggest single issue is cost," Lee said. "Many customers look at cost first, then they look at the workmanship. That's why we're going to Guangxi."[36]

A number of Wal-Mart vendors have expressed concern about rising labor costs in China. Dorel Industries Inc., a Canadian company that designs and sells Safety 1st and Cosco infant car seats, strollers, and other baby products, announced in 2004 that it had begun looking to move production out of central Chinese cities. Dorel's CEO, Martin Schwartz, said that 10 percent to 15 percent increases in wages would not do, even when matched by productivity gains. "These are increases we cannot pass along to our major customers," Schwartz said. "Chinese manufacturers must become more efficient."[37] The talk might just have been bluster, to keep Dorel's suppliers in line. But if this was the case, it has been very effective. Amy Gu, an executive at one of Dorel's suppliers, Goodbaby Corp., which makes strollers near Shanghai, said her company has filled orders at a loss, just to keep Wal-Mart's business in hopes of a payoff down the road. "Dorel will tell us, 'Well, Wal-Mart has given us this price. We need a factory cost of this much,'" she said. "And we have to find a way to deliver it."[38]

Sok Hong, managing director of the family-owned Kong Hong

Garment Co. in Cambodia, admitted to being as worried as any American company about his customers shifting orders elsewhere if they think they can save a penny or two on each unit. "They just care about the price. If you have a cheaper price, they will buy from you," said Sok, whose company exports as many as 30,000 pairs of jeans a month to the United States, nearly three-fourths of them to Wal-Mart. "We don't have child labor at this factory. . . . [But] the buyer doesn't care how good you are."

Where will it end? Wal-Mart says that it is simply acting as an agent of its customers, who want more for less. It insists it is "giving a raise" to poor people lucky enough to have a Wal-Mart nearby; it is helping people out of work make ends meet—even if those customers are poor and jobless because of the practices that deliver those "Every Day Low Prices." Besides, Wal-Mart claims, if it doesn't deliver DVD players for $38.76 or SpongeBob SquarePants T-shirts for $6.44 or any of the other bargains it has every day, someone else will. And if the process of delivering these bargains requires terminating millions of middle-class jobs in Ohio and North Carolina and elsewhere, creating new jobs with poverty-level wages, and putting the United States in hock to China, so be it. More than a few economists agree, as do some of the millions of people who shop at Wal-Mart every day—at least those who bother to wonder how on earth Wal-Mart can make a profit selling Mr. Coffee machines for $19.94.

Others, however, are beginning to question the wisdom of this race to the bottom. "People ask, 'How can it be bad for things to come into the United States cheaply? How can it be bad to have a bargain at Wal-Mart?' Sure, it's held inflation down, and it's great to have bargains," says Steve Dobbins, president and CEO of Carolina Mills, whose business of making thread and yarn for clothes sold at Wal-Mart is continually being nibbled away by lower-cost Chinese competitors. "But you can't buy anything if you're not employed. We are shopping ourselves out of jobs."[39]

THE ANTI–WAL-MART

Discount retailing is a tough business that requires obsessive attention to labor costs, the largest single category of expense for Wal-Mart and its competitors. Even Wal-Mart, that paragon of cost efficiency, makes just three cents of profit on every dollar of sales. "Last year we earned $10 billion in profits, so our critics argue that we should pay more to our associates. But I ask anyone to do the math," CEO Lee Scott said in late 2005. "Even slight overall adjustments to wages eliminate our thin profit margins."[1]

To which the most persuasive rejoinder is: What about Costco?

It's not hard to figure out how Costco Warehouse supplanted Wal-Mart as the big-box employer of choice. Its average wage of $15.97 an hour is 33 percent more than that of Sam's Club, its closest competitor, and 65 percent higher than Wal-Mart Stores'. Costco spends an additional $5,735 a year in health benefits per worker to Sam's Club's $3,500, and it provides coverage to 82 percent of its workforce, compared with Sam's 47 percent.[2] What is surprising—astounding even—is that Costco also is more profitable than Sam's Club. In 2004, Costco reported $13,647 in net profit per employee to Sam's $11,039 per employee. How, in Sam's name, is such a thing possible?

In pioneering its distinctive low-price, high-wage business model, Costco didn't so much beat Wal-Mart at its own game as change the game—or at least its mathematics. The key to Costco's new math of discount retailing is an annual turnover rate of just 23 percent, half of Wal-Mart's. "Taking care of your employees and turning inventory faster than your people is good business," said James Sinegal, Costco's founder and chief executive in what clearly was a swipe at his giant Bentonville rival.[3]

Based just outside of Seattle in Issaquah, Washington, Costco is America's largest warehouse club chain, and its fifth-largest retailer overall. Costco is descended from Price Club, the San Diego chain that Walton had aped in founding Sam's Club. Sol Price, the left-leaning maverick discounter who founded Price Club and who took such delight in baiting Walton over dinner, schooled a talented protégé named Jim Sinegal. In 1983, Sinegal left Price Club and moved up the coast to found Costco with a local partner just as Wal-Mart was launching Sam's Club. In 1993, Price sold Price Club to Costco. "We were good at innovating," Price explained, "but when it came to expanding and controlling, we weren't so good."[4]

Sinegal was good at all of it. A gruffly charming man who resembles the late Quaker Oats pitchman Wilford Brimley, Sinegal is a blue-state Sam Walton, if such a thing is possible. "Here's the difference between Sam's and Costco," said Charlie Munger, who is a Costco director as well as super-investor Warren Buffett's favorite sidekick. "We have a live Sam Walton who's still there, and Wal-Mart doesn't."[5]

Sinegal shared Walton's visceral belief in the primacy of low prices, right down to the insistence that no item ever be marked up more than 14 percent to 15 percent. "The traditional retailer will say: 'I'm selling this for $10. I wonder whether I can get $10.50 or $11,'" Sinegal said. "We say: 'We're selling it for $9. How do we get it down to $8?'"[6] Sinegal, too, could slice fat from crisp dollar bills when it came to operating expenses, and he also brought a barely controlled ferocity to his negotiations with suppliers. Like Walton, Costco's chief traveled compulsively, visiting each of his stores at least twice a year and maintaining a preternatural supply of energy into his sixties by playing racquetball every day, or about as often as Walton played tennis on the court in his yard.

Like Walton, Sinegal kept his office door open to all comers and managed to be demanding without being intimidating. "To walk with Sinegal from his headquarters building to the Costco next door is to hear a nonstop chorus of 'Hi, Jim . . . Hi, Jim . . . Hi, Jim,'" one visitor recalled. "He returns the greetings by using first names, without appearing to consult nametags."[7] Sinegal wasn't any more enamored of unions than Walton had been, but wasn't doctrinaire about it. When Costco opened a store, it modeled its wages-and-benefits package on the contracts of unionized grocery stores in the area. In absorbing Price Club, Costco picked up unionized stores that now employ about 14,000 of the company's 113,000 employees. The current contract with the Teamsters guarantees employees a minimum of 25 hours of work per week and requires that at least half of a store's workers be full-time.[8]

Costco surpassed Sam's Club in sales a few years ago and now controls about 49 percent of the $104 billion warehouse club market in the United States to Sam's 40 percent. Its performance is all the more impressive considering that it operates only 457 stores, about 100 fewer than its archrival. Costco and Sam's both sell pallets of goods out of no-frills stores, but by narrowing its selection to 4,000 items at any one time and skewing its merchandise mix toward high-end goods, Costco attracts a much more affluent clientele than Sam's. "Our customers don't drive 15 miles to save on a jar of peanut butter," Sinegal said. "They come for the treasure hunt."[9]

One could also argue—Sinegal certainly does—that another reason the average Costco store outsells the typical Sam's Club is that it employs a happier, more productive workforce that actually deserves the premium wages it makes. Paying up also serves the cause of customer loyalty by absolving shoppers of any guilt they might be inclined to feel if their savings were coming at the expense of workers.

Wall Street analysts periodically pillory Sinegal for what they consider his excessive benevolence to employees, but it's hard to argue with the numbers that Costco has been racking up. Surprisingly, Costco's labor costs add up to just 9.8 percent of sales, compared with 17 percent at Wal-Mart. (Bentonville does not break out a figure for Sam's Club.) This is a huge differential that speaks not only to the superior salesmanship of Costco's workforce, but also to its longevity. Of the employees who've been with Costco at least a year, a scant 6 percent leave annually, compared with 21 percent at Sam's Club.

In the last few years, Bentonville has experimented with adding more high-end, fashionable merchandise to Sam's Club and Wal-Mart stores alike to compete not only with Costco but also with Target. Mostly, though, Wal-Mart has reacted to the Costco phenomenon in the same way it has always responded to a competitive threat: by trying to muscle its rival on price. To be fair, Sam's Club long was hamstrung by its quasi-independent status in that it was unable to avail itself of its parent's superior buying power or its distribution system, and it wasn't able to compete all out with Wal-Mart discount stores for business. In 2003, Scott bolstered Sam's Club's underlying economics by folding it into Wal-Mart. The warehouse club division promptly cut its prices across the board, and Costco responded in kind. The price war cut into Costco's profit margins, but it managed to maintain its market share and even posted a 22 percent earnings gain in 2004. For Sam's Club, it's time to go to Plan B.

Would Walton have seen in Costco's humbling of Sam's Club a refutation of the business model that undergirds Wal-Mart and its warehouse club unit alike? It's hard to say, but certainly he would have pondered the implications long and hard. Walton's genius lay in disproving conventional wisdom with common sense. Of course country folk were as keen for a bargain as city dwellers, but it took Walton to prove it. The consensus in retailing today—as epitomized by Wal-Mart—is that holding hourly wages to a bare minimum is essential to success, if not survival. Costco's workers are cogs in a big hyperefficient machine, too, but they are well greased and buffed to a bright shine. The ultimate moral of the Costco story may be as commonsensical as any of Walton's old-fashioned maxims: With employees, like most everything else in life, you get what you pay for.

CHAPTER EIGHT

WILL THE LAST INDEPENDENT GROCER IN AMERICA PLEASE TURN OFF THE MONORAIL?

W al-Mart has been a relentless, unstoppable force across the landscape of America. Yet from 2000 through 2005, the company quietly closed nearly 900 stores, far more outlets than Kmart shuttered during its long slide into bankruptcy reorganization in 2003. The fact is that the Wal-Mart discount store—Sam Walton's signature creation—is dying a slow death. The reason? Over the last decade a fearsome new competitor has emerged, against which the traditional Wal-Mart is essentially helpless. Bentonville couldn't be happier about this turn of events, because that competitor is the Wal-Mart Supercenter. Virtually all of the discount stores that Wal-Mart has closed have been reborn in larger and more lucrative form as Supercenters. In 2004, for the first time, Wal-Mart Supercenters outnumbered Wal-Mart discount stores, 1,713 to 1,353; by 2007 the margin is expected to increase to two-to-one.

The triumph of the Supercenter already has enthroned Wal-Mart as America's largest food retailer by far—and Bentonville is just getting started. In 2005, it opened some 250 more Supercenters (160 of which were conversions). Wal-Mart originally thought it had to locate Supercenters at least fifteen miles apart along the fringes of large and midsized cities to avoid internecine competition. In the last few years, though, it has convinced itself that Supercenters can thrive just three to four miles apart in the biggest markets. "In the U.S. alone, we estimate there is room for almost 4,000 more Supercenters," Lee Scott recently told Wal-Mart shareholders.[1]

The great Supercenter expansion augurs an escalation of what already is the biggest food fight in history. America is chockablock with warehouse clubs, supermarkets, convenience stores, drugstores, and corner grocers selling the same stuff Wal-Mart sells, though generally at much higher prices. In most locales, the market for mass consumables is growing at no more than a few percentage points a year. This means that almost every dollar rung up by a new Wal-Mart Supercenter is a dollar that it has taken away from a rival grocer or pharmacy. "Wal-Mart's growing domination of consumers' grocery and drug spending will devastate the competition," Retail Forward Inc. predicts, estimating that two supermarkets will shut down for every Supercenter that opens from 2003 to 2007.[2] This adds up to 2,000 supermarkets, not to mention untold corner grocers and convenience stores.

Wal-Mart's killer business model puts even the largest supermarket chains at a competitive disadvantage in every facet of their business. For a start, the company uses its size to provide brand-name merchandise at the best possible wholesale price. Wal-Mart is able to roll back prices because of the new efficiencies continuously being created by its high-tech distribution system, which minutely tracks everything from power tools to pretzels as they travel from supplier to distribution center to store at a pace no other retailer can match. The effect is not only to lower costs but also to boost sales, since hot-selling items are quickly restocked. Wal-Mart locates stores on the outskirts of a city and brings down its land costs even further by squeezing subsidies out of local government to cover the cost of roads and other improvements. Most important, Wal-Mart's labor cost advantage looms especially large in the grocery trade, where most big chains are locked into contracts assuring even their lowest-paid workers about 20 percent to 30 percent more than their counterparts make at Wal-Mart.

If there is not a Supercenter within a short drive from your home today, one is assuredly on its way. It might take a while, though, for Wal-Mart is Supercentering America in the same way that an invading army conquers enemy territory: city by city. It builds a mammoth distribution center in a market adjacent to one that it dominates, and then methodically fills in the territory defined by the DC with stores.

Oklahoma City was one of the first large metropolitan areas that Wal-Mart thoroughly Supercentered, and it serves as a model of what Bentonville wants to do to every sizable city, with the possible exception of New York City. In 1997, Wal-Mart operated three Supercenters in Oklahoma City and controlled just 6 percent of the grocery market. Today, the company has eight Supercenters and ten Wal-Mart Neighborhood Markets blanketing Oklahoma's largest city, giving Wal-Mart a 35 percent share. (The Neighborhood Market is Wal-Mart's version of a conventional supermarket and is one-quarter the size of a Supercenter; Bentonville introduced the format in 1998 as a more convenient alternative to its flagship store.) Wal-Mart's assault brought down food prices for consumers by a hefty 15 percent, but it has also made making a living in the grocery business a whole lot tougher. Some thirty supermarkets in the area shut down. What had been the number-one supermarket chain, Fleming/Baker's, saw its market share shrivel to 5 percent from 16 percent, despite big cuts in prices and in the wages paid to its workers.[3]

Wal-Mart's financial muscle is unmatched, and its ambition is limitless. Yet in places, the Supercenter juggernaut has been less than inexorable. At times, the company has bypassed a particularly well-fortified city in its path, encircled it, and returned to fight another day from a position of enhanced strength. The most telling example is Cincinnati. By the time the first Supercenter opened in Cincinnati in October 2004, Wal-Mart was well on its way to Super-saturating each of the major metropolitan centers that ring the Queen City: Louisville, Lexington, Indianapolis, Dayton, Columbus, Memphis, and Nashville. Why not Cincinnati, too?

With two million inhabitants, Cincinnati is the twenty-fourth-largest metropolitan area in the United States. The city lies on the northern bank of the Ohio River, which forms the boundary between Ohio and Kentucky. However, culturally it is a Southern city, famously conservative and almost willfully provincial—just like a certain company headquartered in the Ozarks. "When the end of the world comes, I want to be in Cincinnati because it's always 20 years behind the times," Mark Twain supposedly quipped.[4]

In the grocery trade, though, Cincinnati is no backwater. For one thing, it was home to the first U.S. hypermarket. In 1984, the French supermarket company Euromarché had joined with a U.S. partner to form Bigg's, which attracted national attention by opening a 200,000-square-foot hypermart in Cincinnati. Utterly confounded by American shopping habits, the French investors behind Bigg's soon sold out to Supervalu, a big U.S. food wholesaler and supermarket operator. Supervalu scrapped Bigg's plans to build stores in thirty other cities in order to concentrate on Cincinnati, adding ten more stores over the years.[5] Cincinnati was all Bigg's had; it could not afford to cede ground to Wal-Mart (or anyone else) and survive.

Cincinnati also is an important hub for Meijer, the Michigan-based chain that introduced the superstore format to the Midwest in the early 1960s. Meijer, which also operates ten stores in greater Cincinnati, is widely respected in the business as a disciplined, meticulous operator. With $12 billion in revenues, the privately held, family-run company ranks a distant eleventh on the list of America's largest grocers, but it already has proven that it was not afraid to mix it up with Wal-Mart. In 1993, complaints filed by Meijer with authorities in its home state of Michigan had forced Wal-Mart to promise in court to stop making misleading price comparisons, adding to a regulatory backlash that eventually persuaded the company to alter its advertising tagline from "Always the low price. Always" to the less assertive "Always low prices. Always."[6]

First and foremost, though, Cincinnati is Kroger country. Founded in Cincinnati in 1883 by Barney Kroger, The Kroger Co. had outlasted its archrival—The Great Atlantic and Pacific Tea Co., better known as A&P—in classic tortoise versus hare fashion to finally become the nation's largest grocery chain in the 1990s. Today, Kroger owns 2,500 supermarkets, which it operates under two dozen different banners, including Kroger, Fred Meyer, Ralph's, Smith's, Dillon's, King Sooper's, and Fry's. In 2004, Kroger pulled in $56 billion in revenue, ranking twenty-first among all U.S. corporations.

Wal-Mart does not fear Kroger, which it already had taken on and bested in various cities around the country. However, the prospect of doing battle with a company as big, proud, and well-connected as Kroger on its home ground gave even Wal-Mart pause. At the end of 2003, Kroger operated seventy-four supermarkets in greater Cincinnati and had 45 percent of the grocery market, compared with Meijer's 14 percent and Bigg's 10 percent.[7] Wal-Mart's share was 2 percent, thanks to two Supercenters on the metro area's farthest fringe: one in Aurora, Indiana, and the other in Dry Ridge, Kentucky.

Kroger is king in Cincinnati and had been for a century, but uneasy lay the crown by 2004. For two years, the Cincinnati newspapers had been filled with reports of Wal-Mart's real estate maneuverings around the city's suburban fringe. (The company also made one brief, aborted effort to secure a location downtown.) The details often were sketchy, but the message between the lines was unmistakable: Ready or not, here we come. Wal-Mart planned to ring downtown Cincinnati with at least twelve and possibly as many as twenty Supercenters over the next few years. "Wal-Mart is going to come in and just blitz Cincinnati," predicted Stan Eichelbaum, the city's leading retailing consultant.[8] In anticipation of Wal-Mart's belated assault, Cincinnati's established grocers already had turned on one another in a frenzy of cost-cutting and new store openings in an attempt to add market share before the Arkansas invader started wresting it away. The skirmishing quickly claimed a major casualty. In May 2004, the Thriftway chain announced plans to close its twenty-one stores.[9] As recently as 1998, Thriftway had ranked as Cincinnati's second-largest grocer, with an 18.4 percent share.

Today, the Battle of Cincinnati looms large as the ultimate municipal showdown of the nation's two largest food retailers. "Wal-Mart just keeps growing," said David B. Dillon, Kroger's chief executive. "And I don't see any signs of a slowdown in the number of stores."[10] For Kroger, the stakes in Cincinnati are especially high. What hope would Kroger have of holding its own, much less regaining its former greatness, if it cannot stop Wal-Mart from besting it in its hometown?

Cincinnati is equally intriguing as a test case of the place of the independent grocer in the twenty-first century, for it is the home of Jungle Jim's International Farmer's Market, America's most weirdly wonderful supermarket. Jungle Jim's proprietor, James O. Bonaminio, known as "Jungle" to his friends and employees alike, is an independent with a capital "I." When the mood strikes, Bonaminio will don his purple and gold wizard costume—a gift from Procter & Gamble—and roller-skate through the aisles performing "price magic." Or he'll jump in his "Jungleland" ambulance and go off "junking" for a few hours, returning with a ton or two of bargain-priced salvage that he eventually will figure out how to incorporate into his handmade store, as he did with the animatronic Robin Hood recycled from a trade show, the 45-foot trawler he'd pulled out of a swamp, and the 40,000 blocks of wood extracted from defunct highway guardrails.

Bonaminio's business card shows him in doctor's whites performing surgery with a machete on someone labeled "Phill," who appears to be screaming in agony on the operating table as a smirking nurse sticks a needle into him. Bonaminio was known to interrupt meetings with dressed-for-success types by seeking the counsel of a mock hunting trophy—the hindquarters of a deer covertly equipped with a fart machine—mounted on his office wall. "What do you think,

Butthead?" he asked after a visiting delegation of bankers offered him a loan at 7 percent. "Is 7 percent good?" The responding horn blast of flatulence—triggered by the remote control hidden in Bonaminio's hand—blew that 7 percent right out the window. Although Bonaminio never lets business stand in the way of a laugh, the numbers suggest that there is method to his madness. In 2004, he booked $64.5 million in revenue, up from $29.8 million in 1995.

Bonaminio, who got his start selling produce out of the back of a truck in the mid-1970s, has thrived even as the number of independent supermarkets in America has steadily dwindled to the current total of 11,645, according to *Progressive Grocer* magazine's latest tally. (The category includes everything from Mom-and-Pop corner stores to local chains of as many as eleven stores.) The independents' national share of the market has dwindled to 16 percent from 27 percent a decade ago and is generally expected to continue to fall as more and more of them are hammered by the intensifying price wars among the big chain supermarkets and even bigger chain superstores.[11]

Consultants agree that the best way to counter Wal-Mart is to be what Wal-Mart is not. And what food seller is less like a Supercenter than the truly independent grocer? The old corner store faded because it was unable to compete on price and selection when driving long distances to food-shop became a way of life in most of the nation. Consumers flocked to chain supermarkets and to the even larger big boxes that opened later on the edge of town. But that did not mean they rejected the convenience and intimacy that the store down the block offered. For many people over thirty, the phrase "the corner store" continues to be powerfully evocative of an establishment where the person across the counter knew you and would even extend credit if you were a bit short, a place that was as distinctively personal as its proprietor's fingerprints.

If no independent could hope to equal Bentonville's corporate muscle and supply-chain sophistication, neither could Wal-Mart's 1,700 Supercenters pretend to rival the trait that ultimately defined the independent: individuality. To the contrary, Wal-Mart expended enormous effort to make its Supercenters as nearly identical to one another as possible, standardization being the essence of chain-store management.

Although price still rules in the great middle of the food market, and probably always will, affluent consumers in particular increasingly are seeking out alternatives to the big-box bargain hunt, as seen by the surging growth of high-end chains like Wild Oats and Whole Foods, which are thriving despite charging premium prices for organic and prepared foods. At the same time, Americans across all income categories are increasingly drawn to retailers offering a distinctive shopping experience. "In all of our consumer research, we are seeing a complete metamorphosis of consumer behavior," observed John J. Ruf, a partner in the New England Consulting Group (which numbers Wal-Mart among its clients). "Consumers today are on the hunt for the best shopping experience and become loyal to 'inspirational' retail destinations."[12] According to Ruf's definition, "inspirational" retailers come in all sizes, cut across all product categories, and include both chains and independents. What they all share, in Ruf's estimation, is a creativity that gives them a leg up on "surviving in a Wal-Mart World."[13]

Jungle Jim's International Farmer's Market is inspirational retailing at its most madcap. Bonaminio may be a merry prankster of an entrepreneur, but he has thought long and hard about what Wal-Mart's looming invasion of Cincinnati means for his business. "People say, 'Don't worry about Wal-Mart, you are unique.' Bullshit!" boomed Bonaminio. "Independents are different, man; you can't ever let your guard down. You got to understand that it's not just Wal-Mart either. It's the crossfire. You got Kroger, you got Meijer's, you got all these guys shooting. As an independent you're sitting there in the middle of the shooting range. . . .

"I'm fighting for survival! We're all fighting for survival!" continued Bonaminio, his decibel level rising. "I'm fighting for my niche. I'm fighting for who I am. I'm fighting for my people so they get raises. Look," he said, calming down a bit, "business is business, and you have to learn how to compete. Wal-Mart came up with this deal? God bless 'em. If it's not Wal-Mart, it's going to come from someone else anyway. I'm just giving you the particulars. I'm not sitting here crying."[14]

Kroger was the Avis of supermarkets before there was an Avis. The Cincinnati-based company expanded hugely during the great chain-store explosion of the first two decades of the twentieth century, without ever coming close to overtaking its archrival, The Great Atlantic & Pacific Tea Co., the Wal-Mart of its day. By 1929, Kroger operated 5,575 stores across the country, second to A&P's 15,400.[15] (Grocery stores of this vintage were tiny, averaging just 1,200 square feet.) As the modern-day supermarket came of age, Kroger was slow to adjust and suffered the humiliation of being dropped to third place among national grocery chains in 1936 by the emergence of the more dynamic California-based upstart Safeway Stores.[16]

Like A&P, the Kroger Co. was a dinosaur mucking about in the tar pits as smaller, more flexible companies like Meijer in the East and Fred Meyer & Co. on the West Coast combined high-volume grocery selling with discounted general merchandise to create the superstore in the 1960s. Kroger began halfheartedly fiddling with the emerging one-stop-shopping model by opening thirty-three discount stores combining food, general merchandise, and drugs. However, the stores were much too small to make a resounding impact, and Kroger betrayed its inexperience by stocking too much of the wrong sorts of goods.[17] Luckily, a new generation of leaders that took charge in 1970 concluded that Kroger was doomed unless it underwent an extreme makeover. "We did extensive research and the data came back loud and clear. The super-combination stores were the way of the future," recalled Kroger Chairman and President Lyle Everingham. "We also learned that you had to be number one or number two in each market, or you had to exit. . . . There was really no question about what we had to do. So we just did it."[18]

Everingham's laconic recollection underplayed one of the most dramatic corporate transformations of the last thirty years. During the 1970s and 1980s, Kroger methodically reinvented itself "store by store, block by block, city by city, state by state."[19] It closed or remodeled hundreds of outlets, withdrawing entirely from such longtime hubs as Chicago, Milwaukee, and Birmingham. Kroger concentrated its openings in the Sunbelt, where population growth tended to be faster and competition weaker. The new-generation Kroger stores carried a wider array of products, though not nearly as many as a Meijer or a Meyer. These still were supermarkets, not superstores, and they were definitely not discount operations. To the contrary, Kroger widened its profit margins by reorganizing its stores around new specialty departments like delicatessens, bakeries, cheese shops, cosmetics counters, nutrition centers, and flower shops. Many of its moves paid off spectacularly. For example, just two years after it opened its first flower shop in 1980, Kroger became the largest florist in the country.[20] Kroger's long-suffering stockholders finally celebrated as their shares generated returns ten times greater than the market averages from 1974 to 1999.

But by the time that Kroger passed floundering A&P to finally become America's number-one grocery chain in the mid-1990s, the Cincinnati giant already was succumbing to arrogance and complacency. In 1997, Wal-Mart ranked a distant ninth among food retailers, with just $17 billion in annual sales. Kroger's senior executives smugly assumed that they had the Ozarks upstart safely measured in the rearview mirror, only to find themselves quickly choking on Supercenter dust. In 2000, Wal-Mart sped past Kroger into the number-one spot. By 2003, Wal-Mart racked up $138 billion in food sales (including Sam's Club) to Kroger's $54 billion. Although Bentonville's gains came mainly at the expense of smaller operators, Kroger was staggering, losing market share in most every city where it competed with a

Supercenter. Wal-Mart is "the greatest challenge to Kroger since those days when there were no antitrust laws to protect Barney Kroger," said consultant Burt Flickinger of Strategic Resource Group.[21]

Wall Street had expected Kroger to take the fight directly to Wal-Mart after shelling out nearly $13 billion to acquire Fred Meyer Inc. in 1998. The West Coast superstore pioneer operated 800 stores and had performed well against Wal-Mart in the twelve states in which it operated. Acquiring Meyer enabled Kroger to become a more cost-effective distributor of nonfood merchandise. But CEO Joseph Pichler opted not to expand the Meyer franchise nationally, deciding against building superstores under any of the company's other two dozen supermarket brands. Standing pat in the face of Wal-Mart's 30 percent price advantage, Pichler wagered Kroger's future on the proposition that superior product quality and selection, plus convenience of location, would enable its supermarkets to repulse Wal-Mart.

Wall Street emphatically disagreed, sending Kroger's stock into a tailspin from which it has yet to recover. Not until 2002, Pichler's penultimate year as CEO, did Kroger get serious about cutting prices—and operating costs—to counter Wal-Mart. The supermarket giant finally had the "right strategy, possibly three to five years too late," said UBS Warburg analyst Neil Currie. "I think it's going to be very, very expensive for them. But it is the only strategy."[22]

Under new CEO Dillon, Kroger became much more aggressive in all respects. In southern California, the company joined with Safeway Stores and Albertsons to hold the line on labor-cost increases, proving its resolve by holding fast in the record-setting UFCW strike that doomed the union's Wal-Mart campaign. In October 2004, just six months after the California strike was settled, Kroger's UFCW contract with 8,500 workers in the Cincinnati region was set to expire. Again a showdown loomed. Kroger paid its hometown workers an average hourly salary of $11.05, which compared to Wal-Mart's average national wage of $9.68. However, Kroger also covered all of its workers' health-care costs, adding $5.76 to the average workers' hourly compensation, bringing total pay to $16.81 an hour.[23] The company offered a minimal wage hike over the next three years and insisted that employees start picking up part of the cost of their health benefits, as was true with most corporate health plans. Kroger workers reacted angrily to the notion. "They need to put a Wal-Mart sign up, if they're going to act like Wal-Mart," snapped one ten-year veteran of the produce department.[24]

Kroger and the UFCW careened right to the edge of a Cincinnati grocery strike. An overwhelming percentage of the union's members voted to authorize a strike on seventy-two hours' notice, and the company began training replacement workers. In the end, though, the UFCW essentially caved, and the union's leaders did not even bother throwing around the usual "win-win" rhetoric. "Kroger should not kid itself," said Lennie Wyatt, president of UFCW Local 1099. "This contract was ratified for one reason and one reason only: there simply was no workable alternative at this time."[25]

Walking through Jungle Jim's with Bonaminio is like making the City Hall rounds with a charismatic small-town mayor. His well-publicized antics and gloriously cheesy television commercials have made him an icon in Cincinnati. He is an imposing figure—broad-shouldered, six feet one, with the lantern jaw of a comic-book action hero. His dark hair turned silver a few years ago, but he remains fit and brawny at age fifty-five. Everybody knows Jungle or feels like they do anyway. He can't walk through his store without signing autographs, even when he's out of costume, as he is this July morning in 2004. He is showing me around his new flower shop and gift center when a boy of five or six walks right up to him, eyes aglow. "Hi, Jungle Jim," he says.

"Hi! How you doin'? What's going on?" says Bonaminio, bending over to shake the boy's hand. The kid is with his mother and another woman who could be his aunt. "You messin' around or what?"

"Yeah," he replies happily. As the boy walks away, his hand in his mom's, he turns his head and keeps smiling at Bonaminio until he vanishes around a corner.

Bonaminio already has shifted his attention to the flower shop's manager, a petite, feisty-looking woman of about sixty. Her name tag says Jeanne Wallace.

"Looks great, looks great," he tells her. "Go for it, baby! Get 'em. Don't take any prisoners."

Wallace laughs contentedly. "I'm building categories already," she says. "I feel pretty good about that."

"Looks nice," Bonaminio says. "Whatchamacallit did good by bringing you in over here."

Bonaminio is a stickler for a clean, well-ordered store. A dozen times on our walkabout, he is annoyed to discover a minor flaw—an out-of-stock candy shelf, a cracked counter, a dusty beam, an unlocked door that was supposed to be locked—and immediately gets on his cell phone to register his displeasure. In every other respect, though, he gives his thirty managers a lot of room, imposing himself only when they screw up. "She runs the whole thing," he says of Wallace once we are out of earshot. "She's gonna hire, she's gonna fire, she's gonna buy her own things. If she has a great idea, she comes to me and I help her. That's what I do: I block for these people. I don't even come in here unless there's a problem."

Bonaminio hates labor unions as much as Lee Scott does, except that he is honest about it and does not try to mask his antipathy with PR spin. "You know what I'd do if I had a union come in here, I'd milk this son of a bitch. I wouldn't fix nothin'," he says. "Then I'd sell the real estate and thumb my nose at them and say, 'Fuck off.' The day I walk around this store and tell a guy, 'Hey, the floor is dirty, why don't you get a broom?' and he says, 'That's not my job,' then it just ain't worth it to me."

Not that the UFCW or any other union has thought it necessary to attempt to organize Jungle Jim's. Bonaminio·has negated any labor cost advantage he might enjoy in competing with Kroger and Mei-jer's—union shops both—by paying his 400 employees top dollar. A cashier who sticks around awhile can make $14 or $15 an hour at Jungle Jim's, though managerial employees who want a raise often have to beat Bonaminio at poker or billiards to get it. (Lose and you keep your job.) Bonaminio complains that his store is overstaffed, but he can't bring himself to eliminate jobs and fire loyal workers. "You want to take some of them with you to New York? How many do you need?" he says.

Every week or two, one of Bonaminio's floor managers calls up to his eagle's nest of an office above the store to tell him that the Wal-Mart people are back. Usually, there are two or three of them, dressed in ties and jackets. They never identify themselves—much less ask permission—they just show up and start walking slowly through the store, jotting notes and talking into little tape recorders, like Sam Walton used to do. Not everyone appreciates Wal-Mart's intrusive research methods, but Bonaminio does not mind at all. "I think it's hilarious. They do more business in one second than I'll do in a damn lifetime, and they're over here checking me out," he says. However, Bonaminio hasn't returned the compliment in kind: He can't remember ever setting foot in a Wal-Mart Supercenter. "I don't pay attention to other stores," he says. "I get lost."

Wal-Mart's economies of scale put the independent at a great dis-advantage in dealing with suppliers, Bonaminio says. "In the old days, the wholesalers would protect everybody. You had big grocery suppli-ers who came in and said, 'We not only will sell you groceries; we'll give you services. We'll help you with your layout. If you have accounting problems, we have people who will come in and help.' You'd call them up and, boom, they'd have five guys over here tomor-row. They wanted your store to be healthy, and they wanted you to do everything right because they want to sell you groceries. All that ser-vice wasn't free; it was built into the price they charged you. But everybody had to pay it because all suppliers were working through the wholesalers. When a chain would come in and try to cut a special deal with Kraft or Procter & Gamble or someone, they'd say, 'You got to buy through this guy.'

"What happened was Wal-Mart got so big they could just bypass that chain. They could go right to the supplier and say, 'Here's the deal. We want so many truckloads of Miracle Whip. We don't care about accounting service. We don't want any of that other shit. We'll buy so many trucks and it's ours after we pick it up, whatever.'

"So Wal-Mart cuts out the middleman while me, as an independent, I'm still living over here with a wholesaler tacking on 10 percent to 15 percent. Not only that, the big guys get a better price to start. When I'm talking to my suppliers in the grocery business, I'll say, 'How come Wal-Mart can sell it for $1.99 and your best price to me is $2.05?' 'Well, now, they buy from a different division,' they say. Right then and there, I know."

Bonaminio only has one store, but at 280,000 square feet it is by far the largest supermarket in Cincinnati, bigger even than most Supercenters. "You're big in your own right," I say. "Can't you get a price break, too?"

"Yeah, but you got to be able to get to half a truck of what you're buying, which is a lot of product," he replies. "There's no way an independent is going to get a supplier's best deal. You have to rely on your niche—the thing that makes you different. That, and service. The thing is, Wal-Mart is definitely Wal-Mart; it's all about price, price, price, OK? But because Wal-Mart is so definite on who they are, they open a wide field for the niche operator like me."

Like Walton, whom he admires, Bonaminio was a born entrepreneur. The son of a steelworker, he grew up in Lorain, about twenty miles west of Cleveland. A natural salesman, after he left Miami University in Oxford without a degree he struggled as a roadside produce vendor in Hamilton, the town next to Fairfield. Bonaminio couldn't afford to buy his own land, so he had to keep moving; his little stand was a cork bobbing madly on the surface of a suburban real estate market roiled by speculation. It took Bonaminio four years to save the $10,000 that he put down in 1974 to buy the first few acres of the seventy-one-acre site that Jungle Jim's now occupies.

The first thing to understand about Jungle Jim's International Farmer's Market is that it has prospered not because of its location but despite it, defying the first commandment of retailing and of real estate. The store is a hugely inconvenient, four miles from the nearest major highway, Interstate 275, and a long stretch of traffic hell lies between it and Cincinnati's most populous districts. Even so, Bonaminio has never seriously considered relocating and, for that matter, has yet to open a second Jungle Jim's. From the time of his earliest success, Bonaminio was at least as interested in adding onto his building as in adding to his business; to him, it was one and the same. Rob Symjunas Jr., a Cincinnati shopping center developer, once tried to entice Bonaminio into a project by offering him a free building. "I was going to give it to Jungle, but he still wouldn't do it," Symjunas recalls. "Mentally, he is just so focused on that store. It's his baby."[26]

Bonaminio's colossal supermarket is an amalgam of a dozen different buildings that were constructed one after another over three decades and that coexist today under one large and very complicated roof. It is an ingenious labyrinth of a store, constructed largely of recycled materials and filled with oddly angled walls and novel design features. During the two-hour store tour that Bonaminio gives me, he is so eager to point out his favorite props that he all but ignores the wares on his shelves. There is the antique fire truck atop the hot sauce case; the animatronic Robin Hood and Sherwood Forest display above the Great Britain section; the eight-foot-tall, Elvis-impersonating mechanical lion; the 600-pound cheese hanging from a rope inside a glass case; the life-size replica of an Amish buggy; the mint-condition 1919 Boar's Head truck in the deli section; the genuine NASCAR race car wall-mounted outside the front entrance, and on and on.

Bonaminio acquired most of this stuff on junking expeditions. For all the delight he takes in negotiating a bargain price, he will spare no expense in restoring or customizing a salvaged treasure for display in his store. In 1998, he paid $1 for eight, 150-foot-long monorail trains from Paramount's King's Island, an amusement park north of Cincinnati. The trains, which King's Island had used in its African safari ride for two decades, would have fetched a rich price had not the amusement park scrapped the tracks they ran on. To house the trains, Bonaminio put up a pre-engineered metal building designed (by Jimmy Bonaminio, the eldest of Jungle's three kids) to look like a giant snake. He hired General Dynamics to gut the trains and install new engines, brakes, and electrical systems. In 2003, workers began erecting steel pylons to support two miles of track. Bonaminio expects to have sunk about $2 million into the monorail by 2006, when it is expected to be ready to start ferrying shoppers among the store's various entrances and the outer reaches of its huge parking lot.

What sort of return does Bonaminio expect on his monorail investment? He couldn't care less. It's enough for him that Jungle Jim's will be the only supermarket in America with a monorail. "I'm gonna drive that thing even if it kills me," he vows as we peer up at a section of completed track in front of the store.

"Here's the deal. This is what I'm trying to do," Bonaminio says as we walk past the refrigerated, glass-walled room displaying his store's extensive inventory of high-priced cigars. "This is going to sound kind of crazy, all right? What do you hate to do—grocery shopping, right? Everybody hates it. So what's America want to do? We're always trying to find time to be together—husbands, wives, and family. I took a negative and turned it into a positive. I made shopping fun. I have more men shopping with their wives in this store than you can imagine."[27]

Jungle Jim's is not all fun and games; the other distinguishing feature of the niche Bonaminio has carved for himself is an enormous, finely variegated selection of specialty foods, many of them imported from India, Great Britain, Mexico, and seventy other countries around the world. Out of boredom as much as anything, Bonaminio began building a specialty line in the late 1980s, well before the vogue for culinary exotica spread out from America's big cities into the heartland. An Asian section is no longer a supermarket novelty in much of the United States, but Jungle Jim's has separate sections for China, Taiwan, and Hong Kong, not to mention Thailand, Vietnam, the Philippines, Korea, and Japan. About fifty feet of shelf space is devoted to Italian olive oils alone. The hot sauce section includes 1,200 selections ranging in price from $3.99 to a particularly incendiary brand that goes for $229.99. Jungle Jim's carries tens of thousands of items not to be found at a Wal-Mart Supercenter or a Kroger supermarket.

Bonaminio's market draws 50,000 shoppers a week, including regular customers who drive from points as distant as Columbus, Indianapolis, Louisville, and Lexington—all of which are within 150 miles of Fairfield, give or take a dozen miles. (By contrast, the typical urban superstore draws from within a fifteen-mile radius.) Few stores of any kind in America can claim a clientele as ethnically diverse as Jungle Jim's, which bills itself as a "United Nations" of food. "They jam the aisles on weekends in Indian saris and Muslim veils and Yoruba caps, forming a frenzy of international bumper cars," one visitor recalled. "Some drive all day to get to the supermarket, carrying intricate lists of items that yesterday's Ohioans couldn't begin to spell, much less eat: Ghee and rambutan and longan, kimchi and napolitos and durian."[28]

Although high-margin specialty foods generate about two-thirds of its profits, Jungle Jim's relies on the same grocery staples sold by Wal-Mart, Kroger, and every other food retailer for the bulk of its revenues. "We basically use grocery as our loss leader," says Ed Carroll, Bonaminio's general manager. "With Wal-Mart coming in, we want to establish that we are just as low as a lot of the chain stores, which have been a lot sharper in their pricing over the last two years."[29]

Despite its aggressive discounting of staples, Jungle Jim's has seen its annual rate of revenue growth slow to 3.8 percent a year on average since 2002, compared with 11.4 percent from 1996 through 2001.[30] Stiffer competition for the grocery dollar is only partly to blame, Bonaminio says. "I made a lot of mistakes. What happened was I made the store so entertaining that I'm doing a lot more business from out of town. But now it's so big and hard to shop that the local people don't come in. I'm losing my local business." The store's diminishing appeal to the convenience-minded shopper undercuts the one advantageous aspect of its location: Fairfield and the townships that adjoin it rank among the fastest-growing residential areas in greater Cincinnati.

And now along comes Wal-Mart. At the moment, the closest Supercenter to Jungle Jim's lies twenty-eight miles due west in Aurora, Indiana, too far to pose much of a threat. In 2005, though, Wal-Mart is planning to open a Supercenter just five miles north of Jungle Jim's and a second seven miles to the west. The prospect of becoming the meat in a Supercenter sandwich is rousing Bonaminio to bold action. He is wagering most of the profit he has accumulated over the years on what is essentially a double-or-nothing bet: a $12 million expansion designed to make Jungle Jim's the centerpiece of "Foodie Land." It sounds like a theme park (and the monorail certainly will give it the look of one), but Bonaminio prefers the word "campus" to characterize the concept that has been gestating in his overheated brain for more than a decade. "Food is becoming a sport, but nobody's addressing it like that," he says. "There are golf destinations all over America. You fly in and the whole town is golf courses. Nobody's doing that in food. That's what I'm trying to do with Foodie Land."[31]

Bonaminio began putting the Foodie Land plan fitfully in motion a few years ago, and it is about one-third realized. A construction crew is putting the finishing touches on a capacious two-story "special events center" attached to the store.[32] Jungle Jim's will use the events center to sponsor tastings, cooking demonstrations, and food-and-wine festivals. The center's 600-seat auditorium is outfitted with a camera-ready kitchen set to entice the likes of Emeril Lagasse and Mario Batali into broadcasting from the Jungle. Within the events center is a large unfinished space that Bonaminio hopes to lease to a top-flight restaurant operator. He also is trying to interest a national hotel chain in building on his property. "My store has always been a golf course with no clubhouse," he says. "The events center will be my clubhouse."

Even as Bonaminio tries to make Jungle Jim's a more alluring destination for "foodies," he also is making a play to win back the lost locals. In early 2004, he completed a 100,000-square-foot extension to the store to house an expanded beer and wine department and gourmet deli shop. This, in turn, freed the prime space at the store's center for remodeling into what is essentially a compact conventional "American" supermarket within a sprawling specialty store. Here, Bonaminio has collected the everyday items that used to be scattered throughout the rear of the store like an afterthought. To further entice the convenience-minded shopper à la Wal-Mart, he recently added the garden center and flower shop just outside the main entrance and leased space right inside it to a pharmacy, a bank, a post office branch, and a Starbucks. Bonaminio seems sheepish about including the coffee chain. "People say to me, 'Starbucks is not in your image,'" he says. "Hey, I can't do everything in my 'own image.' I'm running a business, not an image."

On September 15, 2004, Wal-Mart fired its first fusillade in the great Cincinnati supermarket war with the opening of a Supercenter in Fort Wright, Kentucky, just five miles south of The Kroger Co.'s headquarters in downtown Cincinnati. Wal-Mart was a long time establishing this toehold in Kroger country. In 1999, the company signed on with a small local developer looking to build a shopping center on the site of a former junkyard. The Fort Wright city fathers were encouraging at first, but turned against the project after 400 people packed a public hearing to protest that a Supercenter would overburden the congested roads in the area. The developer, B&Z Development, worked out a compromise with the city only to be hit by a lawsuit brought by local residents. At Wal-Mart's urging, Regency Centers, a big national developer specializing in supermarkets, bought out B&Z and completed the project.[33]

A few days after the Fort Wright store opened, I called on David Birdsall, Regency Centers' development chief for the Midwest, who operates out of a nondescript building north of the city. At thirty-eight, Birdsall is a battle-hardened veteran of scores of development wars, but he wears his gravitas lightly. Today, he has extra reason to be cheery as he recalls his opening-day visit to the Fort Wright store. "It was insane," he says. "People were camping out, waiting for the store to open."[34]

Regency Centers is a huge company in its own right. Based in Jacksonville, Florida, it is a real estate investment trust, or REIT, that owns 290 shopping centers in twenty-three states. There are larger REITs out there, but Regency controls more grocery-anchored shopping centers than anyone else. It is landlord to sixty-three Kroger, sixty-one Publix, fifty-one Safeway, and twenty-four Albertsons stores. Of the twelve shopping centers that Regency owns in Cincinnati, nine feature a Kroger supermarket. One of its properties, Hyde Park Plaza, houses the highest-grossing Kroger outlet in the country.

Regency Centers is well aware that the Krogers and Safeways of the world see Wal-Mart as their nemesis. So what is Dave Birdsall doing putting a Wal-Mart Supercenter within spitting distance of Kroger headquarters? His job. By the early 2000s, it was no longer possible for Regency Center to sustain its growth at an acceptable rate without doing deals with Wal-Mart, the most prolific builder in grocery retailing by far. "If you can't go to Wal-Mart," Birdsall says, "there's no one else to go to."

Regency Centers' management is convinced that they can have it both ways—grab onto the coattails of Wal-Mart's superstore expansion while continuing to run thriving neighborhood centers anchored by leading supermarket chains. This view is grounded in research. Regency had tracked the performance of the supermarkets in thirty-three of its shopping centers located within three miles of a new Wal-Mart. Of the thirty-three, twenty-five were anchored by the number-one, -two, or -three grocer in the market. On average, these supermarkets had suffered a painful but decidedly non-fatal 2.5 percent decline in sales since the local Supercenter opened. Regency Centers essentially had wagered its future on the belief that this pattern would hold as the Wal-Mart juggernaut rolled on into such cities as San Diego, Tampa, Seattle, and Cincinnati.

The Fort Wright Supercenter is the second Wal-Mart that Birdsall and company have put into greater Cincinnati. The first, a discount store a few miles north of Jungle Jim's, was completed in 2003 and already is being converted into a Supercenter that was expected to open by the end of 2005. "We put a Wal-Mart in by Jungle Jim's, but I can't see the same shopper going to both," says Birdsall, who shops Bonaminio's store a couple of times a month with his wife. "Frankly, his produce is just so much better than anybody else's. If I'm paying 25 cents a pound more for grapes, I don't really care. We're also buying a lot of wine, cheeses—a lot of high-margin stuff. We'll go up there specifically to buy the Boar's Head brand. Maybe we're not the average shopper, but I think a lot of people go to Jungle Jim's not only for the neat stuff, but for the experience."

Birdsall also has a Wal-Mart project underway in Indiana and another in Michigan and is angling to build more Supercenters in Cincinnati. Working with Wal-Mart means that Birdsall is working harder than he ever has before, and not just because Bentonville is meticulous and demanding. "You walk in and tell people you're a Wal-Mart developer and you're the Antichrist," he says with a smile. "You say you're doing a Target development and they'll trip over themselves trying to help out. Nobody seems to get people as riled as Wal-Mart." He thinks that the backlash against Wal-Mart is "patently unfair," but suggests that the company is partly to blame because of its "legacy of leaving ugly-ass buildings all over the place."

Birdsall is an important player on the Cincinnati retail scene but is effectively neutral when it comes to the heavyweight matchup: Wal-Mart versus Kroger. Who better to handicap Cincinnati's struggle for supermarket supremacy?

Kroger's fate is a subject of debate among the retail cognoscenti in its hometown, but on this there seems to be universal concord: There will be no stopping Wal-Mart in Cincinnati. Birdsall predicts that Wal-Mart will take 25 percent to 30 percent of the market within a few years. "In four years, they will be in every major submarket, no question," Birdsall says. "Probably it will take less time than that."

"How many Supercenters will Wal-Mart need to cover the market?" I ask.

Birdsall gets up from his chair, stands before his giant wall map, and begins counting. "About twenty," he says finally. "This is a good, stable market, but there are only so many dollars to go around in Cincinnati, Ohio. Somebody is going to get hurt."

Cincinnati's hometown supermarket giant may have been slow to recognize the threat posed by Wal-Mart's Supercenter expansion program, but there is nothing lethargic now about the defense it is mounting in its hometown. Even as it was besting the UFCW in contract negotiations, Kroger significantly added to its share of the Cincinnati-area grocery market. During 2004, the company bought eight stores from the defunct Thriftway, opened nine new stores of its own, and remodeled a dozen other supermarkets to carry a broader array of food and general merchandise. The new Kroger outlets include a 104,000-square-footer in Anderson Township that is the largest Kroger in the country. (The Anderson outlet is superstore in all but name, containing a Fred Meyer Jewelry Store, a Starbucks, a drive-up pharmacy window, a gas station, and a photo lab.) By mid-2005, Kroger's market share hit 58.1 percent, up from 44.6 percent at the start of 2004.[35] "There's no way Wal-Mart will run us out of town," vows Robert Hodge, the head of Kroger's Cincinnati/Dayton division.[36]

Birdsall agrees with Hodge, though he expects Kroger's market share to decline substantially as Wal-Mart's expansion whips into high gear in 2006 and 2007. "Kroger will hold its own," he says. "They are the hometown boys and are still very good operators. I see them being the convenient neighborhood groceries that they've always been." Eichelbaum, the local retail consultant, thinks less highly of Kroger's management than Birdsall does. Not to put too fine a point on it, Eichelbaum thinks Kroger stinks. "This is a company just waiting to die," he says.[37]

Kroger's gains appear to be coming mostly at the expense of Meijer, which has seen its market share drop to 11.8 percent from 12.6 percent since the start of 2004. Emerging from a protracted bout of cost-cutting designed to make it more price competitive with Wal-Mart, the superstore pioneer announced plans to open five new superstores within its five-state territory in 2005, including three in Cincinnati. "Meijer's expansion here surprises me because they'd lain down and been dormant for a while," Birdsall says. "They're a good operator, but still. How many damn stores can we do here? I think Meijer will be squeezed by Wal-Mart because they don't have the dominant real estate position Kroger has and that Wal-Mart will have."

Birdsall believes that Meijer will survive Wal-Mart's invasion in diminished form, but prophesies doom for Bigg's, the city's home-grown superstore chain. Bigg's took over one vacant Thriftway store but otherwise is standing pat, with a share of 8.4 percent as of mid-2005. "Of all of the chains, I see Bigg's as the most vulnerable," Birdsall says. "Bigg's is a pretty decent operator, but is always competing on price and will get squeezed by Wal-Mart. I'd be very surprised if Bigg's is here in five years."

Birdsall's analysis squares with a Safeway Stores study of the impact of Wal-Mart's entry on established grocers in seven metropolitan areas across the country from 1997 through 2003. The number-one supermarket chain in these markets actually gained 1.5 percent market share on average while the number-two grocer held even. However, the other grocers—the lesser chains and independents alike—collectively lost a catastrophic 17.7 percent of their market share. The Safeway report also documented the dire financial impact of Supercenter entry on all of the supermarkets. The number-one grocer continued to turn a profit, though it declined to $12.3 million on sales of $350 million from $30 million on sales of $400 million. But the number-four grocer in these cities saw a profit of $5 million on sales of $250 million turn into a loss of $13.5 million on sales of $200 million. In all seven cities, the fourth-ranked grocer went under within a year.[38]

In Cincinnati, Birdsall expects Kroger, Wal-Mart, and Meijer to carve up the mass market, with wholesale clubs like Costco and Sam's Club and high-end specialty vendors like Wild Oats, Whole Foods, and Jungle Jim's taking a slice at the margin. Meanwhile, drugstore chains like Walgreens and CVS will continue to expand their food and beverage offerings and win an increasing share of convenience buying. "That's it," Birdsall says. "I just don't see any other grocery operators surviving."

Among the scores of independents that Birdsall is consigning to history's dustbin is Remke Market, a little seven-store chain descended from a Covington, Kentucky, meat market that opened in 1897. Bill Remke, the grandson of the founder, runs the business with the help of his son, Matthew, but in 1996 transferred a majority of the company's stock to its 700 employees. The new Fort Wright Supercenter is smack in the heart of Remke's turf, as is a second store that Wal-Mart is building in Florence. Remke is a technologically progressive but low-key retailer that embodies all the virtues of the old-fashioned neighborhood grocer. Its stores are compact by contemporary standards (the largest of them is 45,000 square feet) and easily navigable. Remke's is the kind of place where the cashiers call you by name and the butchers cut meat to order. Ask for an item, and a clerk will lead you to the spot. "This business isn't rocket science," Bill Remke says. "If you give customers what they want, they'll come back."[39]

But will enough of them come back after they've seen the inside of a Supercenter to keep Remke in the black? Birdsall doesn't think so. "At the end of the day, a majority of people are shopping on price," he says. "There's no getting around it."

The consensus in Cincinnati's retail and real estate circles is that Wal-Mart's inevitable gains are unlikely to come at Jungle Jim's expense, even if Bonaminio falls short with his ambitious Foodie Land venture. "Jungle seems wacky on the outside, but he has a consumer brilliance about him," says Symjunas, president of Cincinnati developer Vandercar Holdings Inc. "He really understands his market."[40]

For his part, Bonaminio is continuing to shove stacks of poker chips into the center of the table. To give shoppers even more reasons to visit his oversized market, in early 2005 he broke ground on a small strip shopping center adjacent to the store. He had pre-leased all of its 65,000 square feet to a dozen shops and restaurants long before it opened in the fall. Brian Gillan, chairman and CEO of Buck$ Dollar Stores, jumped at the chance to put his seventeenth store next to Jungle Jim's, despite its less-than-prime location. "Jungle is an icon," Gillan says. "It's like doing a deal with Sam Walton to open a department within the original Wal-Mart."[41] Except, of course, that Bonaminio is not looking to blanket America with stores.

It turned out that Bonaminio did have one more store in him, though. In March 2005, he finally made a move that he'd been agonizing over for a decade, signing a letter of intent to open a second store. The new, smaller specialty outlet—tentatively named "Baby Jungle"—is supposed to open in 2007 about twelve miles south of Jungle Jim's, not far from Cincinnati's center. Part of what finally persuaded Bonaminio to divide his attention between two locations was the building the developer made available: a 120-year-old warehouse formerly owned by Cincinnati Machine, once the world's largest manufacturer of machine tools. With the warehouse comes a second-hand treasure to rival the monorail. "It has a 25-ton crane that is used to pick up large objects," explained Phill Adams, Bonaminio's right-hand man for technology and design.[42]

Bonaminio's bravado does not extend to making the sort of predictions of certain success to which many entrepreneurs are prone. "No one's doing what I'm doing, and I don't know if I'm going to be able to do it. Ask me in a year," he says with a shrug. "Business is tough right now. But you know what? If you keep at it and give it all you got, it becomes a personal thing. If you don't make it, at least you can sit back and look at yourself and say, 'I gave it a hell of a whack, but it just doesn't work.'"

DOWN AND OUT IN JONQUIÈRE

April 2005

If Sam Walton had been prone to nightmares, they probably would have looked a lot like the Wal-Mart store in Jonquière, Québec, on this Friday evening. Empty shelves outnumber full ones by about five to one. Whole sections have been closed and the remaining merchandise consolidated in the center of the store. The entire contents of the baby department now fits into a single shopping cart left out in the middle of an aisle. Some twenty workers shuffle about forlornly in their blue smocks, tending to a dozen customers searching for a final bargain among the dregs of what had been overflowing abundance a few weeks ago. A tin of oysters is going for $1.10 (originally $1.86), a Johnny Lightning Street Freaks model car is $3 (formerly $3.92), and a quilted lady's car coat is just $10 (having been marked down in stages from $39.98). Here in Jonquière, the ubiquitous Mr. Smiley Face seems downright deranged.

"This is not what a Wal-Mart is supposed to look like," admits Marc St. Pierre, the store manager.[1]

St. Pierre, a short, thickset man with dark bangs and aviator glasses, begins by politely saying that he is not supposed to talk to reporters, that company policy dictates that all comment come from Wal-Mart Canada's chief spokesman in the Toronto head-quarters. St. Pierre can't quite bring himself to clam up entirely, perhaps because we are a very long way from Toronto (and every-where else) and because ministering the last rites to a dying store is dispiriting duty. He would like to return to Québec City, where he worked before he was transferred to Jonquière seven months ago. The store is set to close in about three weeks, but St. Pierre's boss has yet to tell him anything about his next assignment—or if there will be one, for that matter. "I'd be happy if you could let me know," St. Pierre says ruefully.

St. Pierre sent the store's greeters home long ago. In their place are two uniformed security guards who ignore the departing cus-tomers (shoplifting might well be welcome here as a form of accel-erated retail euthanasia) to focus their attention on new arrivals. No doubt they would confiscate a gun if they saw one, but what they are really looking for are cameras. A skeleton crew of downcast employees wandering a shambles of a store is not an image Ben-tonville wants to see splashed across newspapers or magazines. A third security guard patrols the parking lot in a silver SUV, keeping an eye out for shutterbugs. Photographing the outside of the store is allowed, but try to bring a camera inside and this long-haired young man will politely but firmly bar your way.

I didn't come here to take pictures or to shop, but the hockey fan in me cannot resist a set of Montreal Canadiens salt and pepper shakers for $1.89. As I'm checking out, the elderly man in front of me says to the young woman running the register, "It's so sad to see your favorite store like this." She just shrugs.

On the way to my car, I encounter a man who appears to be in his sixties ambling toward the store's entrance. "Are you here to buy something?" my companion asks him. "No," he replies, with a derisive snort. "I'm just here to look at the corpse."

"Remote" is an adjective that does not begin to do Jonquière justice. This rough-hewn, clapboard city of 60,000 rests right at the edge of inhabited Québec. To the north is nothing but forest, mountain, and bay all the way to the Arctic Circle. Québec City is a three-hour drive due south, through a wilderness preserve where moose easily outnumber men and make highway driving an adventure. A media capital Jonquière is not. And yet Wal-Mart's abandonment of this north Québec outpost in the spring of 2005 made news from Tokyo to São Paulo as an object lesson in the lengths to which it will go to throttle the threat of unionization. The company closed its store here a few months after it was certified by the Québec government as the only unionized Wal-Mart in North America.

Canada is important to Wal-Mart, which, with 260 stores, is the country's second-largest retail chain. The company is opening new stores at the rate of thirty a year—a figure that will increase sharply if and when it exports the Supercenter to Canada. Although the allure of "Every Day Low Prices" is as strong above the thirty-eighth parallel as below, the Canadian shopper is far more likely than her American counterpart to belong to a union or be related to a union member. Nearly 29 percent of Canadian workers carry a union card, compared with 13 percent of Americans. Labor laws in Canada are more favorable to unionization than those in the United States and also are more likely to be expeditiously enforced—especially here in Québec, where the unionization rate is a robust 40 percent.

Wal-Mart entered Canada by buying 122 discount department stores from the Canadian subsidiary of Woolco in 1994. (Wal-Mart passed on twenty-two other Woolco stores, including all ten of its unionized outlets.) One was in Chicoutimi, which is a kind of white-collar cousin to the blue-collar mill town of Jonquière. In 2001, these two adjacent cities and four smaller towns merged to form Saguenay, which is the largest city in the Saguenay-Lac St.-Jean region of Québec. It was just about this time that Wal-Mart entered Jonquière, much to the delight of its residents. The opening of the Place du Royaume shopping mall in Chicoutimi a decade earlier had wiped out many a shop in Jonquière, leaving a shopping void that the new Wal-Mart went a long way toward filling. The 190 jobs that the store brought were equally welcome in an area chronically afflicted by one of Canada's highest unemployment rates.

Even so, a company as authoritarian and anti-union as Wal-Mart was pushing its luck entering Jonquière. The Saguenay-Lac St.-Jean is the Ozarks of Québec in the sense that its extreme isolation bred a defiant independence of spirit into what is still a remarkably homogeneous population. Nowhere in the province is support for Québec sovereignty—for separation from English-speaking Canada—stronger than among the Saguenay's French Catholics, every fifth one of whom seems to be named Tremblay. However, the Saguenay, in sharp contrast to the Ozarks, is heavily industrialized. Each of the aluminum smelters and the pulp and paper factories that dot its ruggedly scenic landscape is unionized and has been for decades. The Québec labor movement was more or less born in the Saguenay, and a tumultuous birth it was. In 1942, the army had to be called in when a strike at an Alcan plant spun out of control. Today, a colossal Alcan plant sits right at the edge of Jonquière, the Québec union town par excellence.

The sentiment that drove Wal-Mart's Jonquière workers into the eager arms of the United Food and Commercial Workers is best summed up by a bitter pun popular among them. Québec's official motto is *Québec, je me souviens* ("I remember"). The workers adopted as their own ironic motto *Wal-Mart, je me soumets* ("I submit"). Says Sylvie Lavoie, a forty-year-old part-time cashier and single mother who led the worker rebellion in Jonquière: "Wal-

Mart will only choose somebody for promotion who thinks Wal-Mart, sleeps Wal-Mart, and eats Wal-Mart, and who puts Wal-Mart before absolutely everything—before their family even." Like many of her colleagues, Lavoie stood silently through the mandatory Wal-Mart cheer each morning. "It's not a song, it's a military chant," she says. "I found it to be degrading."[2]

I met Lavoie the morning after my encounter with Monsieur St. Pierre. It is just after 8 o'clock, and she is sitting behind a desk in a union hall less than a mile from the dying store where she worked for four years. Today is the final day for the workers Wal-Mart fired to register for a financial-aid program set up by the UFCW. The union has offered to make up the difference between a worker's unemployment check and his or her lost Wal-Mart paycheck for a full year or until another job is found—no small challenge in Jonquière. Lavoie, who is unemployed herself, is here bright and early to help with an expected last-minute rush and, in a sense, finish what she started.

A pretty, vivacious woman with blond-streaked brown hair and a tiny diamond stud in her left nostril, Lavoie is dressed in blue jeans and a white, cowl-neck sweater that sets off her tan, which seems incongruous in a place that has yet to fully emerge from winter's deep freeze. Lavoie was tending bar in Jonquière when the Wal-Mart store opened. She started as a part-time clerk in the baby department and soon became a backup cashier—a *proud* backup cashier. "My register was always balanced and I had one of the quickest scanning ratios in Québec—close to 700 [items] a minute," she brags. Although Lavoie liked Wal-Mart at first, she was never one to deny her supervisors the benefit of her point of view. "I am not a troublemaker," she insists. "But maybe I had a little more character than the others in saying, 'Look, perhaps there is a fault in the system.'"

As a part-timer, Lavoie did not qualify for health insurance and was almost always stuck working weekends while her parents took care of her little daughter, who was not happy about her mother's absences. She repeatedly applied for the full-time cashier jobs that regularly came open and grew increasingly disenchanted as they were filled by co-workers or by new hires. One day an assistant manager called Lavoie in and congratulated her on being selected for a full-time storeroom job for which she had not applied. She refused to take it.

In 2003, Wal-Mart opened a new store in Alma, about twenty-five miles away, and sent newly hired cashiers to Jonquière for training. Lavoie was outraged to learn that she was being paid less than the new recruits from Alma. As the cashiers in Jonquière got to know and trust one another, they began comparing notes and discovered major pay inequities within their own ranks, too. One day, Lavoie led a delegation of cashiers to the manager's office to complain. "We were a big bunch of girls and we all went together," she recalls. "He laughed in our faces. He told us point blank that there would be no report made and that we weren't supposed to discuss our salaries."

For Lavoie, the last straw came when she and her best friend, a part-time cashier supervisor named Joanne Desbiens, were both turned down for promotions on the same autumn day in 2003. "Joanne came over to my place and she was really crying," Lavoie recalls. "I was a little harder than her; I didn't take it so badly. I just looked at her and said, 'Well, Joanne, I have nothing else to lose.'"

The first approach to the United Food and Commerical Workers already had been made in late 2002 by three of the store's minority of male workers, one of whom had promptly quit in anger and frustration. However, it wasn't until Lavoie and Desbiens signed on that the organizing campaign gained traction, says Herman Dellaire, an organizer for UFCW Local 503 in Québec City. "The difference was that they were cashiers, which is a big department in the store, and much more popular with their co-workers," Dellaire says. "They also had very strong personalities and were not afraid of the store managers."[3]

Local 503 had a strong personality of its own—its president, Marie-Josée Lemieux, who in 1999 became the first woman to head a UFCW local in all of Canada. Lemieux, who was almost exactly Lavoie's age, was a ferociously energetic idealist who made something of a personal crusade out of the Jonquière campaign.

In Québec, unlike the United States, a store can be unionized without an employee election. If a majority of the hourly workers sign union cards, and if those signatures then are certified by the provincial government, the law requires management to sit down with union representatives and negotiate a collective-bargaining agreement. If no agreement is reached, a government-appointed arbitrator can impose a contract. In Québec, the process moves along with an alacrity that tends to blunt the sort of anti-union tactics Wal-Mart puts to such effective use in the United States. In fact, if the necessary number of signatures can be collected covertly, a store can be unionized before management even knows an organizing drive is under way.

Lemieux and Dellaire kept their distance while Lavoie, Desbiens, and a handful of helpers began meeting outside of work with colleagues they knew to be dissatisfied. Discretion was essential, for they knew that there were a few workers who either truly liked their jobs without benefit of a union or were so fearful of losing them that they would oppose unionization. Of the store's 190 employees, 45 were salaried managers, leaving 145 workers in the prospective bargaining unit. Organizers had collected only about 25 of the 73 signatures needed when a co-worker ratted them out to management. The next morning, Lavoie was summoned to the office and handed several of the pink slips cashiers get when their daily accounts don't balance. "After that, they called me in every day to reprimand me for things that were not happening," says Lavoie, who'd never before received a single pink slip. "They followed me absolutely everywhere. They would not let me be."

Lavoie persisted even so, and the store was riven into bitterly

opposed camps as management began holding the usual mandatory anti-union meetings and issuing dire warnings about the
future of the store. Complaints of intimidation and harassment cut
both ways, as pro-company employees told of organizers pestering
them at home at all hours. "[Employees] signed the cards just to get
some peace," says Noella Langlois, a clerk in apparel. "They
thought they would vote against it in a secret vote."[4]

The UFCW fell one signature short of the required number for
automatic certification and decided to take its chances by petition-
ing for a secret vote in April 2004. The move backfired, as the
union was voted down 53 percent to 47 percent. A group of assistant managers and department managers gathered just outside the
front door to celebrate for the TV cameras and to taunt union supporters as they left the store. Many workers who'd voted against the
union were so appalled by this spectacle that they switched sides.
After the required three-month cooling-off period expired, Lavoie
and her allies started over and collected a surfeit of signatures so
quickly that this second campaign succeeded before management
even realized that it was afoot.

The Jonquière store was automatically certified as a UFCW
shop in August 2004, giving a big boost to the union's organizing
campaigns in two dozen other Wal-Mart stores across Canada.
Two months later, just as the UFCW and Wal-Mart representatives were preparing to begin the mandatory contract negotiations,
Wal-Mart Canada issued an ominous press release from its headquarters in Mississauga, near Toronto. "The Jonquière store is not
meeting its business plan," it declared, "and the company is concerned about the economic viability of the store."[5]

Nine days of negotiation between the UFCW and Wal-Mart
produced nothing but acrimony. "When we got to working hours
and schedule, it was never, never, and never," recalls André Dumas,
now the acting president of UFCW Local 503 in Québec City.
Honoring the union's demands would have meant adding thirty

workers to the payroll, retorts Andrew Pelletier, Wal-Mart Canada's chief spokesman. "We felt the union wanted to fundamentally change the store's business model."[6]

The UFCW and the company were glaring at each other from opposite corners of the ring when a Wal-Mart store in Sainte-Hyacinthe unionized in January 2005.This had to be all the more worrisome to Wal-Mart because Sainte-Hyacinthe, a prosperous agricultural center an hour east of Montreal, was no Saguenay-style union redoubt. Louis Bolduc, the UFCW's Québec president, could not resist taunting Wal-Mart at a press conference announcing its latest triumph. "We hope the employer isn't going to tell us that all of a sudden Sainte-Hyacinthe is struggling financially," Bolduc said.[7]

Lavoie and Desbiens were playing bingo on Feburary 9 when a reporter called for comment on Wal-Mart's announcement that it was closing in Jonquière. They were too stunned to manage a response more coherent than *What are you talking about!?* It had never occurred to either woman that Wal-Mart would go so far as to shut down a store that seemed to be busy all the time. Lavoie began frantically calling friends currently on duty but learned nothing useful. "They were all crying," she says.

The tears flowed again when Lemieux died in her sleep of a heart attack a month later. Lemieux, who was just forty years old upon her death, had been complaining of chest pains ever since Wal-Mart announced the shut-down in Jonquière.

Wal-Mart's draconian response to the Jonquière unionists scandalized all Québec. Three of its other forty-six stores in the province were temporarily closed by bomb threats. Bernard Landry, a prominent separatist leader and a former premier of the province, urged Québecois to join him in boycotting Wal-Mart. Newspaper columnists turned the company's name into a scatological pun: "Wal-Marde." A TV broadcaster likened Wal-Mart to Nazi Germany and then apologized, just as Wal-Mart had in Arizona. Jean Tremblay, the feisty, populist mayor of Saguenay, gave media interviews by the dozen denouncing the company as a free-booting scofflaw. "Because you are big and rich and strong, you can close a store to make your workers in other stores afraid? No!" Trombley said. "If you want to do business in Québec—or in Russia or in China—you have to follow the law. And you have to respect the culture."[8]

From his office in Ontario, Pelletier repeatedly insisted that the reasons Wal-Mart gave up on Jonquière were purely financial and had nothing to do with stifling unionism. The store "has struggled from the beginning," the spokesman said. "The situation has continued to deteriorate since the union."[9] In Bentonville, Lee Scott seconded Pelletier's comments. "You can't take a store that is struggling anyway and add a bunch of people and a bunch of work rules," Scott declared.[10]

To which the people of Canada responded pretty much as one: "Liars." A national survey by Pollara Inc., Canada's largest polling organization, found that only 9 percent of Canadians believed that Wal-Mart closed the store in Jonquière because it was struggling financially. In the opinion of nine of ten Canadians, it was *all* about the union. Some 31 percent of those queried said that they would either do less shopping at its stores or stop going to them altogether—a figure that rose to 44 percent among Québecois.[11] In another survey taken six months after the Jonquière pullout, Québecois ranked Wal-Mart eleventh out of twelve retail chains when it comes to meeting their needs and expectations. Only Starbucks did worse.[12]

The harsh treatment Wal-Mart meted out in Jonquière did indeed seem to intimidate its workers elsewhere, reversing the UFCW's organizing momentum. Workers at stores in Brossard, near Montreal, and in Windsor, Ontario, voted against unionization by 74 percent and 75 percent, respectively. In earlier elections in these same stores, Wal-Mart had prevailed with just a 55 percent margin. However, the UFCW pressed on and succeeded late in 2005 in unionizing two Wal-Mart tire-and-lube shops in Gatineau, Québec, and a third in British Columbia. Meanwhile, the contract negotiations in Sainte-Hyacinthe progressively backed Wal-Mart into a corner. Unless the company can break the pro-union resolve of employees, it will face a no-win choice between having a collective bargaining agreement forced on it by the provincial government or closing a second Québec store.

What is a growth-loving, union-hating multinational to do? For a start, Wal-Mart has been trying to rehabilitate its sullied image in the province by stepping up its advertising and softening its public relations. Wal-Mart Canada finally opened an office in Montreal, thus belatedly outsourcing PR responsibility for Québec to French-speaking natives. The Jonquière backlash undoubtedly has hurt Wal-Mart at the cash register, though not nearly to the extent implied by the Pollara poll. The allure of cut-rate prices and convenient locations is not easily resisted, even by tough-talking Québecois, who, in the famous phrase of humorist Yvon Deschamps, are "socialists at heart and capitalists in the wallet."

On the other hand, if Wal-Mart were to close down in Sainte-Hyacinthe as it did in Jonquière, the company might well suffer a public relations and political meltdown that could threaten the viability of its remaining forty-five Québec stores. "They will close all the stores in Québec," predicts Sylvie Lavoie. "The list will be long, because if they close Sainte-Hyacinthe, the boycott will be long, as well."

In Jonquière today, hatred of Wal-Mart coexists with resentment of the UFCW. Carol Neron, a local newspaper columnist, is convinced that the union leaders in Washington, D.C., were aware that Wal-Mart never would have allowed a unionized store to survive, but were only looking for a way to incite public opinion against the company by provoking it into the very action it took in Jonquière. "Many people, myself included, think that our people have been used as cannon fodder," Neron says.[13]

Meanwhile, many local business owners would gladly exchange Jonquière's newfound international notoriety for the obscurity of the pre–Wal-Mart days. André Poulin, who owns a business that supplies high-tech maintenance services to aluminum manufacturers around the world, says that wherever he goes his clients ask him about the UFCW's showdown with Wal-Mart in Jonquière. "In the aluminum business, I know companies that would get a 40 percent tax deduction if they would come here, but now they are not interested," Poulin says. "I don't have any problem with unionizing Wal-Mart, but why did we have to be the first one—the guinea pig?"[14]

In the fall of 2005, the Québec Labor Relations board ruled in favor of the seventy-nine Jonquière workers who had filed complaints that Wal-Mart had illegally dismissed them for pro-union activities. Under the law, the Québec authorities could force Wal-Mart to rehire the employees it fired, but they are more likely to fine the company. Pelletier says that he was surprised by the adverse ruling. "Anybody connected to Jonquière knows how hard we tried to save the store," he says, adding that Wal-Mart probably will appeal once the board issues a final ruling.[15]

For Lavoie and her allies, the labor board's ruling was bittersweet vindication. Even so, finger-pointing and second-guessing persist within the ranks of Jonquière's former Wal-Mart employees. Not long ago, Lavoie's ten-year-old daughter came home crying from school after she had been harangued by the child of a former Wal-Mart manager. A hero to some and a villain to others, Lavoie insists that the injustice of Wal-Mart's labor practices left her no choice but to fight. "Je ne regrette pas," she says. "I regret nothing."

CHAPTER NINE

WHERE WOULD JESUS SHOP?

D rive along Queens Boulevard through the heart of the New York City borough of Queens to the neighborhoods of Rego Park and Elmhurst, and you will see one of the most densely developed—and lucrative—shopping districts in America. In addition to a hodgepodge of commercial development, two large shopping malls flank the spot where the road dips beneath the Long Island Expressway; one of them, Queens Center mall, is among the most profitable in America. In the span of a single mile along the six lanes of Queens Boulevard are many of the best-known names in retailing: Macy's, J. C. Penney, Sears, Marshall's, Gap, Limited, Disney, Old Navy, Circuit City, and Bed, Bath & Beyond. It is safe to say that Rego Park is not hostile to shopping or to chain stores.

But when word leaked out in late 2004 that the biggest retailer of them all, Wal-Mart, was negotiating to open a store in a new shopping complex being planned for open space between the two existing malls, the reaction was swift, visceral, and negative. It could be summed up with the name of one of several grassroots groups that sprung up to oppose the big-box bully's designs on New York: Wal-Mart No Way.

While Wal-Mart had distantly ringed New York City with stores over recent years, its store in Rego Park was to be the first one located within the nation's biggest metropolitan area. For a company that was born in the Ozarks and that grew big by opening stores in under-served, poor, rural communities, New York represents the climactic prize in its conquest of America. What Wal-Mart did not know—or at least did not fully appreciate—was that so many locals would be appalled by its designs on New York. The opposition to the Rego Park store (and, later, to rumored Wal-Mart projects proposed for other boroughs) was not rooted in concerns about traffic congestion or noise, but in ethics and personal values. "Wal-Mart discriminates against women and destroys good jobs, and it would take away busi-ness from local businesses," said one New Yorker, Lupita Gonzalez, summing up the feelings of many. "I don't want it here."[1]

Within weeks, many city council members and congressional rep-resentatives had joined the chorus of opposition, criticizing Wal-Mart for its many well-documented transgressions against progressivism—poverty-level wages, unaffordable health insurance, off-the-clock work, union-busting, child-labor law violations, punitive firings, and demo-tions. "We are not against Wal-Mart because it is big," said Anthony D. Weiner, a New York congressman who at the time was running in the Democratic primary for mayor. "We are against Wal-Mart because it is a bad neighbor on many levels."[2]

Less than three months after news of Wal-Mart's plan for Queens had leaked out, the plan was dead. The mall's developer, the Vornado Trust, concluded that the flak it was taking for Wal-Mart could endanger its entire Rego Park development, which included a pair of twenty-five-story apartment buildings as well as the mall. It said Wal-Mart was no longer part of the deal.

Wal-Mart, which has not lost many development battles, remains determined to have its way in New York. "We'd still be a large, suc-cessful company without being in New York, but there are customers there who need to be served," Lee Scott declared not long after the

Rego Park defeat. "I think New York will be good for us and we'll be good for New York." And make no mistake, Scott added, "We *will* be in New York."[3]

Wal-Mart must attract more educated, upscale customers who don't live paycheck to paycheck if it is to meet the ambitious growth goals it has set for itself. But as it pursues new customers, extending its reach further into more affluent parts of North America, Wal-Mart is finding that its reputation precedes it—and that its reputation is a hindrance. As it seeks to open new stores, Wal-Mart is running into mounting opposition from local residents, including many potential customers, who look beyond its "Every Day Low Prices" sloganeering to see how it delivers those prices. Many of these consumers end up concluding that they cannot in good conscience stand idly by while another Wal-Mart opens in their community. In the words of Peter McKeever, an alderman in Madison, Wisconsin: "This is a business that is not consistent with our values."[4]

In Guelph, Ontario, a city of 100,000 some sixty miles from Toronto, the Jesuit Fathers of Upper Canada opposed the company in a particularly spirited—and spiritual—battle over Wal-Mart's insistence on building a 135,000-square-foot store on a plot of land sandwiched between the Jesuit Centre and two cemeteries. The Jesuits' primary objection was that noise and traffic created by a Wal-Mart would be "incompatible with the peace and serenity people expect at Woodlawn and Marymount cemeteries; and also with the quiet solitude that draws retreatants seeking an encounter with God in prayer at the Jesuit Centre." *Where would Jesus shop? Not right next door.* In testifying at a public hearing, the Jesuit Centre's director, Reverend James W. Profit, added a ringing denunciation of rampant materialism as epitomized by Wal-Mart. "Consumerism masks the need we all have to turn inward to encounter God immanent at our core," he said. "The big box spirituality defining meaning and value in possessions is incompatible with the Jesuit spirituality defining meaning and value in seeking the Divine in all things."[5]

Wal-Mart's Canadian communications chief, Andrew Pelletier, knew better than to engage a learned Jesuit in theological debate. "I apologize if we appear to be a little gun shy," he said. "How are we going to win the debate in the news media: the Jesuits versus the world's largest retailer? You're all going to call us Goliath."[6]

Wal-Mart refused to consider another building site in Guelph, even after the city council voted down the zoning change needed near the Jesuit Centre. True to form, the company persisted in its lobbying and gradually outmaneuvered the Jesuits. The election of a vehemently pro–Wal-Mart mayor tipped the balance in its favor in 2003 and the city council reversed itself the following year and rezoned the site. In desperation, the Jesuits and their supporters tried to concoct a court appeal around a novel notion: In building a store so close to the Ignatius Jesuit Centre, Wal-Mart would infringe on the order's freedom of religion as protected under Canada's Charter of Rights and Freedoms. The argument failed to gain legal traction, making a Wal-Mart groundbreaking in Guelph likely sometime in 2006.

The growing ethical and religious backlash against Bentonville is an ecumenical phenomenon, encompassing not only Catholic orders like the Jesuits and the Sisters of Mercy, both of which pride themselves on a commitment to social justice, but mainline and liberal Protestant denominations, as well. As *Christianity Today* noted in a 2005 article entitled "Deliver Us From Wal*Mart?" the company "has become a lightning rod nationwide in local tempests of moral outrage. Church leaders . . . have joined grassroots activists fearful that mindless global market factors will steamroll human dignity."[7]

About 1,000 churches across the country screened Robert Greenwald's documentary film exposé *Wal-Mart: The High Cost of Low Prices* during its premiere week in November 2005. The most avid of the film's supporters was the United Church of Christ, which had been searching for a way to signal its opposition to Wal-Mart's labor practices short of calling for a boycott, as it had done earlier against Taco Bell in support of tomato pickers in Florida. "A boycott is not workable because Wal-Mart is the only place to shop and [many consumers] now have few other options," said Edith Rasell, the UCC's minister of labor relations and community economic development. However, she added, "The time has come for the UCC to very visibly support the right of [Wal-Mart] workers to organize for a higher standard of pay and benefits."[8]

The anti–Wal-Mart gospel is preached with special verve by pastors of inner-city African American congregations. When Wal-Mart began pushing for approval to build two Supercenters in Chicago in 2004, nine black churches jointly urged a boycott of the company's stores in outlying areas of the city. Among them was the Trinity United Church of Christ, a South Side congregation of 8,500 that promotes itself as "unashamedly black and unapologetically Christian" and whose stained-glass windows depict Martin Luther King and other civil rights activists. Reverend Jeremiah Wright, Trinity United's pastor, excoriated not only Wal-Mart but also its supporters within the black community. "Whenever price means more to you than principle," thundered Wright, "you have defined yourself as a prostitute."[9]

The case made against Wal-Mart from the pulpit of black churches is essentially political, not theological, though inevitably it comes with plenty of quotes from scripture. Wright and like-minded ministers argue that Wal-Mart does not serve the cause of black economic empowerment on balance because it underpays and bullies its employees, especially its non-white ones. (As of mid-2005, Wal-Mart employed 208,000 blacks and 139,000 Hispanics, jointly accounting for 34 percent of its U.S. workers.) Jesse Jackson, whose Rainbow/PUSH Coalition is based in Chicago, likes to use the metaphor of Kool-Aid and cyanide. "The Kool-Aid is the cheap prices," Jackson says. "The cyanide is the cheap wages; the cyanide is the cheap health benefits."[10]

Jackson also is a man of the cloth, and at a press conference in Inglewood, California, he responded to a pointed theological question—"Did not God create Wal-Mart, too?"—with an outburst of biblical reference. "God created Pharaoh, but he empowered Moses to get emancipated. God created Herod, but he empowered Jesus to get resurrected after Herod's forces killed him," Jackson said. "Surely, in free will, we are all God's children. Some of God's children are not fair. God created Adam, Eve, and Cain. But Cain killed Abel because he was greedy. Wal-Mart represents Cain. They are greedy."[11]

Faith-based opposition to Wal-Mart was voiced first not from the pulpit but from within the genteel, big-money realm of professional investing. Over the last two decades, many religious denominations, like many secular investors, have made a concerted effort to align their investment holdings with their values and beliefs. On Wall Street, a new subindustry of money managers and funds emerged to try to meet the growing demand for "socially responsible" investments that also are lucrative. Religious institutions sought to add to their financial clout by joining together to form the Interfaith Center on Corporate Responsibility (ICCR), which now represents 275 Catholic, Protestant, and Jewish groups with $110 billion in investment assets.

The most tenacious of all of Wal-Mart's critics is an earnest, plain-spoken nun from New Jersey named Sister Barbara Aires, the director of corporate responsibility for the Sisters of Charity of St. Elizabeth. Aires, who also sits on the ICCR's board, has been meeting regularly with senior Wal-Mart executives since 1990 to press them on issues ranging from racial and gender discrimination in the United States to the use of child and prison labor in its suppliers' overseas factories. "How does Wal-Mart sustain its low prices? What is it paying its workers? What are the benefits? What is the impact of their business on a lot of other, small businesses?" Aires demanded in 1999. "The company has been growing by leaps and bounds, but it needs to look at these issues."[12] The proliferating public controversies of the Scott era have made Aires' crusade a less lonely one, judging by the clerical collars and crosses in evidence in the crowd that thronged Bud Walton Arena in Fayetteville for Wal-Mart's 2005 annual meeting.

Wal-Mart management is much more respectful of religious investors than of the average secular site-fighter. In 2004, Scott spent

an entire day at the Interfaith Center's offices in New York in meetings with such devoted critics as the Benedictine Sisters of Mount St.
Scholastic, the Congregation of the Passion, the Mennonite Foundation, and the Unitarian Universalist Service Committee. While Wal-
Mart has offered up many a conciliatory word, it hasn't actually done
much of anything to placate its religious critics on the left. "It's nice to
talk, but it's time for action to substantiate that they actually are making progress on the many issues of concern to us," said Vidette Bullock
Mixon of the pension fund arm of the United Methodist Church.[13]

The principal weapon faith-based investors wield against Wal-
Mart is the shareholder resolution. Scores of such resolutions are
voted down at every big American corporation's annual meeting; in
Wal-Mart's case, the announcement of their defeat customarily
prompts derisive hooting and hollering from the majority of stockholders who have come mainly to cheer on their company. However,
the nuns keep returning to Fayetteville every year and are gaining
ground. In 2004, the ICCR crafted a new omnibus complaint, moving that Wal-Mart be required to "develop a public sustainability
report on efforts to protect human rights, worker rights, land and the
environment." The resolution won 14.2 percent of the vote in 2004
and 16.2 percent in 2005. Another resolution demanding a detailed
report on workforce diversity garnered 18.8 percent approval.

These percentages are a more telling measure of shareholder discontent than they might seem, considering that the Walton family
always votes its 40 percent holding against all shareholder resolutions.
"Progress is slow, but it's still progress," said Sister Esther Cham-
pagne, co-president of an association of twenty-seven religious
groups in Québec that enlisted in the fight against Wal-Mart after it
closed the store in Jonquière.[14]

Meanwhile, a growing number of social-responsibility funds have
dumped their Wal-Mart shares in protest against the company's
intransigence. In 2001, Wal-Mart was removed from the Domini 400
Social Equity Index, which consists of 400 big companies screened

for worthiness by KLD Research & Analytics of Boston. Wal-Mart had been the third-largest company in the Domini 400, which KLD introduced in 1990. KLD gave Wal-Mart the boot for buying merchandise from sweatshops in Asia and from suppliers in Myanmar, a country under the control of a military junta notorious for human rights abuses. "Other companies that have been similarly exposed to sweatshop and Myanmar controversies, including the Gap, Liz Claiborne, Nike, Timberland, and Reebok, have taken steps to improve their records on these issues," said KLD in explaining its decision to pull Wal-Mart. "In contrast, Wal-Mart's progress has been minimal."[15]

Religious investors rarely intervene in site fights, even when one of their own comes under attack by Wal-Mart. In Guelph, the Jesuits had secular allies aplenty but neither asked for nor received outside support from their Brothers or Sisters in Christ. In a general sense, though, many religious denominations have added Bentonville's bullying of local communities to their roster of complaints about Wal-Mart. In mid-2005, a group of investors led by Domini Social Investments and the Christian Brothers Investment Services, whose $4 billion portfolio makes it one of the largest Catholic investors, issued a set of guidelines designed to pressure big-box retailers into doing a better job of "environmental and social due diligence" in locating new stores.

The guidelines came with a forty-two-page report filled with instances of Bentonville's bad behavior in its relentless drive to expand. For example, in Dunkirk, Maryland, Wal-Mart circumvented a limit on store size in 2004 by building two stores side by side. Together, the stores exceeded the cap limit by 30 percent. In Honolulu, the company infuriated many native Hawaiians by opening a store before the ancient human remains, or *iwi kapuna*, extracted from the building site had been reburied. A similar outcry occurred near Nashville, Tennessee, when 800-year-old Indian graves were moved to make way for a Wal-Mart and a Lowe's store. However, Wal-Mart did back away from other plans to build on Ferry Farm, the childhood home of George Washington, where, in legend anyway, our first president chopped down a cherry tree and could not lie about it.[16] Simultaneously taking on the ghost of George Washington and the very live and persistent Sister Barbara Aires was too much even for Wal-Mart.

The outpouring of criticism from elements of America's religious establishment has to be galling to the executives of a company deeply imbued with a sense of its own Christian virtue. "I'm not saying that Wal-Mart is a Christian company, but I can unequivocally say that Sam founded the company on the Judeo-Christian principles found in the Bible," former Wal-Mart Vice Chairman Don Soderquist wrote in his 2005 book, *The Wal*Mart Way*.[17]

Sam Walton was an evangelical sort of mogul who artfully spun the fervent Christian fundamentalism of the Ozarks into a distinctive corporate ethos linking personal salvation to Wal-Mart's entirely secular, commercial success. "Wal-Mart publications are full of stories of hard-pressed associates, once down on their luck, who find redemption, economic and spiritual, through dedication to the company," observed Nelson Lichtenstein, a professor at the University of California, Santa Barbara, and editor of *Wal-Mart: The Face of Twenty-First Century Capitalism*. Managers are expected to help associates fulfill their mission by providing "servant leadership"—a phrase of subtle Christian connotation that has appeared with increasing frequency in Wal-Mart literature, most notably in *Sam's Associate Handbook* in 1991.[18] When Scott was promoted to CEO, one of his senior colleagues praised him as "a true servant leader who knows how to build a team and get them to work together."[19]

The upsurge in faith-based attacks on Wal-Mart confounds and angers many born-again Christians, not only in Bentonville but throughout the country. According to *Christianity Today*, they tend to look upon "Wal-Mart as a family-friendly place and a company founded on the biblical values of respect, service and sacrifice."[20] To

many theologians of a conservative bent, the whole social justice crusade betrays an unwarranted (and unacknowledged) hostility to capitalism itself. "The making of a profit, to many of them, appears to be
axiomatically immoral," contended Father Robert Sirico, a Catholic
priest who is president of the Acton Institution for the Study of Religion and Liberty. Sirico argued that "the act of responsibly making
profits is itself a social investment. I doubt that a lot of the folks in
this movement believe that."[21]

For its part, Wal-Mart is not overtly Christian in its marketing or its
public relations. "You will never hear us talking about taking a moral
stand on something or taking an ethical stand on something," insisted
Jay Allen, Wal-Mart's senior spokesman. "What we represent are the
Wal-Mart customers."[22] In other words, Wal-Mart wants to define
itself solely by what it sells. *What we are is what you buy.* Aspiring to the
status of a value-neutral selling machine makes good business sense.
Mass merchandising is hardly the Lord's work, so why should Wal-
Mart risk offending potential customers by defining itself as what they
are not? Management's steadfast refusal to own up to its abhorrence of
labor unions—"We're not anti-union, we're pro-associate"—is intended
in part to keep union members as customers even as Wal-Mart goes to
great lengths to keep unions themselves firmly at bay.

However, Allen's protestations of neutrality are disingenuous. The
fact is, a corporation defines itself at least as much by its actions as by
its words. To a greater degree than any of its competitors, Wal-Mart
has indeed taken a moral stand in its merchandising decisions.
Through its actions, if rarely its words, Bentonville chose sides in
America's culture wars, adopting the same conservative default position that won George W. Bush two terms in the White House: Placate the religious right and take your chances with everybody else.

Wal-Mart was the only one of the ten largest drug chains to refuse
to stock Preven when Gynetics Inc. introduced the morning-after
contraceptive in 1999. Although Preven works only in women who
are not pregnant, Pharmacists for Life and some other anti-abortion

groups considered Preven an abortion pill. They pressed Wal-Mart to ban it. According to Allen, Wal-Mart's decision not to carry the drug was based solely on its poor sales outlook. "If anybody of any belief reads any moral decision [into] that, that's not right," Allen said.[23] However, Roderick L. Mackenzie, Gynetics' founder, says that senior Wal-Mart executives said privately that they did not want their pharmacists to have to grapple with the moral dilemma of abortion. Mackenzie was incensed, but tried to mask his anger in the futile hope that the company would reverse its decision and stock Preven. "When you speak to God in Bentonville," he said sarcastically, "you speak in hushed tones."[24]

Wal-Mart's sanitizing of its media offerings is one of the most unusual—and controversial—aspects of a sales pitch calculated to curry the favor of the socially and religiously conservative. To be sure, selectivity is built into Wal-Mart's business model in the sense that it carries far fewer product offerings than Barnes & Noble, HMV, Blockbuster, and other chains that specialize in media and entertainment. In addition to excluding stuff that does not measure up to the standard of a potential blockbuster, Wal-Mart makes a point of shunning fare that might offend the "family-values" police. A. William Merrill of the Southern Baptist Convention praised Bentonville for its message to Hollywood and the publishing industry: "They have said, 'Don't send us smut.'"[25]

Wal-Mart will not sell any CD with a parental warning sticker, thus excluding most rap and hip-hop releases from its shelves. It does sell some R-rated DVDs and Mature-rated video games, but screens them for content and demands proof that buyers are at least seventeen years old. Because books and magazines do not come with third-party ratings, the printed word poses the biggest challenge to Wal-Mart's buyers. Like countless jurists, they struggle to define indecency but are expected to know it when they see it. "There's a lot of subjectivity," conceded Gary Severson, a general merchandise manager who oversees books, as well as toys, electronics, and sporting goods. "There's a line between provocative and pornographic. I don't know exactly where it is."[26]

Comedian George Carlin chose *When Will Jesus Bring the Pork Chops?* as the title of his bestselling 2004 book to "piss off" all three major religions. He succeeded. Wal-Mart didn't care for the title or the jacket illustration that removed Jesus from Leonardo Da Vinci's famous painting of the Last Supper and inserted Carlin next to the Redeemer's empty chair. Wal-Mart sent back 3,500 copies of Carlin's book that had been shipped to the store either inadvertently or as a provocation.

The cover of Jon Stewart's *America (The Book): A Citizen's Guide to Democracy Inaction* was tailor-made for Wal-Mart, with its bald eagle and huge American flag backdrop. "We thought the flag on the cover would do it for Wal-Mart since they're fond of selling things with flags on them," said Ben Karlin, co-author of *America* and producer of Stewart's *The Daily Show.*[27] But some enterprising Wal-Mart buyer paged through the parody civics textbook and found a portrait of the Supreme Court in which the heads of the justices had been Photoshopped onto naked bodies. As a result, Wal-Mart banned the book, making itself an even riper target of ridicule on *The Daily Show* and its spin-off, *The Colbert Report.*

Lucky for him, Jon Stewart did not need Wal-Mart to sell a million copies of his book. However, most authors and musicians must win a place on Wal-Mart's shelves in order to make the bestseller lists. Wal-Mart's combination of massive size and selectivity has made it a multimedia house of hits nonpareil. By some estimates, it accounts for 60 percent of the total sales of America's top-selling DVDs, 50 percent of top-selling CDs, and 40 percent of top-selling books. "They pile up best-sellers like toothpaste," scoffed Stephen Riggio, chief executive of Barnes & Noble, the largest U.S. book chain, which carries 60,000 titles to Wal-Mart's 500.[28]

Many music labels produce edited versions of albums for sale at Wal-Mart by deleting swearwords or by rerecording a tune with new lyrics. CD covers, too, are frequently altered to Wal-Mart's tastes. Even the late Kurt Cobain, the famously contrary front man of the rock band Nirvana, caved when the retailer objected to paintings of fetuses on the cover of the *In Utero* album. "He remembered growing up in Aberdeen [Washington] and knowing that Wal-Mart was one of the few places you could go to buy music," recalled Danny Goldberg, Nirvana's former manager.[29] Nirvana also changed the title of the *In Utero* track "Rape Me" to "Waif Me."

Wal-Mart banned Sheryl Crow's eponymous 1996 album for lyrics that only the company would have found offensive, as contained in the song "Love Is a Good Thing": "Watch out sister / Watch out brother / Watch out children as they kill each other / With a gun they bought at the Wal-Mart discount stores."

Wal-Mart's censorious impulses are deeply rooted. "At first, it was a question of 'Mr. Sam wouldn't approve of this and Helen *surely* would not approve.' Sam was a good ol' boy, but his wife was pretty close to the vest—Pentecostal almost," said Jon Lehman, the store manager turned UFCW organizer. "I think it evolved from 'Sam and Helen wouldn't approve' to 'our customers wouldn't approve.'" Headquarters was no less protective of the straitlaced sensibilities of its predominantly rural and female workforce. "Stuff came off the shelf when someone complained to the home office, and many times the phone call was coming from the person who put the druggy CD or the sleazy magazine on the shelf," Lehman said.[30]

Even so, it is unlikely that a retailer as keen to grow as Wal-Mart would have remained so ostentatious in its piety had not America tilted accommodatingly to the right, allowing the company to cement the loyalty of its traditional rural and Southern customer base without a net loss of business. In music, for example, the country music explosion that Wal-Mart's market clout helped trigger more than offset its principled refusal to cash in on the hip-hop bonanza. And what did Wal-Mart need with Jon Stewart or George Carlin when it was propelling books by conservative scolds like Ann Coulter and Bill

O'Reilly to the top of the bestseller lists? No retailer has benefited more from the soaring appeal of Christian-themed books, music, and other merchandise than Wal-Mart, which earns well over $1 billion in revenue a year in catering to the seventy-two million Americans who now describe themselves as born again.[31]

However, it appears that Wal-Mart recently has become less reflexively right wing in its media merchandising as it pushes farther into blue-state, big-city America. In 2004, Wal-Mart finally stopped selling the infamous anti-Semitic tract *The Protocols of the Learned Elders of Zion* on its Web site. A faked account of rabbis meeting to plot Jewish world domination, the document was concocted by the Czarist police in Russia in the 1890s. Adolf Hitler liked it so much he made it required reading for the Hitler Youth. Although *The Protocols* was discredited long ago as a racist fraud, Wal-Mart affected neutrality in the disclaimer it attached to the book on Walmart.com. "If . . . *The Protocols* are genuine (which can never be proven conclusively), it might cause some of us to keep a wary eye on world affairs. We neither support nor deny its message. We simply make it available for those who wish a copy."[32]

Wal-Mart ignored various complaints until Rabbi Abraham Cooper of the Wiesenthal Center sent Scott a letter of protest in which he confessed to being "astounded that a reputable company would even give consideration to marketing this flagrantly hateful text." Offering no explanation as to why it plugged *The Protocols* to begin with, Wal-Mart quietly pulled the tract from its Web site the day after Scott got the letter, explaining its action as a "business decision."[33]

Surprisingly, Bentonville pushed back when The Timothy Plan, which touts itself as "America's first pro-life, pro-family, biblically based mutual fund group," objected in 2002 to the presence of *Cosmopolitan, Glamour,* and other "soft-core pornographic magazines" in the racks next to its checkout lanes. "Go into any one of your stores, publicly introduce yourself as [CEO] of Wal-Mart, get on the speaker system and read aloud to your store's customers all the words on the cover of any issue of *Cosmopolitan*," challenged Timothy Plan president Arthur Ally in one of his four letters to Lee Scott. "Then let me know how it goes so I can decide whether or not we have to add your company to our screens list."[34]

In an interview shortly after Wal-Mart's tussle with The Timothy Plan, Tom Coughlin described the checkout display racks as the most problematic real estate in any family-friendly store. "We don't believe we should be censors or any of that type thing, but, you know, my wife had kids in the shopping cart many a year," Coughlin said. "I can remember comments she made to me about my own kids being at the checkout counter and having something inappropriate there. My daughter, who had just learned to read, was asking, 'What does this mean?' It's the kind of thing you don't want."[35] Even so, neither Coughlin nor Scott deigned to respond to Ally, leaving it to a subordinate to politely tell him to buzz off. "It's our intention to continue merchandising magazines in the same manner that we currently do," replied Don S. Harris, Wal-Mart's top merchandising executive, in the last of four letters to Ally.[36]

Ally, who was born in Palestine under the name Ali Rashad and raised as a Muslim, is a man emboldened by uncompromising convictions. "Our moral foundation is crumbling," he said. "We are in a war for the soul of America."[37] Ally unloaded his 9,200 shares of Wal-Mart stock and put the company on the blacklist of morally unworthy corporations that The Timothy Plan distributes to its 10,000 investors and also to 4,000 Christian financial planners. He also solicited letters of support from Morality in Media, the American Decency Association, the American Family Association, and other fellow travelers, bundled them together, and sent them to Bentonville.

Although Wal-Mart never acknowledged the letters, it soon began inserting U-shaped plastic liners into the checkout racks that partially obscured the covers of *Cosmopolitan, Redbook, Glamour,* and *Marie Claire*. The binders blocked offending headlines, but actually accentuated the cleavage that occupied the center of most covers. "It's a big joke," complained Ally, who called off his pressure campaign just the same because Wal-Mart also banished three mildly risqué "lad" magazines—*Maxim, FHM,* and *Stuff*—from its back-of-the-store reading section. Although Ally hadn't complained about the lad titles, he was delighted to see them go. "It is soft-core pornography," he said. "It's very addictive and leads to harder stuff."[38]

To confirm the suspicion that Wal-Mart's decision to yank *Maxim, FHM,* and *Stuff* was rooted not in principle but expedience, all one had to do was take a quick tour of its magazine section. Look, there is a nearly naked Britney Spears on the cover of *Rolling Stone!* Or is it Christina Aguilera? Apparently, Bentonville didn't mind giving the lad magazines the boot because they do not ring the cash register at Wal-Mart and thus could be sacrificed to Ally without also sacrificing much profit. On the other hand, *Rolling Stone* is a big seller at Wal-Mart, as are the women's monthlies that the company grudgingly and ineffectually blindered, even though their cover girls tended to show less skin than did pop princesses Spears and Aguilera on *Rolling Stone.*

It appears, in short, that Wal-Mart is starting to become the value-neutral selling machine Jay Allen claims it already is. Bentonville has come to understand that it needs the secular dollar no less than the Christian dollar if it is to meet its ambitious revenue-growth goals. In other words, Wal-Mart now must find a way to make both God and Mammon serve it.

THE BELMONT SCHISM

Erin Russell lives with her husband and three young daughters in Belmont, North Carolina, a picturesque but down-on-its-luck textile town of 8,705 that undoubtedly will be engulfed by Charlotte's exurban sprawl over the coming decade. Russell, who is forty-one years old, commutes a dozen miles east to Charlotte, where she works as an environmental lawyer for a Swiss corporation. Her husband, John Russell, heads daily in the opposite direction to the city of Gastonia, where he once was a public defender and now is in private practice. Erin, who moved to Belmont when she married John in 1996, is not just a newcomer but also a transplanted Yankee and a Catholic in a very Southern, very Protestant community. But Fredonia, the town in western New York where she grew up, was not much bigger than Belmont, and she was starting to feel pretty comfortable amid its leafy, antebellum charms until 2002 when Wal-Mart decided to build a Supercenter a mile from her front door.

Russell had nothing against Wal-Mart at first. She regularly drove to Gastonia to shop at the Supercenter there. "I loved going to Wal-Mart," she recalled. "You could get everything, it was convenient."[1] However, as an ardent believer in the Catholic social justice tradition, Russell was not the sort of consumer who bestowed her commercial allegiance casually. She had stopped buying Nike products a decade earlier because of allegations of labor abuses in the company's Asian shoe factories. Now that Wal-Mart was coming to Belmont, she decided it was time to research the company's business practices. Appalled by what she discovered about Wal-Mart's wages, its treatment of its workers, its fierce anti-union stance, and its arrogance toward outsiders and its suppliers, Russell added Wal-Mart to the family boycott list and explained her decision at length to her kids. During a trip to Fredonia a few months later, an urgent need to purchase a garbage can arose and the only place open was a Wal-Mart. Erin got as far as the parking lot before six-year-old Grace started to cry. "Grace is my first born and she sees the world in black and white," said Russell, who turned the car around and drove home empty-handed.

Russell, who was pregnant with her third child at the time, founded Citizens for Responsible Growth to try to block the company's entry into Belmont. She went after Wal-Mart with relentless energy and lawyerly thoroughness, advancing all of the standard economic and aesthetic complaints. As an environmental lawyer, she presented the environmental case against Wal-Mart with expert precision. However, Russell went well beyond the traditional critique of Bentonville in her principal argument: that Wal-Mart should not be allowed into Belmont because many of its business practices were immoral and un-Christian. "Do you know that saying, 'What would Jesus drive?'" asked Russell, a self-described liberal Catholic. "My question is, 'Where would Jesus shop?' And the answer is, 'Not at Wal-Mart.'"[2]

Russell contends that Wal-Mart "stands openly against primary social values taught by the Church"—notably those affirming the dignity of work and the rights of employees to an equitable wage and to a voice in the workplace. The Catholic Church has repeatedly come out in favor of labor unions, beginning with Pope Leo XIII's social encyclical in 1891, *Rerum Novarum* ("On the Condition of the Working Person").[3] Russell particularly likes to quote Pope John Paul II's 1981 encyclical, *Laborem Exercens* ("On Human Work"): "Workers' rights cannot be doomed to be the mere result of economic systems aimed at maximum profits. The thing that must shape the whole economy is respect for the workers' right within each country and all through the world's economy."[4]

Russell made religion a central issue in the Belmont fight because Wal-Mart's local development partner happened to be one of the most venerable Catholic institutions in the South: Belmont Abbey. Founded by Benedictine monks in 1876, Belmont Abbey was the first monastery that the Catholic Church established in the postbellum South. In 1910, the Holy See conferred upon Belmont Abbey the status of a diocese unto itself (*Abbatia Nullius Diocesis*)— the first and only time this distinction has been bestowed in the United States. The twenty-one Benedictine monks who live in prayerful isolation within the walls of Belmont Abbey take vows of poverty. That is, "The monk deprives himself of certain goods which could be an obstacle to his total giving of self to God."[5] Such goods will be nowhere as temptingly abundant as they will be if Belmont's new Supercenter opens as planned in late 2006, just a few hundred yards from Belmont Abbey.

Only one thought inhibited Russell as she steeled herself for battle with Belmont Abbey over its partnership with Wal-Mart: Would she and her husband still be welcome at the abbey church? Although the Russells belonged to St. Peter's, a small Jesuit parish in Charlotte, they often attended Sunday Mass at the abbey church as a change of pace. Abbot Placid Solari, the head monk, was always civil if rarely cordial, exchanging nods of recognition with Erin when they met. Even so, once Erin began her campaign against Wal-Mart, the Russells were enveloped by hostility every time they set foot in the abbey. "I got a lot of mean looks and stares from people," she said. "I'm used to it: Lawyers disagree with their colleagues all the time. But the whole process put such a strain on our family. There were times when John would cringe when I told him I was going to a city council meeting."

Fifty-three-year-old Abbot Solari presides over both the monastery and Belmont Abbey College, a four-year liberal arts school that is the only Catholic college between Virginia and Florida. A native of Richmond, Solari joined the abbey out of college in 1974, following in the footsteps of an older brother. Placid Solari taught theology at the college and took advanced study in Rome, earning a doctorate in patristics (the study of the early Catholic theologians). In 1995, Solari was elected abbot by his fellow Belmont monks.

Solari was a Catholic traditionalist who was given responsibility for an institution facing the choice between radical change and slow death. Both Belmont Abbey and its college faced a vexing problem: a dwindling number of recruits. As the number of monks in residence had fallen to twenty-one from a peak population of eighty, the per capita costs of maintaining the monastery had soared prohibitively. Worse, many of the remaining monks were elderly and too infirm to work. Instead of earning salaries as teachers for the benefit of the monastery, they were piling up medical bills. Meanwhile, the college was struggling to lift enrollment to a level that would cover the soaring operating costs that afflicted all institutions of higher learning.

For decades, the monks had lived off the 700 acres of land the abbey owned, tending to a vineyard and raising cattle, pigs, and chickens. After a new four-lane highway, I-85, sliced right through the heart of the abbey's acreage in the early 1960s, the farm died, and the monks tried to offset the loss of income by leasing fifty acres to a developer who put up a strip mall. The center—Abbey Plaza—was poorly managed for the most part and was only a modest moneymaker for the Benedictines of Belmont. When he became abbot, Solari could have quickly converted the remaining acreage into a cash fortune by auctioning it off, but he committed himself to maintaining the abbey's ownership of every acre. "We consider that the property was entrusted to us," he said.[6]

Eventually, Abbot Solari came to the conclusion that the best way—perhaps the only way—to ensure the long-term survival of the institutions entrusted to his care was to develop the remaining 600 acres of mostly forested former farmland that the abbey owned. This realization caused Solari no little anxiety, for in entering the monastery this Catholic intellectual had deliberately insulated himself from the world of commerce. "I wasn't attracted to the business world, which is irony now," Solari said.[7]

Even so, Solari was well aware that the abbey's land had soared in value as Belmont increasingly was drawn into the expanding orbit of greater Charlotte. The highway project that had doomed Belmont Abbey Farm had advantageously positioned the monastery's acreage for future development. "It's funny how things work out," Solari said. "A painful thing turned out to be a benefit for the college in the long run."[8] Work had begun on a second highway, I-485, which would intersect with I-85 about two miles from the abbey's property, further enhancing its commercial appeal.

Assisted by a host of outside advisers, the abbot methodically put together a plan to build a 350,000-square-foot shopping center on a 130-acre tract. Lots of big retailers were interested in anchoring the center, but they insisted on either buying the building site or using it as collateral for a construction loan. According to Solari, Wal-Mart was the only prospective development partner that was willing to build on land leased from the abbey without encumbering the property with a mortgage and was also willing to cover part of the costs of building infrastructure on the site.

Wal-Mart already was well established in greater Charlotte, with seven stores. Gastonia, a city of 66,270 just twenty-three miles from downtown Charlotte, had two Wal-Marts of its own, putting Belmont within ten miles of no fewer than four Supercenters. Was there room for another 180,000-square-foot behemoth in little Belmont? Wal-Mart thought so, and its representatives hammered out a preliminary agreement with Belmont Abbey, subject to the necessary approvals from the city of Belmont.

In choosing to partner with Wal-Mart, Abbot Solari essentially acted alone. There was no formal consideration of the notion either by the abbey or by the college's board of trustees. James Gearity, who was president of Belmont Abbey College at the time, was unaware of the deal until Solari informed him of it the day before it was announced publicly in January 2002. "For a while the abbot was just being coy or cute—'We're in negotiations, but I can't tell you who,'" Gearity recalled. "He certainly played it close to the vest, right up to the very end."[9]

The abbot did take into his confidence Richard Penegar, a retired Gastonia businessman and longtime trustee of Belmont Abbey College. Penegar, who grew up on a local farm, is a courtly, rather soft-spoken man who spent most of his career selling office furniture and also dabbled in real estate development. The Wal-Mart that opened in Gastonia a few years earlier had not hurt Penegar's business, but he was appalled just the same that the city chose to subsidize the Supercenter with a hefty tax abatement. Penegar was all for developing a shopping center on the abbey's property, but he urged Solari to partner with someone other than Wal-Mart. "I've seen the people in Gaston County who have been laid off from textile jobs, and here is Wal-Mart bringing back from overseas the same products we used to make right here," Penegar said. "Wal-Mart is the worst of the worst as far as taking advantage of little people."[10]

Meanwhile, Russell pressed her religious arguments on Solari in several delicately worded letters and e-mails sent after she introduced herself to him at a city council meeting. "You are many times more well-versed than I could ever be in the teachings of the church. My understanding of the teaching may not be as clear as yours," she wrote. "However, it seems to me that what I have learned from the church can clearly support the contention that Wal-Mart is a questionable partner for a Catholic religious order that seeks to live the gospel."

Solari pleasantly surprised Russell by coming to her home one afternoon for a polite if fruitless discussion on the Wal-Mart project. The environmental lawyer wanted to talk ethics and religion; the priest seemed preoccupied with rents per square foot and contract law. As Russell fought on, her dissent became more pointed and more public. "The Abbey owns prime real estate that can be developed without a Wal-Mart," Russell wrote in an open letter to the entire Belmont Abbey community. "Please don't compromise the values of the church by entering into this unholy alliance."

Despite Russell's determined agitating, the Wal-Mart issue never really took hold among Belmont's Catholics. For one thing, Abbott Solari was an intimidating figure who would not be drawn into public discussions of the morality of allying with Wal-Mart. Then, too, Russell's proselytizing drew as many blank looks as angry glares. "A lot of people have not studied the social justice movement and don't know the teachings of the Church on unions or child labor," Russell said. "It's not something you hear in Church every Sunday, so I think there are a lot of Catholics who just wouldn't connect the issue of what Wal-Mart does with their faith in any way."

Even so, it looked as if the Wal-Mart project was going down to defeat when the planning and zoning board denied the abbey the needed variance. There would be no Supercenter in Belmont now unless four of the five city council members voted to override the zoning board. Mayor Billy Joye, a native Belmonter and ardent Wal-Mart supporter, could count on only three votes, so he took the politically audacious but legally permitted step of dissolving the zoning board. The mayor insisted that he took this action not to salvage the Wal-Mart deal, but because several members were guilty of "inappropriate behavior"—mainly in disrespecting pro–Wal-Mart witnesses. It was implausible to say the least, but now all Joye needed to prevail was a simple majority of three votes on the council.

It was all over but the shouting, of which there was plenty when the Belmont City Council convened in January 2004 for a final vote. A hearing that was supposed to last a few hours was extended into the wee hours three nights running to give everyone a chance to vent. The vote, as expected, was three-to-two in favor.

Like most site fights, the battle of Belmont left bruised feelings all around. Mayor Joye settled a defamation suit brought against him by a member of the planning board by offering a halfhearted apology. Still pending is a lawsuit charging the mayor and pro–Wal-Mart council members with "impermissible bias and partiality." Joye shrugs off the suit as the last gasp of sore losers. "You got a very vocal minority in this town," he said. "And if they don't get their way, they sue you."[11] As it turned out, Joye had badly misread political sentiment in Belmont. In November 2005, he lost in a landslide in a mayoral election that was for all intents and purposes a belated referendum on the mayor's handling of the Wal-Mart issue. Joye mustered only 43 percent of the vote to the 57 percent rung up by Richard Boyce, a former Presbyterian minister who had never before run for political office and had lived in Belmont for less than a decade.

Although Russell failed to keep Wal-Mart out of Belmont, she is as determined as ever to keep Russells out of Wal-Mart. From time to time, one of her daughters still will offer a mild protest to the family's Nike boycott. But none of them ever asks why they can't go to Wal-Mart, even as the press of daily events occasionally leads their mother into temptation. "If anything, they are the ones who understand and have no qualms about not shopping there. I am the one who checks e-mail at eight at night only to find out they need to take something to school the next day," Russell said. "Wal-Mart is often the most convenient choice, but for this family it is just not an option."

CHAPTER TEN

THE EDUCATION OF LEE SCOTT

L ike the saying goes, you're not paranoid if "they" really are out to get you. The rumor started one Friday in May 2005, when a few bookshelves and some boxes of books were removed from Lee Scott's office in Bentonville. By Monday, "two sources close to Wal-Mart" had informed the *Arkansas Democrat-Gazette* that the CEO's office had been "emptied out." Over the next few days, word of Scott's impending resignation circulated madly by telephone and Web site, seemingly gaining credence with each repetition. By the following Friday, Scott felt that he had to address the rampant speculation about his future at the weekly management meeting in Bentonville. "I am not going anywhere," he told a few hundred of his most senior colleagues.[1]

Scott had every reason to be upset, but jauntily played his predicament for laughs at Wal-Mart's annual meeting a few weeks later. Departing from his script, Scott began his speech by confessing that as recently as the day before he had expected to miss the 2005 shareholder gathering. "Oh, not for the reason you might think," he said, explaining that he had spilled a drink on his wife's white dress at a social event the night before. "I thought I might be in [the hospital] today," Scott said.[2]

For Scott, the annual meeting offered sorely needed respite from what had been a truly awful year for him and for Wal-Mart. The typically raucous audience of 20,000—dominated as ever by small stockholders and carefully selected employees—gave three standing ovations within the first half hour: for the American flag, for the troops in Iraq, and then for their own embattled warrior, Lee Scott. The endorsement that counted most came when Chairman Rob Walton got up before the crowd and offered the CEO his emphatic and unqualified support. To paraphrase Mark Twain, the rumors of Scott's demise had indeed been greatly exaggerated.

Make no mistake, though, Wal-Mart today is a company in crisis. Wal-Mart had run into serious trouble once before. It performed so poorly through the early 1990s that many outsiders expected David Glass to retire early and work full-time for the Kansas City Royals major league baseball team, which had named him chairman in 1993.[3] However, the predicament that now confronts Scott is far worse and more confounding than anything Glass or Sam Walton, for that matter, ever had to face. For the first time since Wal-Mart's founding in 1962, it can be argued that the vaunted business model that Walton created and that first Glass and then Scott applied on a gargantuan scale has broken down and is in need not of repair but of replacement.

"As it stands right now and for the last few years, Wal-Mart simply isn't performing as a great company," Jeff Macke, an East Coast money manager who is one of the most acerbic of Wal-Mart's many critics on Wall Street, declared in early 2005. "They are the Mike Tyson of retail"—a once great heavyweight champion now prone to embarrassing itself in the ring.[4] Although Macke has stopped short of calling for Scott to step down, he questioned whether the CEO was capable of fixing Wal-Mart. "In terms of the job Lee Scott is doing, ultimately he is going to have to answer," Macke said. "I don't know what he could do to get [Wall Street] back in love with them."[5]

On Wall Street, the nuanced complexities of a company's past, present, and especially its future are reduced to a single number—share price—for all to see. Judged by return to shareholders—today's ultimate measure of CEO performance—Scott has been a D+ student at best. From the day he moved up to CEO in January 2000 to the morning of the 2005 annual meeting, the price of a share of Wal-Mart common stock fell from $64.50 to $47.35. This decline of 27 percent lumped Wal-Mart in with the worst-performing U.S. retail chains over this period and reduced the company's total stock market value (its market capitalization) by $99 billion. For much of Scott's tenure, Wal-Mart had held its own; it was only in the last few years that it began lagging badly behind its closest rivals. While Wal-Mart's stock fell by almost 25 percent over the two-year period ending October 31, 2005, Costco's rose by 35 percent and Target's by 40 percent.

Much as Wall Street's judgment must sting, Scott reached his nadir with the Tom Coughlin embezzlement scandal, which dumped a bucket of toxic sleaze over a company still so straitlaced at heart that it bans the consumption of alcohol at all corporate events and even prohibits its buyers from sampling the wares of its liquor vendors. "For me personally and for this company, the Tom Coughlin issue has been an embarrassment," Scott admitted some months after Coughlin, Wal-Mart's second-highest-ranking executive, resigned as vice chairman and was removed from the board of directors in March 2005. "He has been—was—a friend for years."[6]

Although Scott and Coughlin were indeed longtime colleagues, they were more rivals than friends. Coughlin was so upset when the Wal-Mart board chose Scott over him in 1999 to succeed Glass as CEO that he might well have quit the company had not several members of the Walton family intervened. "They asked me to hang in there, and said that I was an important part and necessary," Coughlin later recalled.[7] It's entirely possible, even likely, that the motivational roots of Coughlin's alleged thievery were sunk in his resentment over not getting the top job he wanted and believed he deserved. After all, he wasn't exactly hurting for money, having received a total of $15 million in salary, bonuses, and other benefits in 2003 and 2004.

In December 2004, Wal-Mart abruptly dismissed four senior executives and three other home-office employees with no explanation, other than that they all had failed "to follow internal company rules." Jim Haworth, the highest-ranking member of the group, was operations chief of the Wal-Mart stores division and a longtime protégé of Coughlin's. Apparently, the impetus for the collective firing was a bacchanalian drinking party complete with strippers, to which executives of vendor companies were invited (yet another violation of company policy). Coughlin, who hosted the party, also lost his job. However, in deference to his status as cheerleader-in-chief and preeminent Walton protégé, the company allowed Coughlin to serve out his board term and spun his ouster as a voluntary departure. Wal-Mart larded the press release announcing Coughlin's retirement on January 24 with flattering quotes from Rob Walton ("I particularly respect the special relationship that he has built with our associates in the field") and Scott ("He is a great example of what a person can accomplish in the retail field").[8]

Just days before Coughlin's retirement became official, he tried to use a $100 Wal-Mart gift card to buy contact lenses in a store. The home-office employee who processed the transaction thought it odd that the vice chairman was redeeming a card he was supposed to have given to "All-Star" store employees. The ensuing investigation ended with Wal-Mart accusing Coughlin of misappropriating at least $262,000 over a ten-year period in order to buy items ranging from an $8,500 all-terrain vehicle, a $6,250 hunting lease in Texas, and a $1,360 pair of custom-made alligator cowboy boots to a $13.09 gun case, a $3.54 Polish sausage, and a $2.57 packet of cold medicine.[9] Coughlin admitted to submitting phony invoices, but insisted that the scheme was part of a covert "union project" he was running for the company. He claimed that he'd used his own money to bribe union officials into fingering pro-union Wal-Mart workers—a potential crime in its own right—and that the company had reimbursed him by covering some of his personal expenses.[10] The company insisted that Coughlin was lying, and the UFCW said it found no evidence that any of its organizers had taken bribes, but given the depth of Wal-Mart's union animus, who could say for sure?

To investigate Coughlin and his alleged accomplices on the home-office staff, Wal-Mart hired two former high-level FBI officials, two former U.S. Attorneys, and the retired director of the Arkansas State Police. Based on their work, Wal-Mart booted Coughlin from its board, fired four headquarters employees whom it accused of helping him (bringing the total number of subordinates the vice-chairman had taken down with him to eleven), and turned over the voluminous evidence it had amassed to the U.S. Attorney's office in Fort Smith. (In November 2005, one of the vice presidents whom Wal-Mart dismissed pleaded guilty in Federal court in Arkansas to three counts of wire fraud.) In a letter to Wal-Mart employees, Scott tried to spin this whole scorched-earth exercise in damage control as a triumph of corporate character: "[T]his demonstrates once again the strength of the Wal-Mart culture. Our standards of integrity apply to everyone, with no exceptions."[11]

But as Scott conceded some months later, the whole sordid episode had taken a heavy toll on morale. "It created a real issue in the company . . ." he said. "It's just a tough thing. There isn't a good explanation for any of it."[12] As for Wal-Mart's public reputation and credibility, it was a toss-up in the end as to which had done more damage: Coughlin's claim that he'd masterminded a covert union-busting bribery campaign within the company or Wal-Mart's own allegations that a top officer, lionized as the embodiment of the Wal-Mart Way, had ripped it off with impunity for a decade. For a company that had always prided itself on squeaky-clean integrity, the Coughlin affair was perhaps the most telling evidence yet of Wal-Mart's newfound fallibility.

Wall Street worries that the accelerating pace of Wal-Mart's expansion is straining management's ability to keep a lid on costs. This is all the more troublesome to investors because cost control long has been a Wal-Mart forte. Take the particularly disappointing results of 2005's second quarter, in which operating expenses rose by $230 million over the preceding year. The rampaging cost of energy was largely to blame, adding $100 million to the company's utilities bill for its stores and inflating the cost of fueling its 7,100 delivery trucks by $30 million. Although surging labor costs presumably accounted for the remaining $100 million, Bentonville declined to disclose the actual number. "There's a lot of concern, focus and frustration . . . as to what exactly is going on here," complained Deutsche Bank analyst Bill Dreher in the fall of 2005.[13]

Wall Street is even more alarmed by another trend: Wal-Mart's loss of sales momentum in the United States. Sales have continued to climb by 11 percent to 12 percent annually only because the company is opening 250 to 300 new stores each year. Strip out the impact of expansion, and the annual growth rate at Wal-Mart and Sam's Club stores now is a meager 3.2 percent, down sharply from 8 percent in 2000, Scott's first year. Meanwhile, Target's "same store" sales rate has jumped to 5 percent from 3 percent. (These are small numbers, but keep in mind that each percentage point translates into many billions of dollars.)

Part of the problem is that existing Wal-Marts are losing business to new Wal-Marts as the company locates its stores closer together than before. At the same time, the company is beginning to pay what promises to be a steep price for having located the great bulk of its stores far beyond the reach of mass transit. The explosion of gas prices above $2 a gallon has made it clear that Wal-Mart's economics are predicated on low-cost gasoline no less than on low wages. According to a study by Retail Forward, 71 percent of Wal-Mart shoppers have altered their driving habits to economize, compared with 65 percent of Target's. Not only are customers making fewer trips to the store, but they have less money to spend when they get there. Like most economists, Scott sees no relief in sight. "I worry about the effect of higher oil prices," he said in the fall of 2005. That is, he fears that "oil prices will erase improvements in employment and real income for a portion of our customer base—an important portion of our customer base."[14]

In maintaining its traditional fixation on low-income consumers, Wal-Mart also has undercut its sales growth by failing to appeal equally to more affluent shoppers who also are walking its aisles in large numbers. According to the company's own surveys, the higher a shopper's income, the more narrowly she shops at Wal-Mart, sticking to basic, low-margin commodities like detergent and socks. Wal-Mart's attempts in recent years to follow Target's and J. C. Penney's lead by adding trendier, more upscale merchandise generally have been half-baked and ineffectual. "Their overall assortment lacks creativity and originality," said Bob Buchanan, a retail analyst with A. G. Edward & Sons. "They have missed on key products many times."[15]

Then, too, an increasing number of Wal-Mart customers across all income groups have been put off by indifferent service, unkempt shelves and aisles, long checkout lines, and other consequences of understaffing and of inept store management. "We've got a lot of stores that do not meet the minimum customer expectation," Eduardo Castro-Wright, a former CEO of Wal-Mart Mexico, acknowledged a month after he was put in charge of the U.S. stores division in September 2005. According to Castro-Wright, 25 percent of all the American stores fall into this bottom-scraping category, double the number of stores rated excellent in the company's monthly consumer-satisfaction surveys.[16]

Finally, the escalating public controversy over Wal-Mart's socio-economic impact on America also has significantly dented its sales. Image matters in retailing more than in most industries, and Wal-Mart's is in tatters. In a national survey taken for *Ad Age* in mid-2005, Wal-Mart ranked second only to Enron Corp. as the "least trustworthy" company in America. (In the same poll, in response to a second question, it ranked second only to General Electric as the country's most trustworthy company, affirming that the United States has polarized around Wal-Mart as sharply as any of the other hot-button issues dividing red state and blue.) By Wal-Mart's own estimate, 40 percent of Americans either are skeptical of the company or hate it outright.[17] For more and more consumers—especially the affluent ones who could benefit the company most—not shopping at Wal-Mart has become a political and moral statement, one made a lot more frequently when a Target or a Costco store is close at hand. "Consumers increasingly have a conscience and are increasingly shifting to competitors," said consultant Burt Flickinger.[18]

Wal-Mart's sales engine is sputtering, but the company's triumphant passage through Hurricane Katrina demonstrated that at least its logistics and distribution prowess is intact. For Scott, Katrina seems to have been the kind of searing, character-testing crisis that the September 11 terrorist attacks were for former New York Mayor Rudy Giuliani. "Katrina was a key personal moment for me," Scott recalled a few weeks after Katrina had devastated the western Gulf Coast, where Wal-Mart dominates retailing with twenty stores in greater New Orleans alone. "The world saw pictures of great suffering and misery. At Wal-Mart, we didn't watch it; we experienced it."[19]

In conspicuous contrast to the federal government, Wal-Mart was well prepared for Katrina, thanks to its Emergency Operations Center. Located just down the road from the home office in Bentonville, the EOC has coped with scores of hurricanes over the years. A full six days before Katrina hit New Orleans, Wal-Mart began shipping bottled water, flashlights, beer, and other essentials to the distribution centers that supplied stores in the storm's projected path. Like everyone else, though, Wal-Mart executives were stunned by the damage Katrina wrought once it made land on August 29. At the hurricane's peak, 126 Wal-Mart stores were without power. The company's reflex response was to make paltry donations of $1 million apiece to the

Red Cross and the Salvation Army and concentrate on safeguarding its stores. But as New Orleans descended into chaos, and as the realization sunk in that some of the thugs terrorizing the city were armed with guns looted from Wal-Mart stores, a shaken Scott called a top-level meeting and decreed that a "measured response" to Katrina was not nearly enough.

Volunteer Wal-Mart truck drivers began hauling emergency supplies to shelters from Texas to Mississippi, often arriving days before relief workers from the Red Cross and the Federal Emergency Management Agency. "We didn't have looting on a mass scale because Wal-Mart showed up with food and water so our people could survive," said the mayor of Kenner, Louisiana, a city of 70,000.[20] The company also donated $17 million in cash to others' relief efforts. In many locations, skeleton crews of Wal-Mart employees fended off looters and distributed merchandise to the needy. A manager in Waveland, Mississippi, cleared a path through her wrecked store with a bulldozer to get at salvageable essentials, which she passed out in the parking lot. By September 16, all but thirteen of Wal-Mart's Gulf Coast stores had reopened. The company had located 97 percent of the 34,000 employees displaced by the storm, provided a third of them with emergency cash, and offered all of them jobs at any Wal-Mart in the United States.

After touring the Houston Astrodome with Scott, former Presidents George H. W. Bush and Bill Clinton singled out Wal-Mart for praise. On *Meet the Press*, the tearful president of the Jefferson Parish section of New Orleans said that if only "the American government responded like Wal-Mart has responded, we wouldn't be in this crisis."[21] Even many die-hard Wal-Mart critics complimented the company, albeit grudgingly. Stacks of fan mail piled up outside of Scott's office while feel-good hurricane tales contributed by employees and outsiders alike proliferated on a company Web log. All in all, this amounted to Wal-Mart's greatest PR triumph ever, and its uplifting impact within the company was all the greater because it had come on the heels of the worst unnatural, man-made disaster in company history: the Coughlin affair.

Lee Scott must still have been somewhere near the top of the emotional roller coaster he rode through 2005 when he got up before an overflow audience at the home office in October and let his long-repressed inner idealist run wild in a speech entitled "Twenty-First Century Leadership." "Katrina asked this critical question, and I want to ask it of you," he said. "What if we used our size and resources to make this country and this earth an even better place for all of us: customers, associates, our children, and generations unborn? What would that mean? Could we do it? Is this consistent with our business model? What if the very things that many people criticize us for—our size and reach—became a trusted friend and ally to all, just as it did in Katrina?"

Just two days earlier, Scott had spoken to an audience of suppliers at a business conference at the University of Arkansas and administered a tongue-lashing straight from the gospel according to the Interfaith Center on Corporate Responsibility or Social Accountability International. "Are you running your factories in a way that promotes environmental sustainability? Are you sourcing from people that causes there to be inclusion and opportunity for women and minority-owned businesses?" Scott demanded before homing in on China. "The factories in China are going to end up having to be held up to the same standards as the factories in the U.S. There will be a day of reckoning for retailers. If somebody wakes up and finds out that children that are down the river from that factory where you save three cents a foot in the cost of garden hose are developing cancers at significant rates so that the American public can save three cents a foot, those things won't be tolerated, and they shouldn't be tolerated."[22]

One can be skeptical about management's desire—and ability—to reform Wal-Mart and still marvel that words like these ever issued from the mouth of one of its CEOs. Was Scott posturing for public relations advantage in these two extraordinary speeches? Yes, undoubtedly, for spinning is part of any CEO's job, especially an embattled one. However, it is probably also true that his view of Wal-Mart's societal role really has evolved beyond the doctrinaire laissez-faire beliefs inherited from Sam Walton and David Glass. Tribulation is a powerful teacher, and over the last two years Scott has been through the sort of ordeal that can indeed change a man.

That said, it would be naïve in the extreme to think that Wal-Mart is going to do anything to benefit generations unborn or anyone else at the expense of its immediate business prospects. The company has taken such a pounding in the court of public opinion of late that for the first time ever it is inclined not to ignore its critics but to try to placate them—some of them anyway, labor unions being the most emphatic exception. As ever, though, it is Wall Street that Wal-Mart seeks to please, for it is only by restoring the company to the stock market's good graces that Scott and his Bentonville cohorts can turn their plethora of out-of-money stock options into personal fortunes and restore the $27 billion in net worth that the Walton family has lost in recent years.

By the end of 2005, Scott was gamely, if belatedly, trying to recast himself from dutiful Walton legatee to bold corporate reformer. "I hope the thing you take with you most of all is that this company, although it is successful . . . is changing today as radically as it ever has in its history," Scott declared in October at Wal-Mart's twelfth annual conference for Wall Street analysts in Bentonville.[23]

Wall-Mart is indeed making substantive changes in some areas, but the retailer certainly is not doing anything as radical as abandoning its low-price sales proposition or downsizing its operations. To the contrary, the company is looking to open as many as 600 new stores in 2006, or about eighty-five more than it added in the previous year. Surprisingly, Wal-Mart managed to get a dozen more Supercenters up and running in 2005 than it had predicted it would, even as the local resistance it encountered across the country doomed scores of projects and put the company far behind schedule in the key state of California. The company managed this feat by putting more building proposals into the hopper than it really needed, anticipating that some would fail to win governmental approval.

In California, Scott acknowledged, Bentonville erred at the start by specifying how many Supercenters—forty—it intended to build. "It was like holding up a red flag to a bull." However, the fourteen Supercenters that Wal-Mart did get into operation in California by the end of 2005 were all "extraordinarily successful . . . some of the best stores we have," he added. Each additional California Supercenter will require winning a lawsuit and will take two to three years to build, but build them Wal-Mart will, the CEO vowed. "It's going to take us much longer to develop California with Supercenters than any of us would have hoped, [but] I think we will get all the stores we need."

The most dramatic changes afoot at Wal-Mart are in the areas of marketing and merchandising. In essence, the company has decided that if it is going to go after middle-income, white-collar, urban-dwelling Americans by emulating Target, it now should do so whole-heartedly. Scott underscored his commitment to taking Wal-Mart upscale by punching a hole in the home office's protective bubble and pulling into Bentonville a handful of experienced outsiders from such sophisticated consumer marketers as McDonald's and Pepsico. John Fleming, whom Scott named Wal-Mart's chief marketing officer in the spring of 2005, had spent nineteen years at Target.

Fleming commissioned a study that divided the U.S. population into three broad categories: the 45 percent of Americans ("loyalists") who shop Wal-Mart stores frequently and in their entirety; the 39 percent ("selective users") who shop far less often and tend to buy only basic commodities when they do; and the 16 percent ("skeptics") who never set foot in a Wal-Mart. Fleming affirmed home-office orthodoxy in insisting that Wal-Mart will never abandon the loyalist. "We will always be the place for low prices," said Fleming, a native Minnesotan who, according to Scott, required heavy persuasion to move to Bentonville. However, it is the selective user who now preoc-cupies Wal-Mart's brain trust. Said Fleming, "We have a tremendous opportunity with this customer to sell them other things, to get them to shop other categories in the store"—particularly in apparel, home furnishings, electronics, and baby goods.[24]

The first fruits of this effort were laid out on Wal-Mart's shelves in time for the year-end shopping crush, including Egyptian-made 400-thread-count sheets for $49, an oversized inflatable snow globe for $129, a Motorola RAZR V3 cell phone for $250, and a Toshiba Libretto laptop for $1,997. Wal-Mart also had changed the look and layout of many of its stores, from the imitation hardwood floors and sleek new fixtures designed to give apparel departments a boutique feel to the massive "digital TV walls" showcasing flat-panel plasma screens. Supercenter interiors are being designed in earth tones, with wider aisles and displays that end a bit above eye level instead of being stacked high with inventory. No doubt Sam Walton would be amazed and probably appalled to see how much capital his company is now investing in the infrastructure of ambience.

Just in time for Christmas, Wal-Mart also introduced to decent notices "Metro 7," its first proprietary line of apparel for "fashion-conscious" women. "The outfits are, in two words: 'Not bad,'" one reviewer opined. "They don't scream Wal-Mart, but they don't whis-per Vera Wang either."[25] To promote Metro 7, Wal-Mart teamed up with teen magazine *ELLEgirl* to sponsor its first-ever fashion show. It was held in New York's Times Square, which is a long way in every sense from Bentonville's town square. The company also signed a two-year contract for 116 pages of advertising in *Vogue*, a sister to the women's fashion magazines Wal-Mart so recently had forced to wear blinders. "Wal-Mart and *Vogue*—three months ago, who would have thunk it," Fleming quipped.[26] Equally startling, Wal-Mart contracted to buy the entire output of an organic cotton farm in Turkey for a new premium line of baby clothes to be introduced in the spring of 2006 as part of "Project Rattle," an attempt to create what senior Wal-Mart style maven Claire Watts calls "the baby store of the future" within the Wal-Mart of the present.[27]

Can a retailer that has defined itself for five decades as America's house of basic bargains now convincingly traffic in fashion, novelty, and discount luxury? Can Wal-Mart restyle itself as "Vogue Mart" without making its loyal blue-collar legions feel unloved and unwanted? These questions will be years in the answering. In the meantime, it's worth noting that for the first time in a long time Wal-Mart is following, not leading, the retail parade. If it is going to get deeper into the wallets of all those "selective users" who now fairly sprint through its aisles to the checkout counters, it is going to have to learn a game that many other retailers already have mastered.

While it chases the upscale American retail dollar with new zeal, Wal-Mart also is pursuing accelerated sales growth abroad, both by adding stores in the nine countries in which it operates and by acquiring its way into new markets. With the United States still accounting for four-fifths of its total sales, Wal-Mart remains much less internationalized than such big foreign competitors as Carrefour SA, which has stores in thirty countries outside its native France, and Metro AG, which is in twenty-eight countries other than Germany, its home. Furthermore, Wal-Mart's foreign business is heavily concentrated in just three countries: Mexico, Canada, and the United Kingdom, which by itself accounted for 47 percent of Wal-Mart's $56 billion in international sales in 2004.

Although Wal-Mart still has miles to go to transform itself into a true multinational retailer, it is heading pretty rapidly in this direction. Sales abroad have risen at a robust 20 percent a year under Scott, double the company's slowing U.S. growth rate. Even so, Bentonville's progress has been erratic, its performance spotty. Only in Mexico, Canada, and Puerto Rico has Wal-Mart been able to establish itself as a potent, solidly profitable operator. Asda, now the UK's number-two supermarket chain, initially thrived after Wal-Mart acquired it in 1999, but lately it has come out on the short end of a price war with Tesco, still the number-one chain by far, and has been shuffling executives and laying off workers. In Japan and Germany—the world's two largest economies after the United States—Wal-Mart has piled up hundreds of millions of dollars in losses in fiercely competitive markets that differ markedly from the United States', each in its own confounding ways.

Basically, Wal-Mart has succeeded to date where it has been able to more or less impose its U.S. model and has struggled to varying degrees everywhere else, including South Korea, Brazil, Argentina, and China, as well as Japan and Germany. The first waves of home-grown executives that Bentonville dispatched abroad were so many missionaries sent to instruct the heathen in the Wal-Mart Way—through translators, of course, since so few of them spoke anything other than English. The sort of arrogance and cultural cloddishness Wal-Mart displayed in Québec have proven especially costly in Germany, which strictly regulates many aspects of retailing—prices included—and allows workers' councils input into all corporate decisions relating to working conditions. "We just walked in and said, 'We're going to lower prices, we're going to add people to the stores, we're going to remodel the stores because inherently that's correct,' and it wasn't," Scott acknowledged in 2001, four years after Wal-Mart entered Germany.[28]

Although Wal-Mart has moved more indigenous managers up into executive positions in many countries in the last few years, the Bentonville-knows-best reflex is not easily suppressed. In the spring of 2005, Wal-Mart caused a furor in Germany by distributing to employees its U.S. ethics manual translated into German. Most American employees wouldn't have thought twice about the manual's caution against supervisor-employee dating. But to Germans, it came off as a presumptuous corporate intrusion into the private lives of employees. Or, as a headline in *Bild*, the largest German newspaper, screamed: "Sex Ban for Wal-Mart Employees." The code also stirred outrage by requiring employees to report violations of company rules by their colleagues or face termination. "To inform anonymously on co-workers reminds most Europeans of the times of dictatorship and repression gone by," commented a German labor confederation.[29] Some months later, Wal-Mart replaced the American woman who had headed its German subsidiary for four years with . . . an Englishman.

Although Wal-Mart has closed a few stores in Germany, Bentonville has repeatedly insisted that it has no intention of pulling out of the country. In Japan, too, the company continues to try to adapt its formula to a country where consumers put more importance on freshness and quality than price. Many Western retailers, Carrefour included, have given up trying to solve the puzzle of Japan, but not Wal-Mart, which gingerly entered the Japanese supermarket business by buying into Tokyo-based Seiyu in 2002. Three years later, Wal-Mart sank another $600 million in Seiyu, lifting its minority stake in the company to a controlling 50.1 percent.

At the same time, Wal-Mart slipped into Central America by purchasing a one-third interest in Central American Retail Holding Corp., a $2-billion-a-year retailer with about 360 supermarkets spread throughout Guatemala, El Salvador, Honduras, Nicaragua, and Costa Rica. When it closes in early 2006, the deal will boost the number of markets in Wal-Mart's international portfolio to fourteen. Bentonville is expected to move next into India, Russia, and Spain, possibly by the end of 2006.

Wal-Mart already has a toehold in what in the long run might prove to be its ultimate growth market—China. With fifty-five stores in China at year-end and plans to open new ones at the modest rate of a dozen or so a year, Wal-Mart has fallen behind other Western rivals, notably Carrefour, which has displayed greater political savvy and willingness to take risks. However, enthusiasm for China is definitely on the upswing in Bentonville. Scott has traveled there with increasing frequency, and in 2004 Wal-Mart's board of directors held a meeting in Shenzhen. "You can build an enormous-sized company in China if you make some fairly aggressive assumptions about what's going to happen to it," David Glass said after returning from Shenzhen. "It's the one place in the world where you could replicate Wal-Mart's success in the U.S."[30]

China's great potential is a function not only of its great size and the sizzling pace of its economy, but also of the odd cultural affinity between the world's largest Communist country and its largest capitalist corporation. While Wal-Mart associates in Germany hide in the bathrooms to avoid the mandatory morning meeting, in China they put on their red shirts and ID badges and cheer like they mean it. "Wal-Mart's management practices have required little tinkering for China," observed one American reporter who toured its Chinese operations in mid-2005. "If anything, the red shirts, mass cheering, incessant pep rallies and veneration of a deceased founder seem characteristics far better suited to the People's Republic than the American South."[31]

China also might well be the one country in the world where Wal-Mart's workers mistrust labor unions as much as Bentonville does. Chinese unions do not negotiate with managements on behalf of workers but rather are arms of the central government that collect dues for the party and monitor the activities of their members. Even so, Wal-Mart resisted growing pressure applied by the All China Federation of Trade Unions, the only entity permitted to organize workers in China. When the Communist Party-controlled federation threatened toward the end of 2005 to sue Wal-Mart unless it permitted unions in its stores, Bentonville apparently concluded that there was no advantage in going to the mat with the ruling party of a country that supplied it with so much of its merchandise. Wal-Mart announced a compromise agreement with Beijing that was largely symbolic but would have rattled the windows and shaken down the walls had it been made in the United States. "Should associates request formation of a union," the company declared, "Wal-Mart China would respect their wishes."[32]

Even as Wal-Mart's aggressive pursuit of new markets at home and abroad alters its business model, the company is holding tight to the status quo when it comes to labor. Change is risky virtually by definition. But Bentonville's if-it-ain't-broke-don't-fix-it attitude toward its workforce could well be exposing the company to greater risk of failure than all of its bold new market-expanding ventures combined.

The best efforts of the David Glass Technology Center notwithstanding, retailing remains a touchy-feely, improvisatory sort of business—a reality that Wal-Mart acknowledges every time it airs one of its television commercials with the tagline, "Our people make the difference." Given the dismal state of so many Wal-Mart stores, this is starting to sound more like blame than praise. Castro-Wright's disclosure that fully 25 percent of Wal-Mart's U.S. stores fail to meet even minimum customer expectations amounts to an admission that the company's workforce is broke after all, since customer satisfaction correlates closely with what the company calls "associate engagement." The financial consequences of this breakdown in employee morale are staggering; according to Castro-Wright, the rate of sales growth at Wal-Mart's 800 best-performing stores is ten times, or 1,000 percent, greater than the 800 worst-performing outlets.[33]

Wal-Mart is running a serious risk of exacerbating this problem by upgrading the quality of its merchandise without also upgrading the quality of its staff. Wal-Mart, as always, is relying heavily on price to close a sale, in defiance of the general rule in retailing that the more expensive and technically complex a product, the more salesmanship required to move it off the shelves. Wal-Mart would have to pay up to attract clerks as knowledgeable about consumer electronics as Best Buy's or as hip to next season's new look as H&M's. However, Bentonville is categorically unwilling to jeopardize its long-standing labor-cost advantage by loosening the purse strings on payday. "Even slight overall adjustments to wages [would] eliminate our thin profit margin," Scott insists.[34] To the contrary, the company promised Wall Street in mid-2005 that it would redouble its efforts to squeeze labor costs.

Even as half of its staff quits every year, Wal-Mart still promulgates the threadbare myth that its workers are so fairly treated by their "partners" in management that they just don't need outside representation. When asked point-blank by a *BusinessWeek* reporter in the fall of 2005 why Wal-Mart is anti-union, Scott replied, "Gosh, I don't think of us as anti-union. I think of us as having a company where we have an open-door policy. In this company, you can talk to . . . whoever you want to about what is happening. You don't have to go to a third party and say, 'Here is my issue.'"[35] The kindest interpretation of Scott's comment—that the CEO was prone to wishful thinking—was obliterated a few weeks later when the contents of a confidential company memo laying out Bentonville's cold calculus of wages and health-care benefits was splashed across the pages of the *New York Times* and other newspapers.

As described by the memo's author, Susan Chambers, Wal-Mart's executive vice president for benefits, Scott's associates were a sorry lot indeed. For a start, they were getting sicker at a much faster rate than most Americans, especially when it came to obesity-related diseases. From 2002 to 2005, the prevalence of diabetes among Wal-Mart workers rose by 10 percent and of coronary artery disease by 6 percent, compared with 3 percent and 1 percent, respectively, for the U.S. population as a whole. And yet less than half of all associates were covered under the company health plan and one-fifth had no health insurance at all. Workers' children were especially vulnerable, with 46 percent of them either uninsured or covered only by Medicaid. Add it all up and Wal-Mart employees on average were spending 8 percent of their income on health care, double the national average.

However, the plight of Wal-Mart's workers was of secondary concern to Chambers, whose aim in writing the memo was to propose changes in Wal-Mart's "benefits strategy" that would rein in the company's health-care outlays without doing further damage to its reputation. Wal-Mart's "increasingly well-organized and well-funded critics . . . have selected healthcare as their main avenue of attack," stated Chambers, adding that "our critics are correct in some of their observations. Specifically, our coverage is expensive for low-income families, and Wal-Mart has a significant percentage of associates and their children on public assistance."[36]

The most inflammatory aspect of Chambers' memo was its implicit denigration of employee longevity at a company that claims to prize loyalty. "The cost of an associate with 7 years of tenure is almost 55% more than the cost of an associate with 1 year of tenure, yet there is no difference in his or her productivity," she wrote. "Moreover, because we pay an associate more in salary and benefits as his or her tenure increases, we are pricing that associate out of the labor market, increasing the likelihood that he or she will stay with Wal-Mart." In the revelatory glow cast by Chambers' comments, the Wal-Mart cheer now looks not only archaic but downright sinister. A company that forces its employees to make daily affirmations of loyalty even as it devises schemes to induce long-timers to leave can only be described as Orwellian.

In the fall of 2005, Wal-Mart remade a second-floor conference room in its Bentonville headquarters into a political-style "war room" with the aim of escalating its public relations campaign to win the hearts and minds of the American consumer. It was set up after the company sought out Edelman Public Relations, a top Washington-based firm that assigned two of its senior executives to the Wal-Mart account: Michael Deaver, formerly communications director for the Reagan White House, and Leslie Dach, one of Bill Clinton's senior media advisers. Among the staffers Edelman dispatched to full-time duty in Bentonville were a half-dozen former political operatives, including Jonathan Adasek, a top director of national delegate strategy for the 2004 Kerry campaign, and Terry Nelson, the national political director of the 2004 Bush campaign.[37]

Wal-Mart's creation of its very own "rapid response" PR swat team was another of those recent developments that would have perplexed and annoyed Sam Walton, who essentially believed that corporate image-polishing was a waste of time and money. Scott had every hope of maintaining Wal-Mart as one of America's most insular public companies, but was forced out of his Bentonville fortress by the maelstrom of criticism that has rocked the company over the last few years. "We used to believe you could run the company out of Bentonville, Arkansas, and if you took care of your business, your employees and your customers, everyone would leave us alone," Scott said in the fall of 2004. "What we're trying to do now is reach out."[38]

After greatly boosting its spending on image advertising and enlarging its in-house PR staff several orders of magnitude, Wal-Mart turned to Edelman for help in coping with a fresh assault launched by its most determined natural enemy: organized labor. Having folded the classic unionization campaign led by Mike Leonard from 1999 into 2004, the United Food and Commercial Workers Union resumed its war against Wal-Mart in the spring of 2005 with a new strategy and a host of new allies. The UFCW joined with the Service Employees International Union to form an anti–Wal-Mart coalition that included some fifty environmental, student, community, and women's organizations.

The coalition in turn spawned two Washington-based pressure groups, Wal-Mart Watch and WakeUpWal-Mart.com, that incorporated the latest techniques of political campaigning in the Internet age to what amounted to the PR equivalent of a guerrilla war against America's largest company. Both groups relied heavily on politicos, though not in the bipartisan spirit of Edelman's Wal-Mart team. Paul Blank, campaign director of WakeUpWal-Mart.com, was political director of the Howard Dean presidential campaign, while Wal-Mart Watch's staff includes Jim Jordan, ex-director of the Kerry campaign. Between them, these two union-financed groups have signed up a few hundred thousand members across the country and even penetrated Wal-Mart's home office. An anonymous Bentonville staffer slipped the Chambers memo into a plain manila envelope and sent it to Wal-Mart Watch, which passed it on to the *Times*.

Even before the Chambers fiasco, Wal-Mart Watch and WakeUp-Wal-Mart.com had succeeded in putting Scott and company squarely on the defensive. "Today, we're the focus of one of the most organized, most sophisticated, most expensive corporate campaigns ever launched against a single company," said Scott in sounding the alarm at Wal-Mart's 2005 annual meeting. "A coalition of labor unions and others are spending $25 million to do whatever they have to do to damage this company. That's a lot of money, that's a lot of firepower, scattered around a lot of territory."[39]

Having finally manned full PR battle stations, Wal-Mart now is spinning its story as aggressively as any candidate for political office ever has—and with far more money at its disposal than any union or public interest group can muster. Make no mistake, Wal-Mart today is not a chastened giant looking to restore its reputation by confessing its sins and accommodating its critics. "Our goal is not to polish our image," Scott said. "Our goal is to have the world understand who we are."[40]

That said, the ordeal of engaging outsiders in debate and discussion has caused Wal-Mart to redefine its self-interest in ways that appear to be changing it for the better. For a start, the company is more inclined to hire outsiders to fill senior management jobs—and less likely to treat executives who leave to work elsewhere as traitors. Wal-Mart also has begun to decentralize its rather imperial real estate office in Bentonville, moving employees into new offices in cities across the country to interact directly with local officials on issues of store location and design instead of hiding behind consultants. The company is showing more flexibility in designing its stores to blend in better with surrounding architecture and to consume less land. Wal-Mart even has gone so far as to initiate out-of-court settlement talks with people who sue the company, instead of automatically hunkering down for all-out legal warfare.

Wal-Mart made a surprisingly credible attempt to elevate the national debate over its economic impact above partisanship in sponsoring a by-invitation-only academic conference in Washington in November 2005. Ten papers were presented, only one of which was financed by Wal-Mart itself. Half of the studies were mildly or strongly critical of the socioeconomic effects of Wal-Mart's business model. "We understood some conclusions might not be favorable," said Bob McAdam, the company's vice president for corporate affairs. "But if everything was one-sided, it would not be credible."[41]

Even more surprising, Scott appears to have emerged an intriguing shade of green as a result of extensive discussions over the past year with left-leaning environmental groups. In the same "Twenty-First Century Leadership" speech in which he invoked Hurricane Katrina as a higher calling, Scott laid out a new corporate environmental agenda so broad and progressive that it would not have sounded out of place coming from Al Gore. "Environmental problems are *our* problems," Scott declared. "The supply of natural products (fish, food, water) can only be sustained if the ecosystems that provide them are sustained and protected. There are not two worlds out there, a Wal-Mart world and some other world."[42]

What has changed is not Wal-Mart's politics, but rather the economics of energy. That is, the soaring cost of oil and its derivatives has created a potentially massive opportunity for the company to do what it does best: save money by devising new ways to stretch a dollar. (Taking on a greenish tinge also should help the company with its wooing of the very customers to whom it is pitching iPod Nanos and luxury sheet sets.) In his speech, Scott committed the company to investing $500 million a year over the next few years to improve the fuel efficiency of its truck fleet by 25 percent, reduce the solid waste produced in its U.S. stores by 25 percent, and create a new store prototype that would consume 25 percent to 30 percent less energy and lower greenhouse gases by 30 percent. In addition, Wal-Mart vowed to press its vendors to reduce waste in packaging, do more recycling, and cut their use of pesticides and other pollutants in everything they do.

Environmental groups reacted carefully, offering qualified praise while saying that they wanted to make certain the company carried through on its new initiatives in publicly accountable ways before clapping Scott on the back. "If they do these things, it's not green-scamming," said Carl Pope, executive director of the Sierra Club, which is a founding member of the UFCW's new anti–Wal-Mart coalition. "If they did what they say they will, it would be a major shift."[43]

In the same speech in which he laid out his environmental manifesto, Scott also departed radically from Walton-era orthodoxy in declaring Wal-Mart's support for an increase in the federal minimum wage of $5.15. For a union-hating company whose founder spent the first decade of his career playing fast and loose with the minimum wage to suddenly come out in favor of one of organized labor's pet proposals seemed like apostasy. "Is Wal-Mart going wobbly?" asked the *Washington Post*.[44] No, it isn't, at least not in the sense of becoming softhearted. But Scott's seemingly out-of-the-blue endorsement of long-stalled legislation to boost the minimum wage was a cry for help from a company that is beginning to realize that it has backed itself into a corner by re-creating a vast swath of the world economy in its low-price, low-wage image.

Despite all the money that Wal-Mart boasts of saving them, the working-class "loyalists" on whom the company's immediate fortunes still hinge are hurting financially. "We can see first-hand at Wal-Mart how many of our customers are struggling to get by . . ." Scott said. "Our customers simply don't have the money to buy basic necessities between pay checks." Why not? Their living expenses are rising much faster than their wages, which aren't really rising at all. Or, as Scott discreetly put it, "There are global forces at work flattening pay scales." Yes, and one of them—the most powerful such corporate force by far—is called Wal-Mart.

It is well within Wal-Mart's own power to raise the living standards of the American worker by raising its own minimal wages and benefits. Despite the fresh thinking going on in Bentonville on some issues, elevating the hourly wage scale is out of the question. "Because we are so big, people forget that we have to compete," Scott said. More to the point, because Wal-Mart is so big and so obsessively focused on parlaying low prices into market share, it has forced both its competitors and its vendors to dance to its single-minded tune, dragging down wages with prices.

Even as it moves up the merchandise food chain into higher-priced, higher-quality goods, Wal-Mart continues to measure its corporate manhood by the gap between its prices and those of its competitors. It simply knows no other way to compete and seems no more capable of altering its path now than a hammer can avoid the nail it was made to pound. In calling for a hike in the minimum wage, Wal-Mart in effect is asking Congress to bolster the spending power of its customers at the expense of the employers who pay even lower wages than it does. (There are some.) Congress almost certainly will not comply, as long as the Republican Party to which Wal-Mart contributes so heavily controls every branch of the federal government. Today, nearly half a century since Sam Walton opened that first store in Rogers, Arkansas, it is far from certain that even Wal-Mart can thrive in a Wal-Mart world.

NOTES

CHAPTER ONE: THE CASE AGAINST WAL-MART

1. Jon P. Goodman, "President's message," www.townhall-la.org.

2. Lee Scott, "Wal-Mart and California: A Key Moment in Time for American Capitalism," February 23, 2005, 1. Available at www.walmartfacts.com/docs/981_leescottspeechattownhall2-23-05_1492524199.pdf.

3. Ibid., 2.

4. Ibid., 7.

5. Al Lewis, "Car Techs Get Crash Course on Unionizing," *Denver Post*, February 13, 2004.

6. Arindrajit Dube, Barry Eidlin and Bill Lester, "Impact of Wal-Mart Growth on Earnings throughout the Retail Sector in Urban and Rural Counties," Unpublished paper, University of California at Berkeley, 2005.

7. David Neumark, Junfu Zhang and Stephen Ciccarella, "The Effects of Wal-Mart on Local Labor Markets," unpublished paper, available at www.globalinsight.com/public-Download/genericContent/neumark.pdf.

8. Michael Sasso, "Critics Push Wal-Mart on Health Coverage," *Tampa Tribune*, June 2, 2005.

9. Steven Greenhouse and Michael Barbaro, "Wal-Mart Memo Suggests Ways to Cut Employee Benefit Costs," *New York Times*, October 26, 2005.

10. Lewis, op. cit.

11. Steven Greenhouse, "In-House Audit Says Wal-Mart Violated Labor Laws," *New York Times*, January 13, 2004.

12. The five are Home Depot, Kroger, Target, Costco, and Dell Computer.

13. Lee Scott, "Twenty-First Century Leadership," October 24, 2005, http: walmart-stores.com/Files/21st%20Century%20Leadership.pdf.

14. Mark Shaffer, "Flagstaff Divided on Big-box Store," *Arizona Republic*, May 15, 2005. For election results, see Shaffer, "Wal-Mart Backers Win a Squeaker in Flagstaff," *Arizona Republic*, May 18, 2005.

15. Interview with author, September 22, 2004. Birdsall is a vice president of development for Regency Centers, a large national owner and builder of shopping centers anchored by grocery stores.

16. Interview with author, March 1, 2004.

17. John M. Broder, "Voters in Los Angeles Suburb Say No to a Big Wal-Mart," *New York Times*, April 8, 2004.

18. Michael Barbaro, "Wal-Mart Chief Defends Closing Unionized Store," *Washington Post*, February 11, 2005.

19. Richard C. Bradford, "Retail: The Wal-Mart Effect," *McKinsey Quarterly*, I, 2002.

20. Peter J. Solomon, "A Lesson from Wal-Mart," *Washington Post*, March 28, 2004.

21. Charles Fishman, "The Wal-Mart You Don't Know," *Fast Company*, December 2003.

22. Tim Johnson and Rick Rothacker, "Deal Seen as Solid for China, Iffy for BofA," *Charlotte Observer*, June 18, 2005.

23. Ted C. Fishman, *China Inc.*, 154.

24. Jerry Useem, "One Nation Under Wal-Mart," *Fortune*, March 23, 2003.

CHAPTER TWO: THEY CALL ME MR. SAM

1. Robert Slater, *The Wal-Mart Decade*, 78.

2. Sandra S. Vance and Roy V. Scott, *Wal-Mart: A History of Sam Walton's Retailing Phenomenon*, 51.

3. Vance Randolph, *The Ozarks: An American Survival of Primitive Society*, 306.

4. Sam Walton with John Huey, *Sam Walton: Made in America*, 112.

5. Ibid., 146. The remark was by John Walton.

6. Ibid., 146.

7. Randolph, op. cit., 303–4.

8. "An American Original," *Chain Store Age Executive*, May 1992.

9. Bethany E. Moreton, "It Came from Bentonville: The Agrarian Origins of Wal-Mart Culture," 59–60, in *Wal-Mart: The Face of 21st Century Capitalism*, Nelson Lichtenstein (ed.).

10. *History of Laclede, Camden, Dallas, Webster, Wright, Texas, Pulaski, Phelps and Dent Counties*, Missouri, 885.

11. Milton D. Rafferty, *The Ozarks: Land and Life*, 246.

12. Walton with Huey, op. cit., 3.

13. Vance H. Trimble, *Sam Walton: The Inside Story of America's Richest Man*, 18.

14. Austin Teutsch, *The Sam Walton Story*, 28.

15. Ibid., 11.

16. Trimble, op. cit., 22.

17. Walton with Huey, op. cit., 14.

18. Ibid., 15.

19. Ibid., 17.

20. Ibid., 69.

21. Ibid., 30.

22. Ibid., 31.

23. Ibid., 32.

24. Ibid., 34.

25. Ibid., 33.

26. Ibid., 175.

27. Moreton, op. cit., 64, 70.

28. Michael B. Dugan, *Arkansas Odyssey*, 477.

29. Walton with Huey, op. cit,, 50.

30. Ibid., 42.

31. Ibid., 42.

32. Trimble, op. cit., 100.

33. Walton with Huey, op. cit., 45, 46.

34. Ibid., 160–61.

CHEERLEADER-IN-CHIEF

1. John Huey, "America's Most Successful Merchant," *Fortune,* September 25, 1991.

CHAPTER THREE: ROCKEFELLER OF THE OZARKS

1. Vance Trimble, *Sam Walton*, 47–48.

2. Susan Reed, "Talk About a Local Boy Making Good! Sam Walton, the King of Wal-Mart, Is America's Second-Richest Man," *People*, December 19, 1983.

3. "The History of Wal-Mart," Walmartstores.com video library.

4. Walton credited Bob Bogle, the first manager of his store in Bentonville.

5. Trimble, op. cit., 91.

6. Sam Walton with John Huey, *Sam Walton: Made in America*, 3.

7. Ibid., xiii.

8. Richard Tedlow, *Giants of Enterprise*, 316.

9. Ron Chernow, *Titan*, 18.

10. Walton with Huey, op. cit., 29.

11. Chernow, op. cit., 48.

12. "Sam Walton: Bargain Billionaire," from the *Biography* series on the Arts & Entertainment network, December 2, 1997.

13. Chernow, op. cit., 174.

14. Walton with Huey, op. cit., 50–51.

15. Ibid., 5.

16. Trimble, op. cit., 147.

17. Walton with Huey, op. cit., 127.

18. Sharon Reiter, "CEO of the Decade: Sam M. Walton," *Financial World*, April 4, 1989.

19. "Small-Town Hit: Sam Walton's Wizardry," *Time*, May 23, 1983.

20. Nelson Lichtenstein, "Wal-Mart: A Template for Twenty-First Century Capitalism," in *Wal-Mart: The Face of Twenty-First Century Capitalism*, 18.

21. Walton with Huey, op. cit., 169.

22. Bethany E. Moreton, "It Came from Bentonville: The Agrarian Origins of Wal-Mart Culture," 79, in *Wal-Mart: The Face of Twenty-First Century Capitalism*.

23. Michael B. Dugan, *Arkansas Odyssey*, 496.

24. Austin Teutsch, *The Sam Walton Story*, 115.

25. John Huey, "Will Wal-Mart Take Over the World?" *Fortune*, January 30, 1989.

26. Walton with Huey, op. cit., 127–28.

27. The richest of them all might have been Sue Cox, who worked as a fabric cutter at the store in Harrison from the day it opened in 1964 until 2004, when she retired with $17 million (the sum included the retirement nest egg of her late husband, also a Wal-Marter).

28. Walton with Huey, op. cit., 131.

29. Huey, op. cit.

30. Walton with Huey, op. cit., 159.

31. Ibid., 159–60.

32. Ibid., 170.

33. Ibid., 52.

34. Stephen Taub, "Gold Winner," *Financial World*, April 15, 1986.

35. Huey, op. cit.

36. Walton with Huey, op. cit., 50–51.

37. Bob Ortega, *In Sam We Trust*, 62.

38. Walton with Huey, op. cit., 91.

39. Wendy Zellner, "O.K., So He's Not Sam Walton," *BusinessWeek*, March 16, 1992.

40. Ortega, op. cit., 130.

41. Walton with Huey, op. cit., 80.

42. "A Discounter Sinks Deep Roots in Small-Town U.S.A.," *BusinessWeek*, November 5, 1979.

43. Walton with Huey, op. cit., 199.

44. Don Soderquist, *The Wal*Mart Way*, 16.

45. Susan Zimmerman, "Wal-Mart Opens First Supercenter," *Supermarket News*, March 7, 1988, 1.

46. Sam Walton with John Huey, *Made in America*, 8.

47. Ortega, op. cit., 214.

48. Interview by author, September 20, 2004.

49. Wendy Zellner, "Mr. Sam's Experiment Is Alive and Well," *BusinessWeek*, April 20, 1992.

50. Brent Schlender, "Wal-Mart's $288 Billion Meeting," *Fortune*, April 18, 2005.

51. Bill Saporito, "A Week Aboard the Wal-Mart Express," *Fortune,* August 24, 1992.

52. Walton with Huey, op. cit., 163.

53. Ibid., 116.

54. Ortega, op. cit., 220.

55. Christiana Cheakalos, "More Than Just a Billionaire; Residents of Arkansas Town Say Goodbye to a Dear Friend, Sam Walton," *Atlanta Journal and Constitution,* April 8, 1992.

CHAPTER FOUR: SO HELP THEM, SAM

1. Interview by author and Wendy Zellner, September 16, 2003.

2. Hank Gilman, "The Most Underrated CEO Ever," *Fortune,* March 21, 2004.

3. Robert Slater, *The Wal-Mart Decade,* 87.

4. Sandra J. Skrovan, "Wal-Mart 2010," *Retail Forward,* December 2004, 30.

5. Bill Thomas is a pseudonym. Ellen Israel Rosen, *The Quality of Work at Wal-Mart,* unpublished paper, 7.

6. Sam Walton with John Huey, *Sam Walton: Made in America,* 137–38.

7. Rosen, op. cit., 27.

8. Walton with Huey, op. cit., 137.

9. Ibid., 137.

10. Interview by author, May 25, 2005.

11. Bob Ortega, "Life Without Sam: What Does Wal-Mart Do If Stock Drop Cuts into Worker Morale?" *Wall Street Journal,* January 4, 1995.

12. Andrea Harter, "Billionaire Bud Walton Dies at 73, Co-Founded Wal-Mart," *Arkansas Democrat-Gazette,* March 22, 1995.

13. Ann Zimmerman, "Wal-Mart Boss's Unlikely Role: Corporate Defender-in-Chief," *Wall Street Journal,* July 26, 2005.

14. Wendy Zellner, "Someday, Lee, Wal-Mart May All Be Yours," *BusinessWeek,* November 15, 1999.

15. Ann Zimmerman, op. cit.

16. Mike Troy, "A Tribute to Tom Coughlin: A Legacy of Leadership," *Drug Store News,* February 14, 2005.

17. Alex Daniels, "Thomas Martin Coughlin," *Arkansas Democrat-Gazette,* December 29, 2002.

18. Liza Featherstone, *Selling Women Short,* 67.

19. Bob Ortega, *In Sam We Trust,* 210.

20. Interview for author by Chris Lydgate, October 4, 2005.

21. Barbara Ehrenreich, *Nickel and Dimed: On (Not) Getting By in America,* 184.

22. John Dicker, *The United States of Wal-Mart,* 30.

23. Lee Scott, "Wal-Mart and California: A Key Moment in Time for American Capitalism," 4.

24. Kris Hudson, "Wal-Mart Investors Fret Over Costs," *Wall Street Journal,* October 25, 2005.

25. Interview for author by Millie Org, October 22, 2005.

26. Interview for author by Millie Org, October 17, 2005.

27. Ellen Rosen, "How to Squeeze More out of a Penny," *Wal-Mart: The Face of Twenty-First Century Capitalism,* 248–49. Kate Moroney is a pseudonym for a worker currently employed by Wal-Mart.

28. Steven Greenhouse, "In-House Audit Says Wal-Mart Violated Labor Laws, *New York Times,* January 13, 2004.

29. Steven Greenhouse, "Labor Dept. Is Rebuked Over Pact With Wal-Mart," *New York Times,* November 1, 2005. Also see Greenhouse, "Wal-Mart Agrees to Pay Fine in Child Labor Case," *New York Times,* February 15, 2005.

30. Ann Zimmerman, "Big Retailers Face Overtime Suits As Bosses Do More 'Hourly' Work," *Wall Street Journal,* May 26, 2004, A1.

31. Steve Greenhouse, "Workers Assail Night Lock-In by Wal-Mart," *New York Times,* January 18, 2004.

32. Steven Greenhouse, "Middlemen in the Low-Wage Economy," *New York Times,* December 25, 2003.

33. Steven Greenhouse, "Illegally in U.S., and Never a Day Off at Wal-Mart," *New York Times,* November 5, 2003.

34. See Ann Zimmerman, "After Huge Raid on Illegals, Wal-Mart Fires Back at U.S.," *Wall Street Journal,* December 19, 2003.

35. Steven Greenhouse, "Wal-Mart to Pay U.S. $11 Million in Lawsuit on Immigrant Workers," *New York Times,* March 19, 2005.

36. *Victor Zavala et al. v. Wal-Mart Stores,* U.S. District Court, New Jersey, 03-Civ-5309 (JAG), First Amended Class Action Complaint and Jury Demand, p. 21.

37. Brad Seligman, "Patriarchy at the Checkout Counter: The Dukes v. Wal-Mart Stores, Inc. Class-Action Suit," in *Wal-Mart: The Face of Twenty-First Century Capitalism,* 236–37.

38. Scott, op. cit., 3.

39. Richard R. Drogin, "Statistical Analysis of Gender Patterns in Wal-Mart Workforce, 2003, 17. www.impactfund.org.

40. Reed Abelson, "Suing Wal-Mart but Still Hoping to Move Up," *New York Times,* June 23, 2004.

41. Dana Knight, "Wal-Mart Plaintiff Tells Story," *Indianapolis Star,* August 22, 2004.

42. 2005 Wal-Mart Stores Proxy Statement, 16. http://www.walmartstores.com/Files/2005Proxy.pdf.

43. Bill Bowden and Lance Turner, "Wal-Mart Tells Employees to Take a Break," Arkansasbusiness.com Daily Report, June 4, 2004.

44. "Wal-Mart Details Progress Toward Becoming a Leader in Employment Practices," company press release dated June 4, 2004.

45. Edward Klump, "Retailer's Insurance Coverage Analyzed," *Arkansas Democrat-Gazette,* October 25, 2005.

46. Susan Chambers, "Supplemental Benefits Documentation," Board of Directors

Retreat FY06. http://www.walmartfacts.com/docs/1436_benefitswhitepaper_352137437. pdf.

47. Abigail Goldman and Lisa Girion, "Wal-Mart Memo Blurs Its Message on Benefits," *Los Angeles Times*, October 27, 2005.

AMERICA'S FIRST FAMILY OF DISCOUNTING

1. Based on a share price of $49.04, on November 10, 2005.

2. July 2005 estimate, *The World Factbook 2005*, the Central Intelligence Agency.

3. Based on a dividend of 60 cents per share, as voted by the board of directors on March 3, 2005.

4. Community Publishers Web site: http://www.commpub.com/history.html.

5. Ibid.

6. Evan Silverstein, "Wyoming Church Holds Memorial Service for Wal-Mart Heir," Presbyterian News Service, July 1, 2005 http://www.pcusa.org/pcnews/2005/05351.htm.

7. Jim Hopkins, "Wal-Mart Heirs Pour Riches into Reforming Education," *USA Today*, March 11, 2004.

CHAPTER FIVE: WAL-MART'S WAR AGAINST THE UNIONS

1. Adam Fifield, "She Was Fired from Wal-Mart for 'Insubordination,'" *Philadelphia Inquirer*, December 26, 2003.

2. Karen Olsson, "Up Against Wal-Mart," *Mother Jones*, March/April 2003.

3. Sam Walton with John Huey, *Sam Walton: Made in America*, 129–30.

4. Bob Ortega, *In Sam We Trust*, 106–7. See also Rhonda Owen, "Wal-Mart Employees Seek Teamsters Union," *Arkansas Democrat*, October 11, 1981.

5. Ibid.

6. Steven Greenhouse, "At a Small Shop in Colorado, Wal-Mart Beats a Union Once More," *New York Times*, February 26, 2005.

7. Leonard Page, "New Directions for the Next National Labor Relations Board," 2001 L. Rev. M. S. U.-D.C.L, Vol. 4: 1063.

8. Unless otherwise noted, all of Lehman's quotes in this chapter are from interviews with the author on September 19 and 20, 2004, or March 18–20, 2005.

9. Ron Browning, "Class Consideration Given to Wal-Mart Case," *The Indiana Lawyer*, March 12, 2003.

10. Although the restraining order applied nationwide, it was authorized by a local Benton County judge named Donald Huffman. Judge Huffman was forced to recuse himself after the UFCW complained that he owned $700,000 in Wal-Mart stock. Even so, the TRO remained in force for eight months, until it finally was dissolved by an Arkansas state court judge in Fort Smith.

11. Interview with author, February 13, 2004.

12. Interview with author, August 23, 2005.

13. Interview with author, September 19, 2004.

14. The UFCW embarrassed Bentonville into overruling Roberts on the sticker issue

by encouraging Sam's Club customers to send protest e-mails directly to Lee Scott. Jay Allen, Wal-Mart's senior vice president for corporate affairs, crafted a statement that avoided any mention of the UFCW. "We are mindful about what our associates put on their name badges, as we want our customers to see clearly the name of the associate serving them," Allen wrote. "Thus, we encouraged our associates to utilize other parts of their work attire to show their patriotism."

15. Cora Daniels, "Unions vs. Wal-Mart," *Fortune,* May 3, 2004.

16. Decision of Keltner W. Locke, Administrative Law Judge, National Labor Relations Board, Division of Judges, Atlanta Branch Office, JD (ATL)-37-03.

17. Steven Greenhouse, "Trying to Overcome Embarrassment, Labor Opens a Drive to Organize Wal-Mart," *New York Times,* November 8, 2002.

CHAPTER SIX: WHEN WAL-MART COMES TO TOWN

1. Kenneth E. Stone, "Impact of the Wal-Mart Phenomenon on Rural Communities," published in Increasing Understanding of Public Problems and Policies (Farm Foundation), 2.

2. Sam Walton with John Huey, *Sam Walton: Made in America,* 182–83.

3. Basker's shopping list consisted of a bottle of Bayer aspirin, a carton of Winston cigarettes, a two-liter bottle of Coca Cola, a box of Tide, a box of Cascade, two different-size boxes of Kleenex, a bottle of Johnson's baby shampoo, a bottle of Alberto VO5, a tube of Crest or Colgate, an Arrow man's dress shirt, a pair of Levi's 501-505 jeans, a pair of Docker men's khakis, a three-pack of Fruit of the Loom briefs, and a three-pack of the lowest priced boy's briefs in the store.

4. Emek Basker, "Selling a Cheaper Mousetrap: Wal-Mart's Effect on Retail Prices," University of Missouri Working Paper No. 04–01, March 2005, 31.

5. N. Currie, A. Jain, "Supermarket Pricing Survey," UBS Global Equity Research, 2002.

6. Emek Basker, "Job Creation or Destruction: Labor-Mart Effects of Wal-Mart Expansion," University of Missouri, March 2004, 17.

7. David Neumark, Junfu Zhang, and Stephen Ciccarella, "The Effects of Wal-Mart on Local Labor Markets," unpublished paper, November 2005, www.globalinsight.com/publicDownload/genericContent/neumark.pdf.

8. Kenneth E. Stone, "Impact of Wal-Mart Stores and other Mass Merchandisers in Iowa, 1983–1993," *Economic Development Review,* Spring 1995, 6.

9. Interview with author, September 15, 2005.

10. Jon Bowermaster, "When Wal-Mart Comes To Town," *New York Times,* April 2, 1989.

11. Stone, "Impact of the Wal-Mart Phenomenon on Rural Communities," 14.

12. Shortly after Stone released his first study in 1988, he appeared before a Chamber of Commerce group in Ottumwa, where Wal-Mart had just opened a store. The manager of the store interrupted Stone's speech from the floor, angrily accusing him of fabricating

his figures. A few days later, he again passed through Ottumwa and decided to check out the new store incognito. Stone removed his tie, left his suit jacket in the car, yet was recognized by the manager the moment he walked through the door. "Say," the manager said threateningly. "I told Mr. Sam about you." Stone did not doubt it, for he had already fielded a barrage of complaints from Bentonville, not from Sam himself, but from Rob Walton, Wal-Mart's general counsel.

13. Kenneth E. Stone, "The Effect of Wal-Mart Stores on Businesses in Host Towns and Surrounding Towns in Iowa," Iowa State University, November 9, 1988, 1.

14. Interview with author, September 15, 2005.

15. Stone, "Impact of Wal-Mart Stores and Other Mass Merchandisers in Iowa," 1983–1993, 25.

16. Interview with author, September 15, 2005.

17. Bob Ortega, *In Sam We Trust,* 166.

18. Philip Matters and Anna Purinton, "Shopping for Subsidies: How Wal-Mart Uses Taxpayer Money to Finance Its Never-Ending Growth," Good Jobs First, May 2004, 7.

19. Ibid., 17.

20. Bowermaster, "When Wal-Mart Comes to Town."

21. Walton with Huey, op. cit., 110.

22. Steve Bishop, "Death of a Town," *Dallas Morning News,* January 26, 1992.

23. Peter T. Kilborn, "When Wal-Mart Pulls Out, What's Left?" *New York Times,* March 5, 1995.

24. Eve M. Kahn, "Thinking Inside the Big Box," *New York Times,* May 12, 2005.

25. Dennis Romero, "Walling Off Wal-Mart," *City Beat,* December 24, 2003.

26. Gayle Pollard-Terry, "Rallying Around Wal-Mart," *Los Angeles Times,* April 24, 2004.

27. Interview with author, April 15, 2004.

28. Fox owned the Fox Theatre at 115 North Market and United Artists owned the United Artists Inglewood Theater at 148 North Market. Fox took over the UA theater and operated both for a time.

29. Nancy Cleeland and Abigail Goldman, "The Wal-Mart Effect; Grocery Unions Battle to Stop Invasion of the Giant Stores," *Los Angeles Times,* November 25, 2003.

30. Interview with author, April 5, 2004.

31. Jessica Garrison and Sara Lin, "Wal-Mart vs. Inglewood—a Warm-Up for L.A. Fight," *Los Angeles Times,* April 2, 2005.

32. Alex Vega, "Wal-Mart Employs Campaign-Style Tactics to Promote Its Expansion," Associated Press, April 26, 2004.

33. V. Dion Hayes, "Wal-Mart Tries End Run Around Balky City," *Chicago Tribune,* January 12, 2004.

34. "A Big-Box Ballot Bully," *Los Angeles Times,* March 29, 2004.

35. Interview with author, April 5, 2004.

36. Interview with author, April 2, 2004.

37. Interview with author, April 2, 2004.

38. Interview with author, April 2, 2004.

39. Erin Aubry Kaplan, "Welcome to Inglewood—Leave Your Aspirations Behind," *LA Weekly*, July 22, 2005.

40. Ibid.

41. "What would Dr. Martin Luther King, Jr. have said about Wal*Mart," pamphlet produced by the Los Angeles County Federation of Labor, AFL-CIO.

42. Recorded by author, April 5, 2004.

43. Recorded by author on April 5, 2005.

44. Jessica Garrison, Abigail Goldman, and David Pierson, "Wal-Mart to Push Southland Agenda," *Los Angeles Times*, April 8, 2004.

45. Earl Ofari Hutchinson, "Inglewood Opens the Wal-Mart Wars," *Los Angeles Times*, April 8, 2004, B15.

46. Constance L. Hays, "At Wal-Mart, The New Word Is Compromise," *New York Times*, September 9, 2004.

47. Ann Zimmerman, "Defending Wal-Mart," *Wall Street Journal*, October 6, 2004.

48. Michael Barbaro, "Wal-Mart Chief Defends Closing Unionized Store," *Washington Post*, February 11, 2005.

49. Nancy Cleeland and Debora Vrana, "Wal-Mart CEO Takes His Case to California," *Los Angeles Times*, February 24, 2005.

50. Interview by Millie Org for author, October 14, 2005.

51. Mark Shaffer, "Flagstaff Divided on Big-Box Store," *Arizona Republic*, May 15, 2005.

52. Interview by Org for author, October 14, 2005.

53. Amy Joyce, "Wal-Mart to Apologize for Ad in Newspaper," *Washington Post*, May 14, 2005.

54. Press Release issued May 16, 2005, by the Anti-Defamation League, www.adl.org.

55. Michael Barbaro, "Wal-Mart's Ariz. PR Executive Resigns," *Washington Post*, June 9, 2005.

CHAPTER SEVEN: WAL-MART'S CHINA PRICE

1. Dale Dempsey, "Market Forces Too Much for Huffy," *Dayton Daily News*, October 24, 2004.

2. Huffy's annual report, Form 10-K, on file with the Securities and Exchange Commission, March 3, 2000.

3. Ron Carter, "City Feels Betrayed by Huffy," *Columbus Dispatch*, June 7, 1998.

4. Greg Barrett, "To the Lowest Bidder Go the Lowest-Paying Jobs," Gannett News Service, Dec. 3, 2003.

5. Greg Barrett, "Forces of Global Economy Usher in Uneasy Change for Low-Skilled Workers," Gannett News Service, Dec. 3, 2003.

6. Sen. Byron Dorgan, "U.S.-China Trade Is a Failed Policy," *The Hill*, September 13, 2005.

7. Bob Ortega, *In Sam We Trust*, 204.

8. Sam Walton with John Huey, *Sam Walton: Made in America*, 242.

9. Ortega, op cit., 207.

10. Interview with Jon Lehman, "Is Wal-Mart Good for America?" *Frontline*, June 4, 2004, and October 7, 2004, www.pbs.org/wgbh/pages/frontline/shows/walmart/interviews/lehman.html.

11. Nelson Lichtenstein, "Wal-Mart: A Template for Twenty-First Century Capital," *Wal-Mart: The Face of Twenty-First Century Capitalism*, 12.

12. Walton with Huey, op. cit., 186.

13. Don Soderquist, *The Wal*Mart Way*, 167.

14. Walton with Huey, op cit., 187.

15. Don Soderquist, *The Wal*Mart Way*, 145.

16. Constance L. Hays, "What They Know About You," *New York Times*, November 14, 2004.

17. Ibid.

18. Kelly Barron, "Spamouflage and Cajun Crawtators," *Forbes*, October 29, 2001.

19. Charles Fishman, "The Wal-Mart You Don't Know," *Fast Company*, December 2003.

20. Jim Collins, *Good to Great*, 26.

21. Mary Ethridge, "Rubbermaid Suffers in Battling Wal-Mart," *Akron Beacon Journal*, July 16, 2000.

22. Ibid.

23. Collins, op. cit., 26.

24. Jerry Useem, "One Nation Under Wal-Mart," *Fortune*, March 23, 2003.

25. Abigail Goldman and Nancy Cleeland, "An Empire Built on Bargains Remakes the Working World," *Los Angeles Times*, November 23, 2003.

26. Michael Barbaro, "Pillowtex Closing Leaves Thousands Out of Work," *The Washington Post*, August 9, 2003.

27. Misha Petrovic and Gary Hamilton, "Making Global Markets: Wal-Mart and Its Suppliers," *Wal-Mart: The Face of Twenty-First Century Capitalism*, 140.

28. Clay Chandler, "The Great Wal-Mart of China," *Fortune*, July 25, 2005.

29. Deloitte Research, "Ideas Change the World," *Deloitte Consulting*, 2003.

30. Nancy Cleeland, Evelyn Iritani, and Tyler Marshall, "Scouring the Globe to Give Shoppers an $8.63 Polo Shirt," *Los Angeles Times*, November 24, 2003.

31. Wal-Mart Stores, 2004 Report on Standards for Suppliers, 1, www.walmart-facts.com/docs/2004SuppStandards.pdf.

32. Steven Greenhouse, "Suit Says Wal-Mart Is Lax On Labor Abuses Overseas," *New York Times*, September 14, 2005.

33. Steven Greenhouse, "Wal-Mart Questions Motives of Lawsuit by Labor Group," *New York Times*, September 16, 2005.

34. Dexter Roberts and Aaron Bernstein, "A Life of Fines and Beating," *BusinessWeek*, October 2, 2000.

35. AScribe Newswire, "NBA, NFL, MLB, NCAA, NASCAR, DISNEY, Hasbro, Wal-Mart Caught Using Brutal Sweatshop in China to Make Popular Bobble-Head Dolls," AScribe Newswire, February 9, 2004.

36. Ibid.

37. Sean Silcoff, "Dorel Faces Cost Hikes in China: Looks Elsewhere in Far East for Cheaper Labour," *Financial Post* (Canada), November 1, 2005.

38. Peter S. Goodman and Philip P. Pan, "Chinese Workers Pay for Wal-Mart's Low Prices," *Washington Post*, February 8, 2004.

39. Charles Fishman, "The Wal-Mart You Don't Know," *Fast Company*, December 2003.

THE ANTI–WAL-MART

1. Lee Scott, "Twenty-First Century Leadership," October 24, 2005, 13. http: walmart-stores.com/Files/21st%20Century%20Leadership.pdf.

2. Stanley Holmes and Wendy Zellner, "The Costco Way," *BusinessWeek*, April 12, 2004, 76.

3. Michelle V. Rafter, "Welcome to the Club," *Workforce Management*, April 1, 2005.

4. John Helyar, "Sol Price on Off-Price," *Fortune*, November 10, 2003.

5. John Helyar, "Costco: The Only Company Wal-Mart Fears," *Fortune*, November 10, 2003.

6. Steven Greenhouse, "How Costco Became the Anti-Wal-Mart," *New York Times*, July 17, 2005.

7. Helyar, "Costco: The Only Company Wal-Mart Fears."

8. Greenhouse, "How Costco Became the Anti-Wal-Mart."

9. Helyar, "Costco: The Only Company Wal-Mart Fears."

CHAPTER EIGHT: WILL THE LAST INDEPENDENT GROCER IN AMERICA PLEASE TURN OFF THE MONORAIL?

1. Wal-Mart 2005 annual report to shareholders, 12.

2. Sandra J. Skrovan, "Wal-Mart Food: Big, and Getting Bigger," September 2003, 2.

3. Ibid., 11.

4. This remark has often been attributed to Twain, but might be apocryphal. "Until the attribution can be verified," advises the Web site twainquotes.com, "the quote should not be regarded as authentic."

5. For the early history of Bigg's see Eugene DiMaria, "Cincinnati Hypermarket May Be First of a Chain," *Supermarket News*, October 15, 1984, and Denise Gallagher, "Bigg's Opens Cincinnati Unit," *HFD, Home Furnishings Weekly*, October 12, 1984.

6. Bob Oretga, *In Sam We Trust*, 268.

7. Randy Tucker, "Kroger Has Been on This Track Before," *Cincinnati Enquirer*, August 1, 2004.

8. Interview with author, September 9, 2004.

9. When Winn-Dixie Stores, Thriftway's Florida-headquartered parent company,

filed for bankruptcy protection in early 2005, the difficulty of competing with Wal-Mart was widely cited as one of the main reasons for its demise.

10. Melanie Warner, "An Identity Crisis for Supermarkets," *New York Times*, October 6, 2005.

11. Food Marketing Institute's summary of *Progressive Grocer* magazine's Annual Report of the Grocery industry, April 2004 and April 1994.

12. John J. Ruf, "Inspirational Retailing: How to Survive in a Wal-Mart World," *The New England Journal of Marketing*, Summer 2004, 13–14.

13. Interview with author, February 14, 2005.

14. Interview with author, July 30, 2004.

15. Tedlow, *New and Improved*, 195.

16. Ibid., 196.

17. Mary Bralove, "Superstores May Suit Customers to a T—A T-Shirt or a T-Bone," *Wall Street Journal*, March 17, 1973. Also, "Plain and Fancy," *Barron's*, May 25, 1981.

18. Jim Collins, *Good to Great*, 68–69.

19. Ibid, 69.

20. Eamonn Fingleton, "250,000 Unpaid Consultants," *Forbes*, September 14, 1981.

21. Lisa Blank Fasig, "A Whole New Kroger," *Cincinnati Enquirer*, December 5, 1999.

22. James McNair, "Wal-Mart's Impact Magnified," *Cincinnati Enquirer*, September 22, 2002. Also, Leah Beth Ward, "Kroger Sees a Shadow Lurking Over Aisle 3," *New York Times*, April 7, 2002.

23. Alexander Coolidge, "Kroger Workers OK Strike," *Cincinnati Post*, October 14, 2004.

24. Ibid.

25. John Byczkowski, "After Agreement, Kroger Workers Angry, Dismayed," *Cincinnati Enquirer*, October 2, 2004, and James McNair, "Unions Unhappy But Cooperative," *Cincinnati Enquirer*, November 6, 2004.

26. Interview with author, March 10, 2005.

27. Interview with author, July 31, 2004.

28. Ted Anthony, "Thinking Globally, Selling Locally," *Washington Post*, November 22, 2001, A57.

29. Interview with author, September 21, 2004.

30. The following revenue figures (in millions), never before disclosed, were provided by George Wissing, Jungle Jim's chief financial officer: 1995, $29.8; 1996, $33.1; 1997, $36.7; 1998, $41.8; 1999, $48.5; 2000, $52.5; 2001, $56.8; 2002, $58.8; 2003, $61.0; 2004, $63.5.

31. Interview with author, September 19, 2004.

32. The events center is at once the newest and oldest part of Jungle Jim's. The timbers used in its construction are of center-cut cedar and date from the late 1700s. Bonaminio took the lumber as well as a few tons of brick of Civil War vintage out of an antebellum Cincinnati factory that was disassembled a few years ago.

33. John Eckberg, "Wal-Mart Supercenter Closely Watched," *Cincinnati Enquirer,* September 15, 2004.

34. Interview with author, September 22, 2004.

35. Alexander Coolidge, "Wal-Mart Doubles Grocery Share," *Cincinnati Post,* August 5, 2005.

36. Randy Tucker, "Kroger Has Been on This Track Before," August 1, 2004.

37. Interview by author, September 9, 2004.

38. Safeway presentation at the International Council of Shopping Centers conference in February 2004.

39. Randy McNutt, "Intimate Yet Innovative, Remke Markets Thrives Without the Hype," *Cincinnati Enquirer,* June 15, 2004.

40. Interview with author, September 19, 2004.

41. Interview with author, February 10, 2005.

42. Ken Alltucker, "Oakley to Get a Jungle Jim's," *Cincinnati Enquirer,* March 10, 2005. Adams started working for Bonaminio as a part-time trash hauler in 1982. When Adams's supervisor decided to leave Jungle Jim's a decade ago, Bonaminio cooked up the surgery photo as a farewell gift and later decided to have business cards made from it.

DOWN AND OUT IN JONQUIÈRE

1. Interview with author and Diane Bérard, April 12, 2005.

2. Interview with author and Diane Bérard, April 12, 2005.

3. Interview with author and Diane Bérard, April 11, 2005.

4. Doug Struck, "Wal-Mart Leaves Bitter Chill," *Washington Post,* April 14, 2005.

5. See www/newswire.ca/en/releases/archive/October2004/13/c9667.html.

6. Clifford Krauss, "For Labor, a Wal-Mart Closing in Canada Is a Call to Arms," *New York Times,* March 10, 2005.

7. Kevin Bell, "Wal-Mart Workers at 2nd Québec Store Join Union," Bloomberg. com, January 19, 2005.

8. Interview with author and Diane Bérard, April 13, 2005.

9. Ian Austen, "Wal-Mart to Close Store in Canada with a Union," *New York Times,* February 10, 2005.

10. Struck, "Wal-Mart Leaves Bitter Chill."

11. Bertrand Marotte, "Wal-Mart Intimidated Unionists, Board Rules," *Globe and Mail,* February 26, 2005.

12. Marina Strauss, "The Secret to Gaining Success in Quebec," *Globe and Mail,* September 27, 2005.

13. Interview with author and Bérard, April 12, 2004.

14. Interview with author and Bérard, April 13, 2005.

15. Ian Austen, "Quebec Rules Against Wal-Mart in Closing of Unionized Store," *New York Times,* September 20, 2005.

CHAPTER NINE: WHERE WOULD JESUS SHOP?

1. Chisun Lee, "The New Movement Against Wal-Mart," *The Village Voice*, August 23, 2005.

2. Press release from Rep. Weiner's office, December 16, 2004.

3. John Heilemann, "Unstoppable," *New York*, August 15, 2005.

4. Karyn Saemann, "Monona Wal-Mart Opposition Organizes," *The Capital Times* (Madison, Wisconsin), May 18, 2005.

5. "Jesuit Objections to Locating Wal-Mart at Woodlawn/Woolwich," www.ignatius-guelph.ca/docs/jesuitobjections.pdf.

6. Peter Kuitenbrouwer, "God and Wal-Mart Forced to Get Along in Guelph," *National Post*, January 7, 2005.

7. Jeff M. Sellers, "Deliver Us From Wal*Mart?" *Christianity Today*, May 2005.

8. J. Bennett Guess, "Justice and Witness Ministries Endorses 'Wal-Mart Week of Action,'" *United Church News*, October–November 2005.

9. Dan Mihalopoulos, "Nobody Neutral on Wal-Mart Proposals," *Chicago Tribune*, May 4, 2004.

10. Dan Mihalopoulos, "Jackson Chimes in Against Wal-Mart," *Chicago Tribune*, April 20, 2004.

11. As recorded by author, April 6, 2005.

12. William Bole, "Stockholders with a Social Conscience," *Our Sunday Visitor*, May 3, 1999.

13. Interview with author, September 30, 2005.

14. Janet Bagnall, "Taking on Wal-Mart: The U.S. retailer's anti-union activities have spawned a network of religious and activist groups to fight the department store giant," *The Gazette* (Montreal), June 17, 2005.

15. Frank Green, "Wal-Mart Removed from 'Socially Responsible' List," *San Diego Union-Tribune*, May 18, 2001.

16. Julie Tanner and Kimberly Gladman, "Outside the Box: Guidelines for Retail Store Siting," Christian Brothers Investment Services and Domini Social Investments, July 11, 2005, 20, 22–26.

17. Don Soderquist, *The Wal*Mart Way*, 45.

18. Nelson Lichtenstein, "Wal-Mart: A Template for Twenty-First Century Capitalism" in *Wal-Mart: The Face of Twenty-First Century Capitalism*, 18–19.

19. Mike Troy, "Scott, Coughlin Set to Lead Wal-Mart," *Discount Store News* 38, no. 2, January 25, 1999.

20. Sellers, op. cit.

21. Bole, "Stockholders with a Social Conscience."

22. Brook Gladstone, *On the Media* (radio program), "Wal-Mart Culture," June 27, 2003.

23. Anthony Bianco and Wendy Zellner, "Is Wal-Mart Too Powerful?" *BusinessWeek*, October 6, 2003.

24. Ibid.

25. David D. Kirkpatrick, "Shaping Cultural Tastes at Big Retail Chains," *New York Times*, May 18, 2003.

26. Bianco and Zellner, op. cit.

27. "Wal-Mart Not Carrying 'America,'" *Publishers Weekly*, October 25, 2004.

28. Bianco and Zellner, op. cit.

29. Interview with Tom Lowry of *BusinessWeek*, September 19, 2003.

30. Interview with author, September 20, 2004.

31. According to Barna Research Group, a Ventura, California-based market research company.

32. Harold Meyerson, "Protocols of Wal-Mart," *American Prospect*, November 2004.

33. Rachel Pomerance, "Wal-Mart Backs Down," *Jewish Times*, September 26, 2004.

34. Jeff Johnson, "Family-Friendly Mutual Fund Drops Wal-Mart," *CNSNews.Com* August 19, 2002.

35. Interview with author and Wendy Zellner, September 15, 2003.

36. Martha W. Kleder, "Mutual Fund Targets Wal-Mart for Selling Sleazy Magazines, *C & F Report* (Culture & Family Institute), August 21, 2002.

37. Leigh Gallagher, "Holy Influence," *Forbes*, December 8, 2003.

38. David Carr and Constance L. Hayes, "3 Racy Men's Magazines Are Banned by Wal-Mart," *New York Times*, May 6, 2003.

THE BELMONT SCHISM

1. Interview for author by Millie Org, April 14, 2005.

2. Ibid.

3. Father Richard P. McBrien, "The Popes and Wal-Mart on Labor Unions," *The Tidings*, December 13, 2002.

4. Joseph Donders (ed.), *John Paul II: The Encyclicals in Everyday Language."*

5. Anselm Biggs, "The Benedictine Life: An introduction to the Benedictine history and the founding of Belmont Abbey," www.belmontabbey.org/benedictine_life/.

6. Ken Elkins, "Monks Ready to Develop College Land," *Charlotte Business Journal*, March 1, 2002.

7. "Abbot Deals When the Spirit Moves Him, *Business North Carolina*, March 2004, tk.

8. Joe DePriest, "Interstate's Invasion Now Paves Way to Prosperity," *Charlotte Observer*, March 10, 2002, 1L.

9. Interview for author by Org, March 16, 2005.

10. Interview by Org for author, April 15, 2005.

11. Interview for author by Org, April 15, 2005.

CHAPTER TEN: THE EDUCATION OF LEE SCOTT

1. Christopher Leonard, "Wal-Mart's Scott Discounts Exit Tales," *Arkansas Democrat-Gazette*, May 21, 2005.

2. John T. Anderson, "Diversity Hiring, Internal Strength Stressed at Shareholder Meeting," *The Morning News*, June 4, 2005.

3. In 2000, Glass bought majority control of the Royals for $96 million.

4. Mark Gongloff, "The Afternoon Report: Blame It On The Rain," WSJ.com, May 12, 2005.

5. Anita French, "Analysts Concerned Over Wal-Mart's Woes," *The Morning News*, May 18, 2005.

6. Scott, 2005 Wal-Mart Twelfth Annual Analysts' Meeting Day I (October 25, 2005).

7. Ann Zimmerman and Kortney Stringer, "Wal-Mart Forces Out Coughlin," *Wall Street Journal*, March 29, 2005.

8. "Tom Coughlin to Retire As Wal-Mart Vice Chairman," December 6, 2004, www.walmartfacts.com/newsdesk/article.aspx?id=579.

9. The company's case against Coughlin and an alleged confederate, Jared Bowen, is spelled out in a July 14, 2005, filing by Wal-Mart outside counsel Eugene Scalia in *Jared Bowen vs. Wal-Mart Stores, Inc.*, Case 6-2320-05-902, U.S. Department of Labor.

10. James Bandler and Ann Zimmerman, "A Wal-Mart Legend's Trail of Deceit," *Wall Street Journal*, April 8, 2005.

11. Zimmerman and Stringer, "Wal-Mart Forces Out Coughlin."

12. 2005 Wal-Mart Twelfth Annual Analysts' Meeting Day I (October 25, 2005).

13. Kris Hudson, "Wal-Mart Investors Fret Over Costs," *Wall Street Journal*, October 25, 2005.

14. Wal-Mart Stores, Second Quarter Earnings Call 2006, August 16, 2005. http://walmartstores.com/GlobalWMStoresWeb/navigate.do?catg=48&contId=4974.

15. Tracie Rohzon, "Wal-Mart Is Going Upscale. Well, at Least a Little," *New York Times*, April 8, 2005.

16. Castro-Wright, 2005 Twelfth Annual Analysts' Meeting Day 1.

17. Andy Serwer, "Bruised in Bentonville," *Fortune*, April 18, 2005. "I look at it this way," said Jay Allen, Wal-Mart's ranking executive in public and governmental relations. "Thirty percent of the country don't care one way or the other about Wal-Mart. Thirty percent love us. Thirty percent have sincere questions about us. And 10% hate us."

18. "Wal-Mart Tries to Win Over Consumers," Associated Press, October 24, 2005.

19. Lee Scott, "Twenty-First Century Leadership," October 24, 2005. http: walmartstores.com/Files/21st%20Century%20Leadership.pdf.

20. Devin Leonard, "'The Only Lifeline Was the Wal-Mart,'" *Fortune*, October 3, 2005.

21. Michael Barbaro and Justin Gills, "Wal-Mart at Forefront of Hurricane Relief," *Washington Post*, September 6, 2005.

22. Greg Levine, "Scott Warns China Wal-Mart Suppliers Re 'Standards,'" Forbes.com, October 20, 2005.

23. 2005 Wal-Mart Twelfth Annual Analysts' Meeting Day I.

24. Ibid.

25. Susana Schrobsdorff, "Vogue-Mart," Newsweek.com, October 26, 2005.

26. 2005 Wal-Mart Twelfth Annual Analysts' Meeting Day I.

27. Claire Watts, 2005 Wal-Mart Twelfth Annual Analysts' Meeting Day I.

28. Wendy Zellner, "How Well Does Wal-Mart Travel?" *BusinessWeek*, September 3, 2001.

29. "Wal-Mart draws ridicule and anger in Germany, but fails to make profits," UNI Commerce, April 12, 2004, www.union-netowrk.org.

30. Hank Gilman, "The Most Underrated CEO Ever," *Fortune*, March 3, 2004.

31. Clay Chandler, "The Great Wal-Mart of China," *Fortune*, July 25, 2005.

32. "Wal-Mart Concedes China Can Make Unions," Associated Press, November 23, 2004.

33. Wal-Mart Twelfth Annual Analysts' Meeting Day I.

34. Scott, "Twenty-First Century Leadership," 13.

35. Robert Berner, "Wal-Mart's Scott: We're Not 'Anti-Union,'" BusinessWeek.com, September 23, 2005.

36. Susan Chambers, "Supplemental Benefits Documentation, Board of Directors Retreat FY06, 7.

37. Michael Barbara, "A New Weapon for Wal-Mart: A War Room," *New York Times*, October 27, 2005.

38. Ann Zimmerman, tk, *Wall Street Journal*, October 6, 2004.

39. Remarks of Lee Scott to the 2005 Wal-Mart Shareholders Meeting, General Session, June 3, 2005, 7. www.walmartfacts.com/docs/1193_leescottshareholders2005_339291970.pdf.

40. Berner, "Scott: 'We're Not Anti-Union.'"

41. Ann Zimmerman, "Wal-Mart Sets Seminar to Assess Economic Impact," *Wall Street Journal*, November 4, 2005.

42. Scott, "Twenty-First Century Leadership."

43. Michael Barbaro and Felicity Barringer, "Wal-Mart To Seek Savings In Energy, *New York Times*, October 25, 2004.

44. Harold Meyerson, "Trouble in Wal-Mart's America," *Washington Post*, October 26, 2005.

INDEX